A.

MW01193994

Amos Alonzo Stagg

College Football's Greatest Pioneer

DAVID E. SUMNER

McFarland & Company, Inc., Publishers
Jefferson, North Carolina

LIBRARY OF CONGRESS CATALOGUING-IN-PUBLICATION DATA

Names: Sumner, David E., 1946– author.
Title: Amos Alonzo Stagg : college football's greatest pioneer /
David E. Sumner.
Description: Jefferson, North Carolina : McFarland & Company, Inc.,
Publishers, 2021. | Includes bibliographical references and index.
Identifiers: LCCN 2021041506 |
ISBN 9781476685762 (paperback : acid free paper) ∞
ISBN 9781476643854 (ebook)
Subjects: LCSH: Stagg, Amos Alonzo, 1862–1965. | University of Chicago—
Football—History. | Football coaches—United States—Biography. |
BISAC: SPORTS & RECREATION / Football
Classification: LCC GV939.S7 S86 2021 | DDC 796.332092 [B]—dc23
LC record available at https://lccn.loc.gov/2021041506

BRITISH LIBRARY CATALOGUING DATA ARE AVAILABLE

ISBN (print) 978-1-4766-8576-2
ISBN (ebook) 978-1-4766-4385-4

Front cover: (top) University of Chicago coach and athletic director
Amos Alonzo Stagg; (bottom) view of Marshall Field during game
action between Wisconsin and Chicago on November 24, 1904
(both photographs from the University of Chicago Library)

Printed in the United States of America

*McFarland & Company, Inc., Publishers
Box 611, Jefferson, North Carolina 28640
www.mcfarlandpub.com*

Table of Contents

To Elise,
my best editor

Preface and Acknowledgments

When I mentioned to friends that I was writing a biography of Amos Alonzo Stagg, a few knew who he was, but I had to explain to most of them a little about his life and why he is significant in football history. While most people have heard of Knute Rockne or Glenn "Pop" Warner, I will argue in these pages that Stagg has had more of an impact on modern football than either of them. In fact, Stagg was chosen the "All-America coach of all time" in 1930 by a unanimous vote of fifteen college coaches. Glenn "Pop" Warner ranked second, and Knute Rockne ranked third in their poll. Read Chapter 9 to learn why Stagg declined the honor.

I did not learn about Stagg until a few years ago when reading the book *Death of an American Game: The Crisis in Football.* Author John Underwood, a former *Sports Illustrated* reporter, wrote about visiting Stagg during his last year of life in a California convalescent center. Underwood had become disillusioned with the rampant commercialism and scandals of college football and saw in Stagg a gentleman who exemplified the lost ideals of amateur athletics of an earlier era.

As I read more books about Stagg, I began to ask some questions. First, why did this football coach keep finding more jobs after he was forced to "retire" at age seventy by the University of Chicago and age eighty-four by the College of the Pacific? He never completely retired from coaching until he was ninety-eight. Both universities that forced him to "retire" from coaching even offered him other jobs with a comparable salary, so he didn't need the money. The second question was how did he manage to stay healthy and live until he was 102? He appeared on the cover of *Time* magazine at age ninety-six to illustrate a story about older, successful Americans. And third, how much did he influence the game of football? Stagg invented or introduced dozens of play formations, innovations, techniques, and even equipment items that are still used today. Stagg's Yale mentor, Walter Camp, is called the "father of American football," which led *Collier's* magazine in 1930 to put it this way: "If Walter Camp is the father of football, Stagg is its Thomas Edison."[1]

The theme that emerged from my research is that of an athletic genius who never gave up, quit, or let an obstacle stand in his way. But I cannot tell his story in isolation from the evolving nature of college football in the late 1800s and early 1900s. He played a significant role in the development of its plays and formations and the founding of the Western Conference (now the Big Ten) in 1895. He wrote a book about football techniques in 1894. He was among the founding coaches of the NCAA in 1905 and spent more than fifty years on its Rules Committee. He was among the first coaches to make frequent use of the forward pass after it was legalized in 1906 and developed sixty-four pass plays for his Chicago team. He was the first coach to use a huddle and put numerals on jerseys to help fans identify the players.[2]

This biography, however, is not hagiography. Amos Stagg is a complex man and not universally admired by football historians. Robin Lester wrote *Stagg's University: The Rise, Fall, and Decline of Big-Time Football at the University of Chicago*. Lester paints a nuanced portrait of Stagg as a football genius whose teams elevated the University of Chicago to national prominence in the 1890s through the 1920s. Yet, he had a leadership style that led to conflicts with faculty members and administration. He protected his turf in the Department of Athletics and resisted interference by administrators or faculty. He became embroiled in disputes with other coaches, who criticized him for pushing the boundaries of recruiting and eligibility rules too far. John Kryk, author of *Stagg vs. Yost: The Birth of Cutthroat Football*, paints Stagg as a ruthless manipulator who would do anything to win, especially against Yost's Michigan teams of the early twentieth century.

Who was the real Amos Stagg? The ruthless, win-at-any-cost coach or the honorable man who lived by the Christian ideals he professed? I believe Kryk's criticisms are exaggerated, but the answer that emerged from my research is that he possessed high moral ideals and a tremendous motivation to excel at whatever he did. He loved his players, loved coaching, loved his family, and loved God. But he was a flawed man. He did not always enforce academic eligibility standards for his players or respect the collegial nature of governance in higher education. He was a perfectionist, and his insistence on perfection made compromise difficult.

Six Stagg biographies have been published since 1946 in addition to his co-authored autobiography, *Touchdown!* Five are mostly uncritical hagiographies. Lester's book, *Stagg's University*, is the most authoritative and respected. He provides an excellent, detailed account of Stagg's role in football's rise and fall at the University of Chicago from 1892 to 1933. Lester's book is, however, largely confined to those years. The goal of this book, therefore, is to write the definitive biography of Stagg from birth to death. It will tell stories about his immense success as a football and baseball player and activities as YMCA leader, Glee Club member, and newspaper reporter at Yale. It will explain his role in founding the game of basketball with his friend James Naismith, a role which helped to earn his membership in the College Basketball Hall of Fame. It is the first biography to critically examine his successes and failures in coaching baseball, basketball, and track at Chicago. It is the first biography to examine in detail his years at College of the Pacific, Susquehanna University, and Stockton College after he left Chicago. Finally, it is also the first biography to tell the story of his seventy-year marriage to his wife, Stella, and her significant role in his football success. Her *New York Times* obituary said, "Mrs. Stagg was said to have been the greatest living woman expert on football during her husband's career."[3]

The size of the "paper trail" left by Stagg during his 102 years is staggering (pun intended). "I was prone to save everything—pictures, programs, clippings, deflated footballs, and the like," he once said.[4] His papers at the University of Chicago Special Collections Research Center include such items as middle school assignments and report cards from the 1870s. The Chicago collection contains thousands of newspaper clippings and letters he wrote and received throughout his life. After he gained fame as a Yale baseball player, newspaper articles about him began appearing all over the nation. A few years after he married in 1894, Stella Stagg began to organize these clippings, letters, football programs, and other memorabilia into albums and scrapbooks. After his death, the family donated them to the University of Chicago, the University of the Pacific (formerly College of the Pacific), and Stagg High School in Palos Hills, Illinois. The University of Chicago collection contains 339 boxes of documents totaling 384 linear feet. I purchased subscriptions to newspapers.com and the *New York Times* archives and drew from thousands of Stagg-related articles between the 1880s and his 1965 death. I found significant amounts of information about Stagg in more than fifty books about the history of college football. I have fact-checked all game scores and team records against official University of Chicago Athletic records that are available online.

I asked Eileen Ielmini, the assistant archivist at the University of Chicago, for a detailed breakdown of the university's Stagg collection, and she reported:

125 boxes of files = 75,000 to 80,000 documents
229 albums documenting his time at the University of Chicago
14 albums documenting his time at the College of the Pacific
17 albums documenting his personal career
10 albums documenting his time before coming to Chicago
75 albums documenting University of Chicago football

27 albums documenting his scouting for other University of Chicago
   sports
6 albums of miscellaneous content
36 photograph albums

With so much information, how did I decide what to use? I established
three criteria. First, is the material original and not published elsewhere?
Second, is the material interesting? Third, is it historically significant and
does it help answer the questions posed earlier? While this book could have
easily been 600 pages, I wanted to make it as readable as possible. I have
tried to take the "middle road" between providing stories and anecdotes to
attract the casual reader and accurate details to satisfy the football historian.

Writing this book has been fun; I looked forward to getting up and
starting work each morning for the past three years. The biggest challenge
was figuring out how to structure and organize the material into chapters.
While I settled on a chronological structure, I also recognized that Stagg's
many interests and activities spanned across decades. Therefore, Chapter 1
begins with an overview of his life, family, and personal interests. Chapter
2 tells about his childhood in West Orange, New Jersey, and the remaining
chapters proceed chronologically.

When I introduce important individuals for the first time, I put their
birth and death years in parentheses, such as Walter Camp (1859–1925).
This information gives readers a sense of their age in relation to Stagg's life
(1862–1965). Because many primary sources date from the nineteenth century, I have occasionally modernized spelling and punctuation. For example, many early documents capitalize nouns that are not proper nouns or
use more commas than generally used in modern writing. However, I have
not added or changed any words from material that appears inside of quo-
tation marks. I have not created any fictitious quotes or circumstances.

Many dollar figures refer to expenses and costs beginning in the 1880s
when Stagg started college that mean little today. Therefore, readers can
use this inflation index to get a better idea of comparable figures in today's
economy.[5]

1880s—dollar amount times 27
1890s—dollar amount times 30
1900s—dollar amount times 32
1910s—dollar amount times 29
1920s—dollar amount times 14
1930s—dollar amount times 16
1940s—dollar amount times 19
1950s—dollar amount times 11
1960s—dollar amount times 9

For example, Stagg's starting salary at the University of Chicago in 1892 was $2,500, which multiplied times twenty-eight is comparable to $70,000 in today's money. When his salary was raised to $4,500 in 1905, it was the equivalent of $180,000 in today's money. Head coaches at major universities today earn more than a $5 million annual salary, which illustrates how popular culture's demand and expectations for coaches have dramatically increased.

For twenty-five years, I was the head of the magazine journalism program at Ball State University in Muncie, Indiana, and wrote three popular textbooks about magazine writing and publishing. Several friends have asked how I became interested in writing about football. After retiring from teaching, I wanted to write about topics with more popular appeal. I played four years of high school football in Florida and enjoy watching games. Football helps form character, and I believe it helped form mine, especially teamwork, endurance, and inner fortitude. Football gave me lifelong encouragement to stay physically fit, which helped me survive cancer ten years ago. Stories about football players and coaches such as Stagg are filled with drama, conflict, disappointment, failure, hope, inspiration, fortitude, endurance, and faith. Football is a metaphor for life. Despite football's well-deserved criticisms, I believe its benefit to players and the public outweigh its abuses and risks.

In my last book, *Fumbled Call*, I wrote in the introduction, "Writing a book is like building a house brick-by-brick. Each 'brick' in a book is a fact or quote. If you are building a house, you can order all the bricks delivered to your site all at once. If you are writing a book, you have to go out and find the bricks—one or two at a time in dozens of locations." Yet, the mystery of the hunt is not as laborious as it sounds. New facts lead to new questions, which means going out and searching for more "bricks." For example, I made one trip to the University of Chicago Archives for the main purpose of reading the 1906 minutes of the University Senate because I was curious about what the Senate did that made Stagg threaten to resign. Answering questions like this and solving historical mysteries is why I enjoy research so much. Research for earlier books has taken me on trips to archives at Yale, Vanderbilt, Princeton, Emory, Fisk, the University of Georgia, and publishing companies such as Time Inc. and Condé Nast.

For her support and assistance, I owe many thanks to Ms. Eileen Ielmini, assistant archivist at the University of Chicago Special Collections Research Center. The center offered me a generous Robert L. Platzman Research Fellowship that helped pay for five visits. Ms. Jennifer Baniewicz, social studies teacher and archivist at Amos Alonzo Stagg High School in Palos Hills, Illinois, helped me access the school's extensive collection of Stagg papers during three visits. Michael Wurtz, university archivist and history professor at the University of the Pacific, located, scanned, and sent more than 200 pages of Stagg documents. He also reviewed Chapter 12 about the University of the Pacific for accuracy. Meg Garnett, special collections librarian at Susquehanna University, provided many Stagg documents from the university's archives. Elaine Nelson, head of Interlibrary Loan at Ball State University, helped find and borrow forty-five football history books from other universities. I found an online collection of Stagg correspondence and documents from the Springfield College Archives in Springfield, Massachusetts. University of Chicago economics professor Robert Topel and archivist for the Olympia Hills Country Club contributed primary documents about Stagg's role in its history.

John W. Boyer, Chicago's dean of the Undergraduate College and professor of history, reviewed Chapter 12 about the university's early history and made some helpful suggestions. Finally, my wife, Elise, is a better copy editor than me and read every word of the manuscript at least three times to help correct typos and improve clarity. She is a wonderful help, friendly critic, and enthusiastic supporter of all I write.

1

Stagg, the Man

His character and career have been an inspiration since his own undergraduate days for countless Americans of all ages. Few men in our history have set so persuasive and shining example as teacher, coach, and citizen.—President John F. Kennedy

At age eighty-four, shortly after he was forced to retire for the second time, Amos Alonzo Stagg narrowly escaped from a train wreck that killed four and injured eighty-two passengers. The wreck occurred near Fresno, California, when a gasoline truck-trailer plowed into a San Francisco-bound train and exploded, sending a 150-feet geyser of flaming gasoline into the sky. The train struck the trailer, wrapping it around the front of the engine and dragging it 300 yards before stopping. Eight members of the San Francisco Shamrocks ice hockey team were among the injured.[1] Stagg was returning home from an NCAA Rules Committee meeting in New Orleans. Because he was sitting in a rear car not caught in the flames, the indomitable Stagg stepped off the train uninjured, determined to continue his coaching career.[2] He went on to coach football for another fourteen years.

Stagg was coaching the University of Chicago football team in 1922 during a year that it won only one game. Friends reported to him that some critics and fans wanted him to resign. "You can tell those fellows that they can come out here ten years from now if they're still alive, and they'll find me on the job."[3] He was right.

Stagg grew up in a poor family with eight children but worked his way through Exeter Academy and Yale University. His extraordinary baseball and football abilities thrust him into the national spotlight while still a student. He achieved fame as a Yale baseball pitcher before earning All-America honors on the 1889 football team. He spurned lucrative baseball offers from six pro teams so he could study for the ministry at Yale's divinity school. After a year at the divinity school, however, he recognized

Amos Alonzo Stagg (1862–1965) at age 89 with his induction certificates into the National Football Hall of Fame as a player (Yale) and coach (University of Chicago and University of the Pacific). University of Chicago Photographic Archive, apf1-07867, Special Collections Research Center, University of Chicago Library.

he could have a greater influence on young men on the athletic field than in the pulpit.

Under Stagg's leadership, the University of Chicago emerged as one of the nation's most formidable football powers in the late 1800s and early twentieth century when his teams compiled a record of 227–112–26. His teams won seven Big Ten Conference championships (1899, 1905, 1907, 1908, 1913, 1922, 1924) and two national championships (1905, 1913), outscoring opponents 5,827 to 2,724 points.[4]

Table 1: Stagg's Life Chronology

Birth	August 16, 1862
West Orange, N.J.	1862–1883
Exeter Academy	1884 (Spring)
Yale University	1884–1888

Yale Divinity School	1888–1890
YMCA School	1890–1892
University of Chicago	1892–1933
College of the Pacific	1933–1947
Susquehanna University	1947–1953
Stockton Junior College	1953–1958
Death	March 17, 1965

When the university forced him to retire at the age of seventy, he started looking for another job. He accepted the head coaching job at the College of the Pacific in Stockton, California, where he coached for fourteen years. He was again forced out of a job by a mandatory retirement. So he moved to Pennsylvania where he joined his son, Amos Alonzo Stagg, Jr., as "advisory coach" at Susquehanna University and coached for another six years. In 1953, he returned to Stockton because of his wife's declining health. He became an assistant coach for the Stockton Junior College team, coaching kickers and punters.

Amos Alonzo Stagg doesn't fit into neat stereotypical labels. He was heroic in many respects but flawed in others, and football was only one part of his life. He held strong views on many subjects. He was a practicing Christian and affiliated with Presbyterian, Baptist, and Methodist churches at different eras in his life. He was a teetotaler and public supporter of prohibition. He didn't allow his athletes to smoke and dismissed them from the team when they did. He held progressive views on race and welcomed minority athletes onto his teams. He held great contempt toward professional sports and discouraged his athletes from playing for professional teams after graduation. He never had much money and gave it away generously.

Marriage and Family

Amos and Stella Stagg were loyal and devoted to each other for almost seventy years. While she never worked outside of the home, she was her husband's secretary and chief assistant coach. "My multitudinous duties required continuously long hours of work, daytime, evenings and Sundays, which I have been able to do only through the unpaid, voluntary and sacrificial efforts of my devoted wife," Stagg wrote in his autobiography, *Touchdown!*[5]

In 1922, Amos Stagg, Sr., received a letter from the University of Chicago comptroller asking him to reduce the size of his staff to stay within the budget. Stagg refused, arguing that besides his two secretaries, his wife did a great deal of office work for him. He wrote, "May I add that for the past twenty-eight years, Mrs. Stagg has gratuitously given many thousands of hours in helping to run the work of the department. I have endeavored to run the department with the utmost economy possible, personally working nights and Sundays and until such time as Mrs. Stagg can be relieved from certain work which she has been doing, It doesn't seem to me quite fair to ask for further reductions in our force."[6]

Stella Robertson Stagg (1875–1964) was an athletic woman who enjoyed playing tennis, basketball, and golf. Amos Stagg once said, "I was attracted by the scrappiness she showed in a basketball game" when she was a University of Chicago student. He also gave her tennis lessons soon after they were married. During many summer months, they played three hours of tennis daily and golfed or cycled in the afternoon.[7] Their marriage was often described as "storybook." They raised a daughter and two sons, both of whom became college football coaches and athletic directors. Their daughter, Ruth, was the youngest, born in 1904. Years later, she told an interviewer that although her father was very strict, "He loved us; I am positive of that."[8]

Stella Stagg won a local women's tennis tournament in 1898 soon after winning a summer tournament at the Chautauqua Institution in New York. The *Chicago Tribune* reported, "Mrs. Stagg had fine control and called forth frequent and long applause from the sideline spectators by her playing and vicious cross-courting. She displayed fine headwork … again and again placing the ball where her opponent was least expecting it."[9] Two days later, the *Tribune* reported, "Her tennis was the best she has ever put up in a championship event, and yesterday it was even better than on the initial day of the tournament…. The onslaught of Mrs. Stagg was terrific."[10]

Amos Stagg, Jr., recalled that his father and mother were musically talented. "I remember when he [his father] would put his arm around me, and he would sing tenor, and I would sing the melody. Then, he would turn and sing melody, and I would sing tenor. He was a beautiful singer, and my mother was a beautiful pianist. Over and over they would have faculty members in when I was young. Maybe half a dozen women gathered around the piano and sang these beautiful songs. It made for a very lovely family life."[11]

Stagg Jr. expressed deep admiration for his father because he saved his life by staying up for twenty-six hours when he contracted diphtheria as a seven-month-old infant. Diphtheria causes a thick covering in the back of the throat, which can lead to loss of breath, heart failure, and death. "I came down with diphtheria when there were no antibiotics and had it very bad. For twenty-six continuous hours, my father [stayed with me], picked

Amos and Stella Stagg at the University of Chicago in 1930. University of Chicago Photographic Archive, apf1-07761, Special Collections Research Center, University of Chicago Library.

me up and walked with me every time my face would get black; he turned me over and he swatted me.... It brought out great anger, and I would fight it and managed to get my breath again. It's a terrible thing to strangulate. Somehow or another, I lived through it. I was one person probably marked for death, but it didn't happen because of my father," he said in a 1985 interview.[12]

From the time he refused a cash gift from his minister before he left for Exeter, Amos Stagg lived a frugal lifestyle and refused to borrow money. He graduated from Yale without any debts. He and Stella lived in a Chicago apartment from 1892 until 1915 until they had saved enough to pay cash for a modest house at 5539 Kenwood Avenue near the university.[13] "The fear of debt is apt to be drilled deep into the innards of one who was at close grips with poverty in his youth as I was," Stagg wrote.

After their three children were grown, Stella became his chief assistant, scouting future opponents and keeping detailed records of every game. She managed his voluminous correspondence, typed his letters, and sometimes answered them herself. She clipped and organized thousands of newspaper articles about Stagg and his teams and pasted them into dozens of scrapbooks that are still preserved today in archives at the University of Chicago and University of the Pacific.

A slender, petite woman who weighed less than 100 pounds, she struggled with health issues throughout her life, which her husband occasionally mentioned in correspondence. He referred in a couple of letters to her "breakdown." When she was forty-nine in 1925, Stagg wrote to a friend: "Dr. Greer says that Mrs. Stagg has no really organic trouble, but she has what he calls a tired heart. That combined with over-worked nerves, he thinks, is responsible for her present weakened condition. He told her several years ago that she ought to take it easy but unfortunately, she did not act on his advice.... She now lies down several times during the day."[14]

Because of his nationwide fame, Stagg received a huge amount of correspondence, sometimes 100 letters a day, which contained every imaginable kind of request. He and Stella tried to answer every letter, although not always quickly. For example, Stagg received a letter in 1928 from a prison inmate offering to sell a "hand-beaded horsehair belt" for $7.50. The inmate wrote, "Our warden has extended to those of us whose conduct may permit, the privilege of making during spare time articles such as indicated above and placing them on the market where those who feel kindly disposed may have the opportunity to purchase at a fair price." Stagg replied in a courteous note and ordered one enclosing a check.

He received hundreds of requests from sports writers, editors and graduate students who wanted to tap his rich knowledge of football history. "One of my jobs seems to be to pass out information of a historical character. I get a good many letters wanting information in the various branches of athletics that I have coached. In some cases, to reply to them and to be perfectly certain of the facts necessitates checking up and that often takes considerable time," he wrote a friend in 1941.[15] "We have become more-or-less specialists on helping people out with their master's theses and sometimes one for a PhD. There are a large number of boys majoring in physical education, and they seem to think that we can furnish data for their theses, and between us we have helped quite a number. She does the typing. I could not get along without her help in the secretary work for I get an immense lot of letters, and I try to answer them all," he said.[16]

Allison Danzig, a *New York Times* sportswriter from 1923 to 1968, published his epic *The History of American Football* in 1956, the most comprehensive history of college football until then. He credits Stagg as his primary source of information and help in writing the book. "Time and time again I went to him for information, often to clear up discrepancies or conflicts in the views of other coaches as to the origins of formations, plays, techniques, devices, and so forth. Never once did Mr. Stagg fail me, even when the health of his devoted wife ... was failing."[17]

Like father, like sons. Both Amos Alonzo, Jr., and Paul played quarterback for the University of Chicago; both became assistant coaches at the University of Chicago and later head football coaches and athletic directors at other universities. Amos Alonzo Stagg, Jr. (1899–1996), graduated from the University of Chicago in 1923 and earned a master's degree at Columbia University. He was a quarterback for the Chicago team from 1918 to 1922 and later an assistant coach under his father. When his father left the University of Chicago in 1933, the younger Stagg retained his post until 1935 when he was hired as the head football coach at Susquehanna University. He was Susquehanna's head football coach from 1935 to 1942 and 1946 to 1954 with the interruption due to World War II.

Paul Stagg (1909–1992) earned a geography degree from the University of Chicago in 1932, a master's degree in physical education from Columbia in 1934, and a PhD in physical education from New York University in 1946. He quarterbacked the Chicago team from 1929 to 1931. After his father accepted the coaching position at the College of the Pacific, Paul Stagg became his assistant coach at Pacific from 1933 to 1934. He left that position in 1934 to become head football coach at Moravian College (1934–1936), Springfield College (1937–1940), Worcester Polytechnic Institute, (1941–1946), and Pacific University in Forest Grove, Oregon (1946–1960).

The two brothers coached against each another in two games. In 1935, Amos Junior's Susquehanna Crusaders and Paul's Moravian Greyhounds played to a 0–0 tie in Bethlehem, Pennsylvania. The following year, Moravian beat Susquehanna, 26–16, in Selinsgrove, Pennsylvania. Ruth Stagg Lauren (1903–1978) earned a bachelor's degree at the University of Chicago in 1925. She married a Chicago businessman and spent the remainder of her life as a wife and homemaker. She maintained a private profile, and little else is known about her.

Recreation—Golf and Tennis

Stagg was an accomplished golfer and tennis player, and his hobbies revolved around maintaining his physical fitness. He and Stella played tennis every morning eight months of the year.[18] In 1899, he won the university's Handicap Tournament and became "the champion golfer of the University of Chicago."[19] When he was sixty-seven, the *Tribune* reported, "Many days he runs the five blocks from Bartlett Gym at a fast dog trot, and he can sprint a block when necessary with the speediest of his pupils." When he was sixty-nine, the *New York Times* reported that the senior Stagg defeated his son Paul in "several hard sets of tennis under a hot sun." Stagg told a reporter, "They've been retiring me every year for a long time, but as yet I have no plans for retirement. I'm going to coach as long as I'm in good health. Just now, I feel great."[20]

He frequently played golf at the Olympia Fields Country Club south of Chicago and the Pinehurst Resort in North Carolina when vacationing. His scores generally ranged from eighty-five to ninety-one, with an occasional round in the upper seventies.[21] A 1913 *New York Times* article reported that he barely lost during a playoff on the nineteenth green at a Pinehurst tournament.[22] Three years later, Stagg was recruited to become the first president of the Olympia Fields Country Club and played a significant role in its early growth. By 1916, Stagg was a national football celebrity, and the founders recruited him to help publicize the club and recruit new members. Board minutes record that Stagg was unanimously elected the club's first president on January 11, 1916, a position he held for four years. He first suggested the name "Olympia Fields" because of its beautiful location. "Stagg gave the club a patina of class, even when it was as much a pasture as golf course," club historian Tim Cronin wrote.

The club eventually hosted two PGA Championships, two U.S. Opens, and five Western Open championship tournaments. Real estate broker Charles M. Beach and his friends Charles Smalley and James Gardner founded the club in 1915 when the Chicago area already had fifty golf courses. "He [Beach] saw that most every club had a waiting list and that public courses were crammed beyond belief, and saw room for one more course," Cronin wrote.[23]

The club's 676 acres in a remote wooded location eventually contained four golf courses, a club house, swimming pool, and tennis courts. The Illinois Central Railroad built a station especially for the club and put on "fast trains" from the city at 1:15 and 4:00 to accommodate increasing demand for the twenty-eight-mile trip to the club.[24] That made it convenient for Stagg and other city residents to arrive quickly. "The fact that our club owns the property on both sides of the track for a considerable distance is an assurance that we never will be annoyed with switch tracks or manufacturing plants," Stagg wrote in the club magazine, *The Olympian*.[25]

The club grew rapidly in its first three years and reached 1,200 members. In recognition of his success as president, the board of governors in 1919 created a special "A.A. Stagg Membership," which granted him full lifetime membership, which was "at all times exempt from dues and assessments." The club's popularity resulted in rapid growth in the surrounding area and the establishment of the town of Olympia Fields, which was incorporated in 1927. Today, the Olympia Fields Country Club has an "A.A. Stagg Room" and hosts an annual "Stagg Tournament" for members and guests.

Stagg playing tennis on his 68th birthday in 1930. University of Chicago Photographic Archive, apf1-07864, Special Collections Research Center, University of Chicago Library.

During World War I, Chicago area golfers debated whether they should use caddies to carry their clubs, which they discussed at an executive committee meeting of the Chicago District Golf Association. The opposition to caddies originated because of the war and those who felt that young men should be encouraged to enlist in the military instead of holding jobs. Stagg agreed, but also hoped that the agitation for "caddyless" golf would dissipate the "prevailing idea" that it was not good form for a player to carry his own clubs. He told the executive committee, "I have made it a practice to carry my own clubs at Olympia Fields in order to break down the rather aristocratic idea that a player must hire a caddy or be looked upon as a violator of some unwritten code."[26]

Eating Habits

A clue to Stagg's longevity is seen in his eating habits. He was a fierce opponent of alcohol and tobacco and a proponent of simple diets. "Keep the hot dogs in the stands where they belong. I never had one in my life," he told his team captain, Andrew Wyant.[27] Walter A. Davenport, editor of *Collier's Weekly*, wrote Stagg in 1926 asking for his favorite food and how he prepared it. "[We] would like to publish your answers along with those of other notable citizens. The chief aim of such an intimate referendum is to discover, if it exists, the most popular American food," Davenport wrote. Stagg replied tersely, "I can say that bread and milk, or crackers and milk is my favorite food and, of course, it doesn't require any preparation. When I was less ancient and in active athletic training, I had a hearty appetite for steaks and roast beef. So far as I know, I am in good health, but I have found it advisable to eat comparatively little meat."[28] He tasted coffee once when

Stagg on a three-wheeled motorcycle he used to coach from the sidelines while battling sciatica, 1914. University of Chicago Photographic Archive, apf1-07824, Special Collections Research Center, University of Chicago Library.

he was a teenager. "At once I abjured it, and I have not drunk it since," he said.

In his 1893 book, *A Scientific and Practical Treatise on American Football*, Stagg listed these foods on the "proscribed list" for football players: "Pies, cakes, salads, all forms of pork, veal, rich dressing, fried food, ice-cream, confectionery, soda water, so called soft drinks (and it is needless to say drinks of a stronger nature), tea, coffee, and chocolate should be cheerfully and absolutely given up." He also wrote, "The practice of drinking water during the game is exceedingly bad and never should be permitted." That advice, like some of the "proscribed foods," is outdated today.[29]

In 1907 he told a reporter he had eaten "practically no meat" for two years and encouraged his Chicago athletes to adopt a vegetarian diet. "The Chicago director advocates a vegetable diet for championship athletes and as a result of his newly discovered vegetarianism, the Midway team may show ... the superior advantages to be gained by abstaining from meat," the reporter wrote. Stagg told him, "The diet should be one-tenth proteins, four-tenths fats, and one-half carbohydrates. This is not so complicated as it sounds."[30] Some academic studies since then have found a correlation between vegetarianism and longevity.

While Stagg was not a lifelong vegetarian, his meat consumption was always modest. "I have found it advisable to modify my diet around my 78th year," he wrote to his Yale classmate Henry L. Stimson, who was FDR's Secretary of War. "I have been eating less meat and more fruit and fruit juices in the last couple of years. I have eaten more salads than ever before in my life. At eighty, I started to drink a modest variety of buttermilk, which I had never cared for or been accustomed to use."[31] To celebrate his eighty-ninth birthday in 1951, he ate a meal consisting of pea soup, two ears of corn, peaches and milk.[32]

Health Issues

While he remained in overall good health throughout his life, Stagg suffered for years from a damaged sciatic nerve, which caused severe pain in his back and legs. Sciatica's primary symptom is pain caused by damage to the sciatic nerve that runs from the lower back down each leg, which spreads to the hips. Some seasons he was forced to coach from the sidelines using a three-wheel motorcycle and in later years an electric auto.

He irritated the sciatic nerve in spring 1903 while hitting flies to his baseball squad one afternoon. Shortly after the football season ended that year, he suffered from pneumonia, which for a time threatened to be fatal. On December 21, he left for a month-long trip in the warmer climate of New Mexico "in search of 'health and vigor'" according to a report in Chicago's *Inter Ocean* newspaper.[33] The newspaper reported that Stagg took the trip only after his physician and family persuaded him to do so. During his absence, the track team was coached by the former track star Fred Moloney.

He suffered a fall in 1904 that aggravated the sciatic nerve damage. While carrying his young son through ice and snow, "a heavy fall of snow in the morning had melted rapidly when the sun burst through and the streets were so sloppy that I had to carry the five-year-old boy ... from my home to the gym. Near the gym I took a run to clear a broad pool, landed on ice on the far side, and in a desperate effort to recover my balance, I threw certain bones in my back out of place," he wrote in *Touchdown!*

After the 1904 season, Stagg felt compelled to take additional time off. The *Chicago Tribune* said, "Coach Stagg has been a sick man for several weeks ... on the verge of a collapse." A week later, the *Tribune* reported, "Alarming reports concerning the condition of Coach Stagg last week, when it was thought ... he might be compelled to abandon further work with the football team this fall, if not for all time."[34] Two years later, the same newspaper reported that he wasn't able to coach the baseball or track teams in 1906 because of continued sciatica attacks.[35]

For years after the football season ended, at least until 1930, Stagg took extended rest periods at sanitariums in Arkansas, Colorado, Florida, Indiana, Michigan, New Mexico, North Carolina, and elsewhere. He wrote to a friend, "My trouble in March 1904 was caused by a sacroiliac joint strain which resulted in sciatica. It took several years to conquer it. In the effort I went to Mt. Clemens, Michigan, and took the baths. I also had a masseur work on me because I was crooked [all] over."[36] In a letter to another friend, he wrote, "Whenever I feel a slight inflammation of the sciatic nerve, I soak heavy bath towels in hot water and lay them in the small of my back."[37] The cost of these trips was considerable. Stella once recalled, "From 1903 to 1909, practically all our money went to get Lon over it."[38]

The sciatic nerve pain continued in 1910 forcing him to coach his football team from a three-wheel motorcycle driven by his son. In 1912, it forced him to take another leave of absence after the football season. These frequent absences were not without consequences. In 1913, an editorial in the *University of Chicago Magazine* called for Stagg to resign or be relieved of all duties in the athletic department except coaching football. Written by Dean James Linn, the editorial stated, "The daily newspapers have given wide publicity to the fact that for the second consecutive year, Coach Stagg has been forced to leave the university for the winter quarter in search of health.... For two years he has gone south to live an outdoor life and regain his health.... Isn't it about time that he be formally relieved himself or was relieved of all duties except football coaching?"[39]

Another recurrence came soon. "The sciatic attack returned in 1914, forcing me to coach the team from a motorcycle side car, in which I pop-popped about the field. Another recurrence in 1919 led the alumni to present me with an electric automobile, from which I coached that year's eleven."[40] When his sciatica recurred, he used that car on numerous occasions to move up and down the practice field. After he left Chicago, he donated the electric vehicle to the Chicago Museum of Science and Industry where it remains today.[41]

Whether Stagg was ever cured of sciatica is not known, but newspapers and archival records do not report recurrences after 1930 nor subsequent years at other universities. He continued to play tennis, mow his lawn, rake his yard, and do part-time coaching at Stockton College until he was ninety-eight.

Stagg cleaning his Baker electric car, which he used to coach during the 1919 season because of his sciatica injury. The car, a gift of the Alumni Association, remains today at the Chicago Museum of Science and Industry. University of Chicago Photographic Archive, apf1-07885, Special Collections Research Center, University of Chicago Library.

Social Causes—Fighting Tobacco

Stagg hated smoking long before science discovered its fatal consequences. On several occasions, he dismissed players from the team when
he caught them smoking. In one case, he caught a player smoking on the
train on the way to a game. He gave the player $10, told him to get off at the
next stop, take the next train home and not return to the team.[42] He was
also a public opponent of tobacco and cigarette smoking during the 1920s
when U.S. cigarette sales increased by almost 500 percent. A newspaper
article reported that the American Tobacco Company planned to spend $12
million to promote the sale of "Lucky Strike" cigarettes in 1929. Company
president George W. Hill told the newspaper: "The basis of our advertising appeal during the coming year will be ... directed primarily to men and
women interested in avoiding overweight to preserve a slender figure....
Moderate cigarette smoking, it will point out, replaces the desire for excessive sweets without impairing the appetite for healthy nourishing food."[43]
Stagg was not alone in his opposition. Notre Dame coach Knute Rockne
told the advisory council of the Boys and Girl Anti-Cigarette League that
American Tobacco Company offered him $2,000 to sign a testimonial that
Notre Dame athletes always used Lucky Strike cigarettes because they did
not hurt their wind. He refused.

Stagg was frequently asked to make public statements against smoking. In 1916, the managing editor of *The American Boy* wrote to ask
Stagg for a statement to discourage boys from smoking cigarettes. Stagg
replied, "There is no question but that cigarette smoking by boys is decidedly harmful.... It is very rarely that a boy amounts to anything in athletics who has the tobacco habit.... In all sports in which endurance is a
large factor, the tobacco user is a failure, and coaches and trainers therefore universally insist upon abstemiousness. We absolutely prohibit the
use of tobacco by the members of all athletic teams at the University of
Chicago."[44]

Asked by *The Instructor* magazine for a statement against smoking,
Stagg replied, "Only this spring I threw off the baseball team a young
man whom I caught smoking. He has since twice deeply apologized to
me and says he has 'learned his lesson.'"[45] *The Young Crusader* quoted
Stagg as saying, "A few years ago two of our athletes were dropped from
the baseball and track teams on the day of our most important contests
with the University of Michigan for smoking cigarettes on the sly." Stagg
said at the time he felt it would mean losing the game, which indeed
happened. He said Michigan's one-run victory in the baseball game was
because of a mistake made by the substitute for the player he expelled
from the game.[46]

The Rev. W.F. Baldwin, a missionary in Nome, Alaska, wrote and asked Stagg for "a general letter to … the Eskimo young men pointing out the evil of cigarette smoking and drinking booze."[47] Among other points, Stagg stated, "I have no doubt at all that smoking and drinking by a high school boy is distinctly damaging physically and morally.… Few people smoke without inhaling, which means that eight times as much of the nicotine poison goes into their systems, according to recent experiments by a German scientist. One of the leading physicians of Chicago has personally told me that since he started smoking, his pulse has gone up ten to twelve beats."[48]

Social Causes—Supporting Prohibition

The eighteenth amendment, which was ratified in 1919, took effect in 1920 and prohibited the manufacture, sale, and transportation of alcoholic beverages in the United States. Since it didn't prohibit the actual consumption of liquor, millions of Americans took advantage of illegal bootlegging and purchased liquor through secret drinking establishments, better known as "speakeasies." Prohibition contributed to the rise of gangsterism, personified by Al Capone, and violent turf battles between criminal gangs involved in illegal liquor sales.

Organized efforts to repeal Prohibition began in the mid–1920s with the rise of temperance organizations, which favored retaining it. Since Prohibition originated with an amendment to the U.S. Constitution, it could only be repealed with another amendment. Stagg, who said he had never consumed an alcoholic beverage, was recruited by temperance organizations in 1926 and 1930 to testify before House and Senate committees considering a constitutional amendment to overturn the ban against alcoholic beverages. Mrs. Lenna Lowe Yost, legislative director for the National Women's Christian Temperance Organization, invited Stagg to testify on behalf of their organization in 1926. He accepted her invitation and testified three weeks later.[49]

Stagg was one of twenty-seven witnesses during three weeks of Congressional testimony. Eleven witnesses, including Stagg, favored Prohibition, while sixteen were in favor of repealing it. Supporters of the repeal were mostly political leaders and public officials who understood the popularity of alcohol. Supporters of Prohibition were bishops and other religious leaders, a few public officials, a judge, and the governor of Pennsylvania.

In a three-page typed statement, Stagg described the effect of alcohol abuse in the poor neighborhood where he grew up in West Orange, New

Jersey. He said there were about a dozen families in his neighborhood. "I saw at least nine of the heads of those families drunk on various occasions. It was a regular thing on Saturday nights and not infrequently in mid-week for several of our neighbors to get drunk." These drunk men occasionally beat their wives and children, he said.

He went on to describe the effects of alcohol abuse in his Chicago neighborhood. Before Prohibition, he said, "I have seen scores and scores of drunken men staggering along the street." Since Prohibition, "the number of drunken men I have happened to see on Fifty-Fifth street you could count on the fingers of one hand." Finally, he said he has consulted with some of Chicago's "leading social workers" who all claimed there has been a "tremendous gain in social conditions" and "economic conditions have greatly improved as a result of people not spending money on drink."[50]

The *New York Times* reported on the hearings, saying, "Probably there has never been another hearing in either house of Congress quite like the one that ended a week ago yesterday. Certainly, there has never been another one that exceeded it in the intensity that animated the two sides of this bitter all-American controversy."[51]

Stagg testified again before the House Judiciary Committee on March 12, 1930. He said, "Since Prohibition has been put into effect, hundreds of thousands more children have had had a fairer start in life than before, than existed in pre-prohibition days. I can say with absolute confidence that it is not a problem at the University of Chicago, that only a very small percentage of the students drink at all." He was immediately challenged by some Chicago students. Dexter Masters, editor of the campus humor magazine *Phoenix,* told the *New York Times* that about 40 percent of the men drank and "women drink in almost the same proportion." John Hardin, news editor of the *Daily Maroon,* said several students had been dismissed and some fraternities had their social privileges revoked because of campus drinking problems.[52]

The only other recorded instance of Stagg's political involvement did not come until thirty years later in 1958 when he endorsed California's "Proposition 3," which passed. Three-fourths of the $200 million bond referendum supported the expansion of state universities, while one fourth went to mental hospital and prison expansion.[53] As a public figure, Stagg usually kept his political views to himself. The only time he ever endorsed a political candidate was in 1912 when he was an elector to the Progressive Party convention that nominated Theodore Roosevelt for an unsuccessful third term. There is no other record that he expressed any political views except for his opposition to the repeal of Prohibition.

Views on Race

Sol Butler, sports editor of the *Chicago Bee*, wrote Stagg in 1926 for the purpose of "making an inquiry of prominent coaches and distinguished athletes on the relation of race and color to sports." Butler described the *Chicago Bee* as "the second-largest colored newspaper in America." He asked Stagg to answer three questions:

1. Do you believe in mixed games? By mixed games, we mean two things—a. Do you believe that a white team should play against a colored team? b. Do you favor white and colored members on the same team?
2. Do you think Negroes make as good athletes as whites? If inferior or superior, give your reasons.
3. Do you favor colored athletes in some games but not in others? If so, what games? For instance, it is customary to see an occasional colored member of a football or track team but seldom on the baseball, basketball, boating, boxing and tennis teams.[54]

In answering the first question, Stagg said that he welcomed the presence of "colored athletes" on athletic teams, but "a good many hotels will not rent rooms to colored boys. In the same way, most hotels object to colored boys eating in the dining room…. Most times it is necessary to make special arrangements for their accommodations." Stagg said he thought other team members were "very fair and decent in their treatment of a colored boy who is a member of their team."

In answering the second and third questions, Stagg replied, "It is clearly demonstrated that in track and field athletics colored men are splendid athletes. Occasionally, one finds a colored athlete who is a wonderful player in football, but they are less likely to be good in that sport, where fearlessness, aggressiveness, and dogged determination played a large part in their selection of positions." He was obviously wrong but admitted that the "number of colored boys who have tried for our teams has been comparatively very small."[55]

This was the situation at the University of Chicago in the 1920s when there were no athletic scholarships, and few athletes of any race could afford the university's high tuition. In the research for this book, only one Chicago athlete—track star Henry Binga Dismond—was identified as Black. There may have been more since Stagg told the sports editor, "Occasionally, one finds a colored athlete who is a wonderful player in football" and "In track and field athletics colored men are splendid athletes." This research found no evidence that Stagg was prejudiced against minorities. He certainly favored women's athletics, hired women faculty members for his department, and organized women's teams in several sports soon after he arrived in Chicago.

Religion

Although his father didn't attend church, Stagg's mother took the children to Sunday School at First Presbyterian Church in West Orange. Stagg later wrote, "Through the efforts of my Sunday School teacher in presenting God's truth to a careless, indifferent, mischievous boy, I decided to confess Christ before the world." He joined the church and made a profession of faith on May 23, 1877. This decision, more than anything, motivated Stagg to aspire to attend college. "How the joy in my newborn faith ... brought about a spirit of earnestness and consecration which bade me strive to get an education that I might serve him better.... Deep down in the darkest corners of my heart I hid the yearning perhaps I might go to college and afterwards become a minister," he wrote in a letter.[56]

He was influenced to enter the Presbyterian ministry by a young lady named Grace Livingston, who was the daughter of the church's pastor. He later described her as "one of the loveliest and most zealous Christian girls that it has ever been my good fortune to meet.... She encouraged me in my aspiration for the ministry and urged that.... I go to college. I was further encouraged by my older sister, Pauline," Stagg wrote.[57]

As general secretary of the Yale YMCA, he gave frequent talks on "The Christian Athlete" and spoke at YMCA meetings, Bible studies, and other Christian events. But he was never denominationally or theologically rigid. While studying at Exeter, he attended Episcopal and Congregational churches. During his University of Chicago years, he and his family were members of Hyde Park Baptist Church. He made generous annual financial pledges, served on the board of deacons, finance committee, and "Welcoming Committee."[58] After the Stagg family moved to California, they joined the Stockton Methodist Church. He told a newspaper reporter, "I was born and reared a strict Presbyterian. I changed to a Baptist without immersion. I attend a Methodist church today because I like the breadth of views of the pastor. I could never be a stickler for meaningless, rigid doctrine."[59] From its earliest days, the Hyde Park Church was more liberal than most Baptist churches, and William Rainey Harper, the first University of Chicago president, and other faculty members and administrators were members.

Writing to his former Hyde Park Baptist pastor in 1943, Stagg said, "Through you and other great teachers, we have understood that there are no denominations in heaven. That is a source of comfort to the Stagg family since the father and mother are Methodists, Alonzo and Arvilla are Lutherans, Ruth and Alton are Baptists, and Paul and Virginia are Congregationalists."[60]

Stagg received a letter in 1929 from the secretary of the Bible Guild in New York asking about his favorite Bible verses. She said, "The Bible Guild is collecting the opinions of well-known Americans on the Bible passages that have given them the greatest personal help and inspiration," adding that the Guild planned to publish them "to stimulate Bible reading especially among those who may not realize its value."[61]

Stagg filled out the enclosed form listing Ecclesiastes 9:10 ("Whatever thy hand findeth to do, do it with thy might"); Matthew 7:12 ("All things therefore whatsoever ye would that men should do unto you, even so do ye also unto them: for this is the law and the prophets"); and John 14:27 ("Peace I leave with you; my peace I give unto you; not as the world giveth, give I unto you. Let not your heart be troubled, neither let it be afraid"). He added this explanation: "These three verses have come most often into my mind and have influenced my life … more than any other single ones," he told her.[62]

Stagg was generous in making donations to needy causes and people but could not fulfill every request. "My heart is willing, but family conditions say otherwise," he responded to one letter in 1928. "For many years I have given away over one fourth of my salary. There is an unfortunate situation in two branches of my family which throws a heavy burden on me. This involves several elderly people. I want to do something, so I am going to ask you to let me off with a check for $25, which is heretofore enclosed."[63] That is approximately $375 in today's currency.

Stagg's active involvement with his family, current and former players, Chicago alumni, church activities, golfing, social causes, and Yale and Exeter alumni associations gave him a vast network of thousands of friends and acquaintances. Consequently, he is not an easy man to write about. If you insert "Amos Alonzo Stagg" into newspapers.com, a proprietary database of more than 1,000 newspapers, the search returns 135,879 articles. Putting it into a Google search yields 386,000 results. Those totals do not include the 339 boxes of Stagg archival documents at the University of Chicago. Discovering the inner man and finding a narrative to his life is a compelling challenge. I will say he possessed an unquenchable drive to achieve and prove himself. He grew up in a large, poverty-stricken family, and his ambition to outshine his peers ran throughout his life and helped him sustain a remarkable, if sometimes controversial, coaching career. This story begins with the obstacles he overcame simply to graduate from high school four years later than most of his peers.

Growing Up in West Orange, 1862–1883

The children had to help; I can hardly remember a time as a boy when I did not have chores to do.—Amos Alonzo Stagg

When Amos Alonzo Stagg was born on August 16, 1862, Abraham Lincoln was president, the Civil War was raging, Stonewall Jackson was marching on Manassas, and the average male lifespan was forty years. College football was unknown. When Stagg died on March 17, 1965, Lyndon Johnson was in the White House, the Civil Rights Movement was raging, and Martin Luther King, Jr., was preparing to lead the fifty-four-mile Selma to Montgomery march. During Stagg's 102 years, telephones, electric light bulbs, phonographs, automobiles, airplanes, radios, motion pictures, and televisions were invented, and twenty men served as president of the United States.

Stagg was born in West Orange, New Jersey, about eight miles west of Newark. The family's two-story home at 384 Valley Road was on land purchased by their ancestors two centuries earlier. His father, Amos Lindsley Stagg, was a shoe cobbler who maintained his business at his house. "Father had his little shoe shop at the right side of his house.... Father made boots and shoes for people and repaired shoes and heels," Stagg wrote.[1]

"I was sixth in number of the five girls and three boys born into our family. There being so many mouths to feed, my father had a very hard time for a number of years.... At times there was little in the house to eat," he wrote in an unpublished autobiography, *Stagg of Yale*.[2] Stagg's older siblings included Warren Burson (b. March 22, 1848); George Randolph (b. October 26, 1850); Sara Ella (b. February 9, 1853); Harriet Erma (b. December 1, 1855); and Pauline Hannah (b. June 25, 1859). His younger siblings included Mary Ida (March 2, 1865); and Maurice F. (b. November 16, 1867).[3]

In an 1894 letter, Stagg described his parents: "Mother had all the sweet, womanly qualities, which go to make up an ideal mother. Father was strong physically and mentally and was a veritable Brutus for right and justice…. My father gave strength and energy to the children, and my mother gave sweetness and gentleness to their dispositions." He described his mother, Eunice Pierson Stagg, as a "midget in size" who weighed only eighty pounds.[4]

Harvesting Salt in the Meadowlands

For eight summers, Stagg, his father, and brother used scythes to cut and harvest salt hay (a species of cordgrass native to the Atlantic coast) in an area known as the New Jersey Meadowlands. Wading through the water, Stagg described the work as brutal: "The cut hay had to be raised above tidewater. When it got wet in the cocks, we would run long, smooth black walnut poles beneath the cock and carry the heavy wet hay to piling. There was no letting go of the poles to swipe at the mosquitos." He said the mosquitos "bred by billions in those salt meadows nine miles long and three miles wide and stung our half-naked bodies maddingly."[5] He also cleaned stoves to earn extra money and carried out thousands of buckets of ashes for neighbors.[6] The money that Stagg and his brother earned went to help support their family, not for personal spending money.

Stagg also helped maintain a large garden where his family grew more than a dozen vegetables that provided "a large and vital part of our living," he said. "I acquired a thorough knowledge of gardening and was able to plant and take care of the garden quite well. From fifteen to twenty-one, I helped my father at all kinds of farm work."[7] Stagg said in 1946: "Our home life had to be one of cooperation. The children had to help; I can hardly remember a time as a boy when I did not have chores to do in connection with bringing water from the well, chopping wood, carrying coal, weeding the garden, digging, hoeing, and assisting in the planting."[8]

While attending grade school in West Orange in a one-room schoolhouse, he developed an early love for sports. One of the first sporting matches Stagg saw was a wrestling match at the Orange ballpark. He was awed by the massive muscles of the wrestlers and became determined to develop his physical strength. He carried buckets of coal to strengthen his shoulders and arms and ran every day to and from the school, which was about three-fourths of a mile each way.[9]

Stagg developed a disgust for alcohol from his early surroundings. He wrote in his autobiography about the men in his neighborhood: "In bad luck, men drowned their sorrows at the bar; in good luck they celebrated there. When too warm, they drank; when too cold, they did likewise. In high spirits they let off steam at the saloon; when bored, they bought high spirits from the bartender. We saw our drama first-hand and in the raw from the saloon, and the show was continuous."[10]

Introduction to Baseball

He started playing baseball around age thirteen and later recalled, "To develop my wind, I ran to and from school until I would rather run than walk. I swam and skated on a pond where the Edison plant now stands. I played first-hand base and third-hand base and was the treasurer of the gang when we saved our scant pennies to buy a league baseball." He added, "It took us kids many months to accumulate $1.25 to buy a ... baseball. I was treasurer of the club known as 'the Green Leaves.' When we finally reached our goal, our joy knew no bounds. I recall my contribution was making and selling kites at one and two cents each. Kite flying was my favorite pastime during the summer months."[11]

Although he played first base, he really wanted to pitch. He told a story about learning to pitch a curve ball: "I had been trying to pitch a curve ball which then was just coming into vogue. I was doing my practicing with my cousin in the rear of his yard, and the day I first accomplished the curve, I recall running pell mell to my mother in the kitchen and yelling, 'I've got it, I've got it.' She said, 'Got what?' I said, 'the curve.' 'Oh,' mother said, evidently relieved."[12]

When Stagg was seven in 1869, Princeton and Rutgers played the first game of collegiate football. In its early years football resembled British rugby, from which American football gradually evolved. "There was no such thing as football as it is known today," he once said. "Each spring my father bought two shotes [young pigs] and fattened them until November slaughtering. Each autumn I'd beg for the bladders and we'd inflate them by blowing through a quill." Kicking these real "pigskins" was his early introduction to the sport that was first known as "foot ball" and eventually "football."[13]

Stagg's behavior wasn't perfect in grade school. He recalled, "I was bad in school, and Miss Coburn sent me home with a note to my father." Using a leather strap from his shoe repair shop, his father "gave me a good strapping ... on the seat of my pants. Each blow hurt painfully, and I bawled at the top of my voice." He said the spanking "cured me" and his father never had to punish him again.[14]

Stagg's grades at St. Mark's, a middle school in West Orange, were high. When he was fifteen, his fall 1879 report card showed an average grade for all subjects of 97 percent; his spring 1880 report card showed a 99 percent average. But because of frequent interruptions to work, he was eighteen before he finished middle school. West Orange did not have a high school, so attending the neighboring Orange High School required a $60 annual tuition even though the Stagg family's back fence sat on the dividing line between Orange and West Orange.[15]

"I then went to my father and told him of my yearning to get a better education (I did not speak to him of going to college then)." Stagg asked his father if he could still live at home without having to pay for room and board so he could work and earn the $60 yearly tuition. His father consented. "I then worked early and late, often times from five am to eleven and twelve pm filling in my hours with every kind of work I could get to earn my schooling."[16] He continued to play for the sandlot team calling themselves the "Green Leaves" and then earned a spot as a pitcher on the Orange High baseball team "by virtue of my small stock of curves."[17]

High School Graduation

After finishing in three years, Stagg graduated from Orange High in 1883 at age twenty-one in a class of four. That fall he watched his first football game, Princeton versus Yale at Manhattan Field in New York City. "I had no real expectation as yet of being in college the following year, and no certainty it would be Yale if I did go," Stagg wrote.[18] The assistant principal at Orange High, Alton H. Sherman, was a Yale graduate who suggested to Stagg that he was sufficiently intelligent and motivated to attend college. Stagg didn't think he could because he was so poor. Sherman encouraged him to consider it because he knew it was possible for students to work their way through college with scholarships and part-time jobs. Stagg said Sherman "gave me a great deal of encouragement and caused me to dream more of the possibilities of my going [to college], and I began to shape my studies with that view in mind."[19] Amos Stagg, Jr., said in a 1985 interview, "Going to college seemed like going to the moon in those days; about one to two percent of high school students went to college."[20]

Stagg began to investigate colleges and wrote to Noah Porter, the president of Yale, inquiring if there was any possibility of financial aid. Porter replied in a handwritten letter: "To good scholars the college has given from the Ellsworth Fund of $175 a year. Beyond this the college can do little or nothing, but opportunities for self-help present themselves and are soon discovered by those who keep their eyes open to discern them."[21] But Stagg found a copy of Yale's entrance examination and quickly realized he had no chance of passing it. The June 1884 entrance exam contained sections about Greek, Latin, and mathematics. Four questions about Greek history included:

1. Form a chronological table about key events in the history of Athens.

2. What were the chief Greek colonies west of Greece?

3. Give the dates, consequences, and chief parties of the battles of Chaeronea, Leuctra, and Salamis.

4. What were the principal causes and consequences of the Peloponnesian War? When and where under whose leadership was it begun? When and from what cause was it ended?

The math section asked the applicant:

1. To bisect a rectilinear angle, that is, to divide it into two equal angles.

2. Is a right-angled triangle the square which is described on the side subtending the right angle, equal to the squares described on the sides which contain the right angle?

3. If two isosceles triangles are on the same base, will the straight line joining their vertices … bisect the base at right angles?

4. AB and AC are any two straight lines meeting at A; through any point P draw a straight line meeting them at E and F, such as AE may be equal to AF.

After reading the exam, Stagg again felt discouraged. However, his friend George Gill told him about the special college preparatory program at Phillips Exeter Academy in New Hampshire. Gill was the son of the mayor of Orange and had entered Phillips Exeter in the fall of 1883. The one-year program with courses in Latin, math, history, and English prepared students for the intimidating entrance exams at Yale and other prestigious schools. Gill wrote and told him the school granted tuition scholarships to many students based on need. "He gave me a glowing account of the life at Exeter and told me of other young men who were working their way at that school and urged my trying; I determined to go back with him after Christmas time."[22]

Stagg's father encouraged him to go to Exeter, but his mother "could not hear of such a thing…. She pictured to herself all the evil which would befall her son and sought me most earnestly and tearfully not to go."[23] With his father's support and a grieving mother, however, Stagg left home on a cold January morning in 1884 and boarded a train for Exeter, New Hampshire.

3

Exeter and Yale, 1884–1890

No college man of that time would hesitate to name Stagg as the most popular college man in America. Not only was he the most popular in his own college, but he was disproportionately popular in other colleges. —George W. Woodruff, Yale classmate

For his first twenty-one years, Amos Stagg never spent a night away from home nor traveled farther than New York City.[1] He didn't even have proper winter clothing to wear at Exeter. "Gill gave me one of his suits. It cost my stubborn pride a wrench to take it. Anyway, I would accept no more favors, and I leaned backward in that determination." Stagg even refused to accept a cash gift from his minister. "When I came to say good-bye to Doctor Storrs, my minister, I saw that something was hidden in the hand he offered. I suspected, and rightly, that was a bill, and I shook his other hand."[2]

Stagg had saved $21, which he took to Exeter to begin the spring semester. He rented a poorly heated attic room, which he shared with roommates. For three months during a grueling winter, he barely survived and lived only on his savings. In the evenings, he wrapped himself in blankets from his bed to keep warm. He walked to Greek, Latin, and math classes without a heavy overcoat. He lived on a diet of crackers, stale bread, and milk that cost three cents a quart. He cut back on his expenses and recorded every cent in a small pocket memorandum. Stagg said he spent just sixteen cents for his daily rations (about $4 in today's money). "I made my luncheon and supper on one pound of soda crackers that cost me five cents. Similarly, that was my diet for my first two meals at Yale. Later I found that stale bread went further and tasted as well. That and milk at three cents a quart was the food on which I boned Latin, Greek, and mathematics for three months."

Exeter Academy

Stagg's austere lifestyle made him feel out-of-place among his mostly affluent classmates. Phillips Exeter Academy in Exeter, New Hampshire,

31

was established in 1781 by John Phillips, the son of a Presbyterian minister, who made his fortune as a merchant and banker. The academy historically educated the children of upper-class New England families. The academy's 1884 handbook said that the purpose of the instructors was to "lead pupils to cultivate self-control, truthfulness, a right sense of honor, and an interest in the pursuit of the moral atmosphere of the school. Boys whose influence is felt to be injurious to good scholarship or good morals will be removed from the school." However, the school was generous in awarding tuition grants based on need, proficiency, or general merit.[3]

Eventually he found a job sweeping out the chapel for fifty cents a week. It wasn't much, but it slowed the drain from his meager savings. One afternoon, Professor Faulhaber, the German teacher, stopped him after class and asked if he was interested in a job. Faulhaber told him that his home required numerous chores like sweeping, cleaning, and chopping wood. When Stagg said yes, Faulhaber offered him the job in exchange for a free room. The job along with his chapel pay covered living expenses and enabled him to save for the next semester's tuition.

With the extra income, Stagg found time to try out for the Exeter baseball team. The school had no professional coach, so the team was managed by a student "tutor" who was also the captain. While his teammates quickly recognized Stagg's pitching ability, the captain put Stagg in the outfield. The

The Exeter baseball team, 1884. Jacketless Stagg is in the top row, upper right. University of Chicago Photographic Archive, apf1-07861, Special Collections Research Center, University of Chicago Library.

captain, who also pitched, enjoyed the attention and accolades of pitching and didn't want to yield the position to anyone else. But the team was losing every game, and team members revolted and demanded that the pitcher-coach quit or be fired. Stagg was chosen by his teammates as the new captain and pitcher for the final three games of the season. Stagg's steady arm and fast ball turned the team around and won the last three games.

His baseball reputation spread quickly. In the summer of 1884, the president of the Dartmouth Athletic Association wrote and invited Stagg to enroll and play baseball, saying: "There is no first-class college in New England where a man can get along on less money. A large number of fellows pay their own way, receiving of course considerable aid in the way of scholarships."[4] W.N. Cragin, president of the Dartmouth Baseball Association, also wrote Stagg the same summer, saying, "I have taken the first opportunity to write you with the view of persuading you to come to Dartmouth if it can be done. We already have an excellent catcher in view and shall probably get him, but we are as yet unprovided with a pitcher. I think we could guarantee you a place on our team as a pitcher."[5]

Since Dartmouth had no divinity school, Stagg stuck to his goal of studying for the ministry at Yale. He had enjoyed his six months at Exeter. He wrote his sister, Ida, saying, "I feel more like a man and have more self-reliance now that I have left my home. Exeter has done a great deal toward rounding and filling out in me the qualities that every mature person ought to have."[6] He wrote a friend, "Those six months were probably the most trying in my whole life, and they stand out strongly in my memory for the lessons they taught me of initiative, perseverance, and independence."[7]

Yale Freshman Year

Beginning in high school, Stagg had his heart set on studying for the ministry at Yale. Besides its divinity school, he later revealed another reason he chose Yale. "I had once longed to go to Princeton, but [a teacher] told me to go to Yale because he thought there the boys would not look down on me if I had to work my way, and that they would lend me a helping hand.... I never remember the time when I felt that any member of the class felt that I wasn't just as good as he was."[8] At twenty-two, Stagg was considerably older and poorer than most of his 142 freshmen classmates. He arrived in New Haven on June 1, 1884, with $32 to his name. He took the entrance exam shortly after that and passed. But like Exeter, he lived on a starvation diet that could not sustain him long. The tuition was $50 a term, and Stagg received a $20.20 credit because he was a future divinity student.

He wrote about his first semester: "I found an unheated garret room for which I paid one dollar a week. Not yet having found work, I allowed myself five cents for breakfast, ten cents for the noon meal, and five cents for supper. It was a starvation diet, and I fell ill for the first time in my life. Chills and fever overtook me on the way to class. There was no college hospital and Jesse Lazier … led me to his room, put me in bed and called a doctor. The doctor was not long in recognizing undernourishment and ordered me to drop my nickel-and-dime meal nonsense."[9]

The doctor asked what kind of food he was living on, and Stagg told him about his diet of crackers, milk, and stale bread. The doctor said he had a form of scurvy and ordered him to eat healthier meals. He pulled two dollars from his pocket and gave it to Stagg, who reluctantly accepted it but promised to repay it.[10] Some friends helped him get a job in an eating club that helped tremendously. Three members of that Yale eating club included his friend, George Gill from West Orange; William H. Seward III, grandson of Lincoln's secretary of State; and Henry L. Stimson, who became a lifetime friend and cabinet secretary in the Taft, Hoover, FDR, and Truman administrations. Life at Yale was starting to look up.[11]

Playing Baseball

Stagg was relatively small and weighed about 160 pounds. One newspaper described him this way: "He is scarcely over five feet, six inches in height, but a more muscular frame than his would be difficult to find, even among professional athletes of the country … his body is as hard as a rock, and when clad in uniform, he presents the perfect picture of a middle-weight gymnast."[12] With extra jobs and more free time, Stagg joined the Yale baseball team and was soon elected president of the Freshman Baseball Association. Playing third base, he finished the year with a 347 percent batting average and 806 percent field average. But teammates soon discovered his pitching ability. During his sophomore year, he pitched and won nine games and lost two, beating both Harvard and Princeton twice.

Thanks to his pitching, Yale won five consecutive championships from 1886 to 1890. He won thirty-four games, lost eight, and tied one, striking out 241 batters and allowing 262 hits. Against chief rivals Harvard and Princeton, he beat Harvard fifteen times and lost four, and defeated Princeton fourteen times and lost three. On May 26, 1888, he struck out twenty Princeton batters in a game and only allowed two hits. The *New York Times* reported on this game: "Stagg eclipsed all his former brilliant feats on the diamond today…. He not only pitched so effectively as to enable his opponents to bat the ball safely but twice, but he made the remarkable record of twenty strike-outs…. Stagg's performance has never been equaled between teams of equal quality, and it will go on record as one of the most memorable of intercollegiate games."[13]

President Grover Cleveland's wife, Frances, attended this game. Although Cleveland nor his wife were Princeton alumni, they had a home in Princeton, and the former president later became a Princeton trustee. Mrs. Cleveland wore the orange and black colors of Princeton to the game, which infuriated Stagg and motivated him to pitch one of his best games. In *Touchdown!* he wrote, "Mrs. Cleveland entered the grandstand wearing the orange and black of Princeton. As wife of the President of the United States, it seemed to me that she should have been neutral in word and deed … and I pitched my arm off in resentment."[14]

A month later, Stagg pitched the Yale baseball team to its third consecutive conference championship with a win over Harvard in a game attended by 12,000 fans. The *Yale Daily News* reported, "New Haven tonight is the scene of hilarious joy, bands are playing, rockets ascending, and cannon crackers booming. By a score of 5 to 3 Yale's ball nine defeated Harvard thus winning the championship for the third consecutive year…. Stagg was the recipient of great honors, and while he was not at his best, he deserved all he got, which were a ride on the shoulders of all his friends, a hearty three cheers, and a floral piece representing a baseball with 1888 on it in flowers."[15]

Stagg (right) and Yale catcher Jesse Dann. University of Chicago Photographic Archive, apf1-07991, Special Collections Research Center, University of Chicago Library.

Stagg had an overactive conscience at times, especially during his early years. When he spoke to a Christian association meeting in Boston, Stagg reported that while playing a game against Harvard, the umpire declared him "not out" when he believed he should have been called "out." His conscience told him that the decision was wrong, so the next time he came to the plate he purposely struck out. The *Boston Globe* questioned the wisdom of this decision: "The question arises: was it right for him thus to hazard the fortunes of his side?"[16] That would be a good discussion question for an ethics class.

While he was baseball captain, Stagg invented a sliding apparatus that helped the Yale team lead the league in stolen bases in 1888 and 1889. Until then, players stole bases by sliding head-first, which was risky and dangerous. "I rigged up an apparatus of my own design to improve our sliding.... The men ran, dived, and slid along this device to learn how to avoid ripping themselves open," Stagg wrote. He also had the front side of baseball pants quilted to avoid abrasions from sliding.[17] A *Yale Courant* editorial commented that these improvements had "elicited the praise of expert professionals" and Stagg deserved special recognition: "To the captain in particular to whom we are indebted for the innovations that led to this new device."[18]

Stagg played Yale baseball for six years—four as an undergraduate and two as a graduate and divinity school student. He pitched on five championship teams and was elected team captain. Author and Yale English professor, William Lyon Phelps, called Stagg the greatest college pitcher that Yale and the country had ever seen. Phelps said he never saw "a man with such a memory of the weaknesses of the men he faced."[19] Six National League teams offered Stagg a pitching contract. Frederick Stearns, president of the Detroit team, wrote Stagg, saying "Would you play ball professionally provided the inducement was a sufficient one, and would you sign a Detroit contact for the remainder of the season, or would you sign a contract for the two summer months until your college opens again?"[20] Jim O'Rourke of the New York Nationals wrote and offered him $4,200 for a three-month season, saying, "Your real friends are urging their every effort to have you better your financial condition by accepting the advantages which the present opportunity presents."[21]

In the nineteenth century, a pro baseball career was not held in high esteem. H.B. Jewett, a friend of Stagg's, wrote to advise him against accepting any baseball offer: "I felt it my duty as a man somewhat your senior in years and larger experience in life to kindly enter my protest against your accepting any of them. It is a question whether the profession is an honorable one or not ... but as a whole, I think it is not considered reputable. With your education and many fine traits of character something nobler must certainly be in store for you."[22]

Stagg later commented, "I never did a wiser thing than refusing the $4,200 a season offered me by the New York Nationals in the 1880s when that sum just about represented the national wealth to me. If it is money the college man wants, he ought to be able to make more on a real job than by peddling a physical skill."[23] He said he refused the offer for two reasons: loyalty to Yale and the "character" of professional baseball:

> The professionals of [that] day were a hard-bitten lot, about whom grouped hangers-on, men, and women, who were worse. There was a bar in every park, and the whole tone of the game was smelly. I have never regretted my decision. I managed to get along financially. I have never borrowed a penny from an individual in my life, nor have I bought an article on the installment plan.... I have never capitalized on my name because I did not like the feel of it.[24]

Stagg's baseball success at Yale earned him national fame. G.W. Woodruff, Stagg's Yale teammate and later a successful football coach at the University of Pennsylvania, wrote of Stagg: "No college man of that time would hesitate to name Stagg as the most popular college man in America. Not only was he the most popular in his own college, but he was disproportionately popular in other colleges.... Mr. Stagg's hold of the public attention was so remarkable that it was inexplicable." Woodruff said any boy might not be able to tell you who the president of the United States was, "but he could tell you who was the pitcher of the Yale baseball nine."[25]

Playing Football

Yale's football team was a member of the Intercollegiate Football Association, which consisted of Yale, Princeton, Harvard, and Columbia. Yale began its winning football tradition years before Stagg arrived. Its first team played in 1872 three years after the first college game between Rutgers and Princeton. Between 1872 and 1900, Yale won 198 games and lost only nine. Until 1915, Yale's teams never had a losing season. The legendary Michigan football coach Fielding Yost (1871–1946) once said, "Yale was the first to have the true feel of the game, a game which means spirit, body contact, and team play, all the finest elements of competition. Of course, many others have come along since, but it was Yale that set the earlier pace."[26]

When their freshman year began, Stagg and his high school classmate, George Gill, planned to try out for the rowing team. "Gill was disposed to the [rowing] crew, and where Gill went, I was inclined to go.... We were

Yale's 1888 championship football team. Stagg is in the second row, far left. University of Chicago Photographic Archive, apf1-07804, Special Collections Research Center, University of Chicago Library.

on our way down Chapel Street to the boathouse when we met a friend of Gill's, a football partisan, who argued us into turning back and ... reporting for football. I had no opinion. I knew nothing of either sport," Stagg said.[27] He played on the freshman team in 1884 and made the varsity team in 1885. However, he sat out on football during his junior and senior years because the baseball team captain asked him not to play to avoid the risk of injuring his pitching arm.

He re-joined the football team in the fall of 1888 in divinity school where he played right or left end. The 1888 team earned the consensus national champion recognition with a perfect 14–0 record, outscoring opponents 704–0. That season included three wins against Wesleyan by the scores of 76–0, 46–0, and 105–0. Other opponents included Amherst (two wins, 39–0, 70–0), MIT (68–0), Penn (two wins, 34–0 and 58–0), Princeton (10–0), Rutgers (65–0), Stevens (69–0), and Williams (30–0). In its closest game of the season, it defeated Harvard, 6–0. The Yale team did almost as well in 1889, finishing with a 15–1 record and 665 points against its opponents' thirty-one points.[28]

Table 2: 1888 and 1889 Yale Football Seasons

1888			1889		
Team Played	*Yale*	*Opp*	*Team Played*	*Yale*	*Opp*
Wesleyan	76	0	Wesleyan	38	0
Rutgers	65	0	Wesleyan	63	5
Pennsylvania	34	0	Williams	36	0
Wesleyan	46	0	Cornell	60	6
Amherst	39	0	Amherst	42	0
Williams	30	0	Trinity	64	0
M.I.T.	68	0	Columbia	62	0
Stevens Institute	69	0	Pennsylvania	22	10
Pennsylvania	58	0	Stevens Institute	30	0
Crescent A.C.	28	0	Crescent A.C.	18	0
Amherst	70	0	Cornell	70	0
Wesleyan	105	0	Amherst	32	0
Princeton	10	0	Williams	70	0
Harvard	6	0	Wesleyan	52	0
TOTAL POINTS	704	0	Harvard	6	0
SEASON RECORD	14–0		Princeton	0	10
			TOTAL POINTS	665	31
			SEASON RECORD	15–1	
Source: John D. McCallum, Ivy League Football Since 1872 *(Stein and Day, 1977).*					

The 1888 team captain was William H. "Pa" Corbin, who played center. The ends were Stagg and Frederic C. Wallace; the tackles, William C. Rhodes and Charles Gill; the guards, William Heffelfinger and George W. Woodruff. William C. Wurtenberg was the quarterback; Lee McClung and William Graves, halfbacks; and William T. Bull, fullback. William W. "Pudge" Heffelfinger became Stagg's best-known teammate from the 1888 and 1889 teams. He went on to become football coach at the University of Minnesota from 1895 to 1910. Heffelfinger said of Stagg, "[He] was one of the greatest athletes I've ever known. As a pitcher, he could have made the big leagues in a breeze…. In addition to being a great pitcher and a great football end, he had a great force of character we all respected."[29]

In the 1880s, football teams wore no head protection. Full-sleeved canvas jackets were laced tightly up to the neck. They wore padded moleskin pants with stockings that reached the knees. Stagg developed the idea of inserting a sponge into each pant leg to create more knee protection. He practiced falling on a football twenty to thirty times a day to become proficient in recovering fumbles. The Yale practice field was more than a mile from campus, so the team traveled to and from the field in a horse-drawn wagon. Instead of riding in the wagon, Stagg ran alongside the wagon to develop his leg strength and endurance.[30] Stagg said in *Touchdown!* that he never suffered any football injuries except for a "perpetually skinned nose, due to the sandpaper-like surface of canvas jackets, bruised knees, and sore arms."

During football's early years, scoring was quite different from today. In 1883, a touchdown earned only two points, while what is now known as a field goal counted for five points. A kick over the goal post after a touchdown counted for four. Consequently, a team's main incentive for scoring a two-point touchdown was the opportunity to kick afterwards for four points. In 1884, the value of a touchdown doubled to four points, to five points in 1898 and finally to six points in 1912. The kick after a touchdown went from four to two in 1884 and one in 1898. Meanwhile, the value of a field goal fell from five to four points in 1904 and then to three in 1909, where it remains today.[31]

Table 3: Numerical Values of Scoring Plays in College Football, 1883–1912

Year	Touchdown	Point after*	Field goal*	Safety
1883	2	4	5	1
1884	4	2	5	2
1898	5	1	5	2
1904	5	1	4	2
1909	5	1	3	2
1912	6	1	3	2

*The point after a touchdown was originally called a "goal from touchdown" and the field goal was originally a "goal from field."

Source: Paul Stagg, "The Development of the National Collegiate Athletic Association in Relationship" (PhD diss., New York University, 1946).

Walter Camp's Influence

Walter Chauncey Camp (1859–1925), a Yale graduate and former player, was the "advisory coach" at Yale from 1888 to 1906 while holding another full-time "day job." He attended practices and met with team leaders in the evening. It was typical during that era for alumni of a university to serve as volunteer advisers and coaches for the teams on which they had played. At Yale and most nineteenth century colleges, Stagg wrote, "There were no coaches, trainers, rubbers, or even a water boy. Occasional graduated players were drifting back to advise the football team, but the captain was still a captain, not a coach's foreman. He chose the team, ran it, and was not always above playing favorites."[32]

No other football player or coach had more of an influence on Stagg than Camp. During Camp's first four years as advisory coach (1888–1892), the team's record was 67–2. For most of his career, Camp held a full-time job with the New Haven Clock Company, where he became president in 1903. Camp was a halfback on the Yale football team from 1878 to 1881, which included his first two years of medical school. During his playing years, the team's record was 25–1–6.[33] He quit medical school after flunking the anatomy and surgery qualifying exams in his freshman and sophomore years.[34]

It's hard to conceive how Camp found time for an executive position in an 800-employee company, successfully lead the Yale football team, and achieve a national reputation as a widely published author. But he had help. His wife, Alice Sumner Camp, was his de facto assistant coach. "Allie" was the younger sister of the popular Yale professor William Graham Sumner, who held Yale's first faculty position in sociology and is considered the founder of the field of sociology. She supervised the team's practice sessions when Walter could not attend. One player noted that she "made careful note of the plays, players, and anything that should be observed in connection with the style of play and individual strengths and weaknesses." Known by players as "Mrs. Walter," Stagg recalled, "She was more coach than he. She was out for practice every afternoon and made a detailed report from notes at night to her husband." Her contributions to the team were recognized at the twenty-fifth reunion of the 1888 team with a photo of both Alice and Walter Camp on the cover of the souvenir program with the inscription "Head Coaches, 1888." Stagg's future wife, Stella, would follow her model of becoming his top assistant.

The editor of *Harper's Weekly* visited New Haven to interview Camp and wrote of him: "There is only one man in New Haven of more importance than Walter Camp, and I have forgotten his name. I think he is the president of the university." Camp is widely recognized today as the "Father of Football" because he was more responsible than anyone else for establishing the rules that transformed British-style rugby into American-style football. His influence on today's football rules cannot be overestimated. While still a Yale student in 1878, he was invited to join the Rules Committee of the Intercollegiate Football Association, which included schools now comprising the Ivy League. He died of a heart attack while attending an NCAA Rules Committee meeting in 1925.

One of the features in rugby competition is the scrum (short for scrummage) which is a method of restarting play when players pack close together with their heads down trying to gain possession of the ball. Stagg later called the scrummage "a weird and unscientific institution." He said the difference between British rugby and American football was "the British play a game for the game's sake; we play to win."[35]

The scrum didn't make sense to Camp either because it didn't seem logical for a team to gain ten or twenty yards and then risk losing the ball in a free-for-all scrum. When a team advanced the ball down the field, Camp thought it should be rewarded for maintaining possession. In describing the difference between rugby and football, Camp wrote in the *Yale Courant*: "Instead of a mass of men with no definite positions, kicking indiscriminately at the ball and their opponents, we have a game perfectly systematized. A position for every player and a duty for every position."[36]

While playing and coaching at Yale, Walter Camp originated the quarterback position. Stagg explained how the names of other offensive positions evolved in *Touchdown!* The player holding the position known today as "center" who hikes the ball was first called a "snapper back." The players on either side of the snapper back guarded the quarterback and were thus called "left guard" and "right guard." The players on the end of the offensive line were called "end men," later shortened to "left end" and "right end." The two players between the guards and ends eventually became known as "left tackle" and "right tackle."[37] In the backfield, the fullback stood about eight yards behind the center, the left and right halfbacks about four yards, and the quarterback stood behind the "snapper back" to take the ball. Today's backfield formations have become more complex, and those who hold these positions, other than quarterbacks, are usually called "running backs" or "flankers."

Camp also originated the concept of the "first down" that gave a team an opportunity for another series of plays after gaining five yards. He persuaded the Rules Committee to adopt this idea. The committee later extended the required distance from five to ten yards. Serving on the Rules Committee from 1878 until his death in 1925, Camp's other innovations included reducing the number of players on a team from fifteen to eleven, defining the line of scrimmage, creating offensive signals, and the first-down requirement that a team give up the ball after failing to advance five and later ten yards.[38] Camp persuaded the Rules Committee to adopt a scale of numerical values for touchdowns (six), points after touchdown (one), field goals (three) and safeties (two)—all of which remain today's standards. He also wrote a nationally syndicated sports column, more than 250 articles, and thirty books about football. He was honored on a thirty-seven cent U.S. postage stamp in 2003.[39]

The system of downs was the most significant innovation Camp introduced to college football. Roger R. Tamte, author of *Walter Camp and the Creation of American Football,* said, "The system of downs and distance—four downs to gain ten yards (which for many years was three downs to gain five yards)—was an absolute unknown when Camp created it. As natural as the idea seems today, it was quite unobvious when Camp suggested it. His fellow rule makers thought it was crazy and unworkable and tried to prevent its enactment."[40]

Stagg was chosen for the first All-America team in 1889, an idea that originated with Caspar Whitney, publisher of *Week's Sport* magazine, who asked Walter Camp to choose the team. Whitney was the first to describe Walter Camp as "the father of American football." The first All-America team was published in the December 18, 1889, issue. All eleven choices came from Harvard, Princeton, or Yale. Princeton dominated with five players; Yale had three, and Harvard had three. Stagg was chosen along with Yale teammates William Heffelfinger and Charles Gill. *Sport* lasted only two years, but Whitney continued publishing the All-America team listings as sports editor for *Harper's Weekly* and later at *Collier's Weekly.*[41]

Stagg's friendship with Camp continued until Camp's death. They served together on the Rules Committee for twenty years. Stagg learned from his mentor and followed in his footsteps as a strategist and inventor of plays, formations, and equipment. While still playing at Yale, Stagg created the first of his many football inventions—the tackling dummy. Common today in football practices at all levels, the dummy is a stuffed canvas bag originally hung from the gym roof a few feet above the floor. It gives players the opportunity to practice tackling and blocking. Stagg created it by rolling up a mattress and hanging it from the roof. He wrote, "The previous year the Rules Committee had lowered the tackling line to the knees, but the Yale squad continued to tackle high and poorly. To drill the new technique into them, I rolled a mattress up to an approximation of a man's body, suspended it from the gym roof and laid other mattresses flat beneath it. With this equipment, we ran the team through long tackling practices."[42]

Camp also influenced Stagg in his leadership style. Both as team captain and coach, Camp believed in "the czar principle." It required unquestioned leadership by the leader to whom team members gave their complete loyalty. Camp credited Yale's athletic success to the fact that the "one-man element of management and direction was the more certain to produce in the long run the best results." Although Stagg never used the term "czar principle," he followed Camp's "one man" style of leadership throughout his career.[43] Stagg wrote in *Touchdown!* of "the necessity for a military obedience on the football field. A player must obey orders like a soldier where orders have been given, and, like a good soldier, act swiftly and surely on his own in an unforeseen contingency."[44]

Writing for the Newspaper

Besides playing baseball and football, Stagg became a writer for *Yale Daily News.* In one week during his freshmen year, he published three articles and an editorial. "The competitive pace to get articles published became 'hotter each day' and every man hastily scans the paper with hope and fear to see whether his contribution is published. I tell you it is exciting...," he wrote to his sister Pauline.[45] During his senior year, he held a paid editorial position that paid $425.[46] His writing ability became a profitable talent later when he started receiving frequent requests to write articles about football and baseball.

For example, G.H. Dickinson, sporting editor of the *New York World,* wrote to Stagg in 1889, "*The World* would like from your pen, to be published May 5, 3,000 or 4,000 words on the art of pitching. If you can supply the article will you kindly send it to me by next Wednesday?"[47] That same year, *Harper's Young People* asked Stagg to write four articles on baseball. Titled "Baseball for Amateurs," the series explained a step-by-step process on how young people could become better players by using effective techniques and preparation.

Three years later, A.J. Johnson, publisher of *Johnson's Universal Cyclopaedia,* wrote Stagg and asked if he would write a 1,725-word article on "the great national game of base-ball" for the next revision of his encyclopedia. He told Stagg, "You are the best-known specialist on the subject, [and] we shall hope that you will favor, not only us, but the American people who are already so favorably acquainted with you, and who must continue to regard you as their idol in athletic sports."[48] Stagg wrote the articles and received $15 and a set of the new edition.

Joseph Shipley, editor of *The Springfield (MA) Union,* asked for an article about Yale football in 1890. "The Yale-Harvard foot-ball game comes on Saturday of next week," he wrote. "Would you be kind enough to prepare for *The Union,* to be published over your own signature, an article descriptive of modern foot-ball with some account of the successive seasons of games which have been played.... I would like further to know if you could furnish [an article] to be used before Saturday, an account of the present Yale team and of their probable chances for success."[49]

Singing in the Glee Club

The Yale Glee Club was another extracurricular activity for Stagg. He wrote to a friend that although he had no musical training, "I sang first tenor on the Yale Glee Club for three years, 1887–88, 1888–89, and 1889–90.

I must have had a natural tenor voice for I never had any musical training, and we had no musical instrument in my home. All of the singing I did was at Sunday School and church."[50] Stagg wrote his brother Paul in 1889: "I want to invite you up to the Glee Club Concert on Monday night. I have four tickets which I offer at your disposal. I think that you will enjoy the concert for we have a rattling good club."[51]

A St. Paul, Minnesota, newspaper reported on the Glee Club's visit to that city, saying, "The audience which assembled to hear their concert last night was enormous in proportions and unbounded in admiration. Every seat was taken, every box was occupied, and many people were standing." Another newspaper reported, "A.A. Stagg, the famous pitcher of the Yale University nine, is a member of the.... Yale Glee Club and was in town last evening with his organization. He is equally at home singing a high tenor in college glees or sending in puzzling curves on the ball field."[52]

Stagg's appreciation for the fine arts extended to sculpture as well as music. The Yale student newspaper reported that he spent several days modeling for an art student to create a sculpture of a baseball pitcher. The article read, "For several days past an art school student has been modeling a statuette of a baseball pitcher. Stagg of the Yale nine has posed several times to enable the student to perfect the model and the work has been pronounced a complete success. 'The Pitcher' will be on exhibition during the Art School reception this evening."[53]

YMCA General Secretary

With his goal of becoming a minister, Stagg became active in the Yale chapter of the Young Men's Christian Association (YMCA) during his freshman year. Its mission was "to promote growth in grace and Christian fellowship among its members and aggressive Christian work especially by and for students." Organized in 1879 as the Yale Christian Social Union, it affiliated with the international YMCA movement in 1881. By the mid–1880s, the YMCA movement was booming. The 1885 annual report stated it had chapters on 181 campuses with more than 10,000 members, which was one third of the total college population.[54]

The Yale chapter built its own facility in 1886, which it named "Dwight Hall" after Timothy Dwight IV, Yale's eighth president from 1795 to 1817. Dwight Hall's purpose was to serve as a "home away from home" for Christian students and a focal point for campus religious activities. The three-story building contained a large reception area, four meeting rooms, an organ, auditorium seating 500, and living quarters for a few students. Its activities included prayer meetings, Bible studies, lectures by Christian leaders, summer conferences, and local mission work.[55] Dwight Hall remains on the Yale campus but is known today as the "Center for Public Service and Social Justice."

The Yale YMCA helped sponsor summer Bible conferences in Northfield, Massachusetts. Stagg attended his first conference in 1885, which attracted more than 400 students from ninety colleges. During the 1890s, more than 100 Yale students attended each year. The founder of the conferences was Dwight L. Moody (1837–1899), the prominent nineteenth century evangelist and founder of Chicago's Moody Bible Institute. The conferences were largely informal and filled with Bible instruction and music. "We want to stir you up and get you in love with the Bible, and those of you with a voice in love with music," Moody told one conference.[56]

Stagg wrote to his sister Ida in 1886: "We have just had a YMCA convention of New England colleges. Delegates numbered around 125. Such lovely meetings. Everybody is chuck full of enthusiasm. The addresses were simply fine. If such conventions could be held often, they would do a world of good. We had lovely singing. The boys sang with all their hearts."[57]

During his college years, Stagg was an evangelical Christian. In his junior year, he expressed joy in a letter to his sister Pauline that their elder sister had finally become a Christian at age thirty-seven. But he expressed hope that Hattie, another sister, might do the same. "I wish that Hattie might come around now … won't you write along with me and try to influence her, dear sister. It is our duty. We must have a complete family circle in Christ."[58]

Stagg was elected as general secretary of the Yale YMCA at the end of his senior year, a position he held for the next two years of graduate study. As general secretary, he coordinated and supervised Christian work on campus. He was the third general secretary and the first to hold the position for two years. General secretaries were chosen by a YMCA graduate committee from among recent Yale graduates. His tenure as general secretary became best known for the establishment of the Grand Street City Mission, which opened on September 3, 1888.[59] The mission promoted temperance and targeted "railroad men, shop men, longshoremen and loafers." Sunday night services averaged forty in attendance and included singing and Christian testimonies from Yale students. The mission sought to motivate the men to lead disciplined, productive lives. Stagg described the mission's accomplishments: "A year ago, we established a mission in the lowest quarter of New Haven. We chose it as the best field for us, where there was no one else to do the work—where our work was needed…. [Students] go among those poor wretched men right out of the gutter, leading desperate lives, in drunkenness, immorality; every bad thing. They sit down by them and listen to the story of their lives, get into sympathy with them, try to get them to give up their bad ways and point them to Christ."

Yale Divinity School

While serving as YMCA general secretary, a part-time position, Stagg took Divinity School and graduate school courses. "Most of my classes in these two years were with Prof. William R. Harper, who had classes in Biblical literature and Hebrew," he wrote to a friend. Hebrew was his most difficult subject, which he said required six hours of study a day just to get through it. In a 1925 letter to Walter Camp, he described Harper as an "inspirational teacher," but said Hebrew was a subject that "now seems to me the deadest and most uninteresting language which developed out of the tower of Babel. It took a lot of will power for me to study Hebrew."[60]

Other experiences during these two years led him to question his preaching ability. "The more often I spoke in YMCA work, the deeper sank in the conviction that I was not cut out for the job," he said. The most frequently cited incident that led Stagg to question his preaching ability came after speaking at a national YMCA conference in Lake Geneva, Wisconsin, in 1889. He followed John R. Mott (1865–1955) on the speaker's platform. Mott was the national secretary of the Intercollegiate YMCA who later earned the 1946 Nobel Peace Prize after a distinguished public service career. Following his speech, Stagg was sitting in his tent at the conference feeling discouraged about the talk he had just given. He heard Mott and another speaker pass by outside while Mott said to his friend, "I can't understand why Stagg just can't make a talk." Stagg wrote in *Touchdown!*, "Here was expert confirmation of my own doubts and escape from addressing student mass meetings."[61]

When Stagg spoke at the Harvard YMCA, the *Boston Globe* also criticized his speaking ability: "No one who has seen him standing bareheaded on the ballfield using all of his energies to puzzle the Harvard hitters, can ever forget Stagg. But Stagg looked like a different man last night as he spoke to the young men who had assembled in the Young Men's Christian Association hall. He appeared almost frightened. He stood with one hand resting on the desk and the other in his pocket. His voice was tremulous at times, and he could be heard with difficulty."[62]

Stagg's decision to forego the ministry and pursue an athletic career did not come easily. "I fought against going into physical training as a life work. It was a long hard fight for me because my whole earnest purposeful life had worked toward another channel for accomplishing the most good." He saw "the ministry only as a field in which to do that." Prior to that decision, he said, "I must confess that I thought it [athletic work] as too low a vocation; that while I loved it and believed in it…. I spurned the thought of giving my life to such work."

Stagg never excelled in the classroom nor received academic honors at

Yale. He was basically an average student and by his own admission ranked in the bottom half of his class. But describing him as an "average" Yale student in the 1880s belies the college's demanding curriculum. A required semi-annual exam for juniors in June 1887 consisted of about ten questions in each of seven subjects: astronomy, English literature, geology, German, physics, political economy, and psychology. Students were given two hours to complete the test in each subject. A sample question from each subject appears below.[63]

Astronomy: Prove that the sun's apparent diameter varies approximately in the inverse relation of its distance and show how the eccentricity of the earth's orbit may be thence determined (e = 1/60).

English literature: What were the terms of the oath to be taken by Portia's suitors in Merchant of Venice? Describe the casket scenes, showing how each suitor is led to the choice he makes, and explain how each character is tested in each case.

Geology: How does the vegetable life of the Triassic period differ from that of the Carboniferous age; and the vertebrate life of the Carboniferous from that of the Devonian age?

Physics: Describe the conditions under which a current may be induced in a coil of wire by another current, the direction of the induced current and the source of its energy in each case.

Political economy: Give the history of legal tender cases before the Supreme Court.

Psychology: Describe the product of sense-perception: (1) the stages of its formation; (2) the faculties involved in its construction; (3) when it may be regarded as finished.

A few months before graduation, he told his sister how much Yale had meant to him. "My! but it will be hard to leave this dear old spot—it sometimes seem to me the dearest place on earth because I have received the greatest inspirations to noble effort and manly Christian living; here I have made my lifelong friendships with the noblest men."[64]

Stagg graduated from Yale on June 2, 1888. The athletic and leadership talents he displayed at Yale were prescient of the success and national recognition he would later receive. From an early age, he was driven. This driving ambition would remain with him throughout life. His friendship with his Divinity School professor, William Rainey Harper, brought together two unusually gifted men who would shape each other's lives and careers. Walter Camp taught him the skills he needed to succeed as a football coach, and William Rainey Harper gave him the place to use them. Before that occurred, however, Stagg spent the next two years in Springfield, Massachusetts, where he began his football coaching career and helped shape the new game of basketball.

4

International YMCA School
at Springfield, 1890–1892

I realized in divinity school that I wasn't a good preacher and decided I would have to make another choice. I enrolled in the Springfield YMCA school to learn how to become a coach. —Amos Alonzo Stagg

For graduate study, most Yale graduates would not have chosen the International YMCA Training School in Springfield, Massachusetts. It was essentially a vocational training school that lacked the prestige of the old New England universities. However, after Stagg decided he wasn't cut out for the ministry, he decided the next-best thing he could do was to become a YMCA director. In this work, he could have a moral and spiritual influence on young men through coaching and directing athletic activities. Here he met James Naismith, who created the game of basketball while they were students at the school now known as Springfield College. These two men whose paths crossed for the first time in Springfield would have a profound influence on American college athletics.

Stagg later said, "I realized in divinity school that I wasn't a good preacher and decided I would have to make another choice. I enrolled in the Springfield YMCA school to learn how to become a coach."[1] The head of the school's athletic department, Dr. Luther Gulick (1865–1918), had often visited and spoken at Yale, where he invited Stagg to consider attending the school. Naismith, a graduate of McGill University in Toronto, chose the YMCA School for the same reason. Naismith and Stagg were members of the entering class of four students in 1890 and became lifelong friends. Naismith played on the football team that Stagg organized and coached, and Stagg played on the basketball team that Naismith organized and coached. Stagg and Naismith were chosen as inaugural members of the Basketball Hall of Fame in 1959.

The school was founded in 1885 and originally called the School for

Christian Workers. It prepared young men to become general secretaries or directors of YMCA organizations. In 1912, it adopted the name International YMCA College and in 1954 was renamed Springfield College. Gulick, who was three years younger than Stagg, was a New York University Medical School graduate who became the founding superintendent of the school's Physical Culture Department. Gulick believed that body, mind, and spirit—visualized in the three sides of a triangle—should be developed to achieve "the whole man complete as God made him." He designed the YMCA's triangle logo, which the organization still uses today.

Student and Faculty Member

At Springfield, Stagg enrolled as a student his first year and was promoted to faculty member his second year. "I entered as a student in a class of four and later was made a member of the faculty with the formidable title of 'instructor in the theory and practice of training,'" Stagg wrote. He asked Gulick if he could "get up a football team." Gulick agreed and appointed him to the faculty with a $350 annual salary as the school's first football and baseball coach. In the fall of 1890, he organized, coached, and played on the football team, which won five games and lost three. Stagg later wrote, "On this team, I played half back and captained and coached it. I did the same in the Fall of 1891. In the Spring of 1891, I organized, coached, and pitched on a baseball team at the school. I did the same in the Spring of 1892." The official name of the school, "The International Young Men's Christian Association Training School," was too cumbersome for reporters who started calling the team "The Christians" or "Stagg's team." Stagg's two-year football record at the YMCA school was ten wins, eleven losses, and one tie.[2]

On December 12, 1890, Stagg's team played in history's first indoor football game at Madison Square Garden in New York. His team played the Yale consolidated team, which consisted of five members of Yale's current team and some of its football alumni. About 2,000 fans watched the game, which was part of a series of events sponsored by the Staten Island Athletic Club. The *New York Times* reported that James Naismith made the first touchdown for the YMCA team after recovering a Yale fumble and "making a clean run to touchdown." Stagg's team led for most of the game, but Yale eventually won 16–10 after a last-quarter touchdown.[3] This narrow loss was an amazing performance by an upstart team against the East's most powerful team, which had only lost one game in the previous thirteen seasons.[4]

During the next season, Casper Whitney, the sports columnist for *Harper's Weekly,* said of the YMCA team: "Here is a school that contains just forty-two boys and yet out of these Stagg has succeeded in developing a team that has made those of Harvard and Yale play ball."[5] Whitney's "play ball" comment about the Yale and Harvard games was generous. Although Yale barely won the 1890 game, it defeated the YMCA School 28–0 in 1891 and 50–0 in 1892. The YMCA School lost to Harvard 34–0 in 1891. The *New York Times* reported on the Harvard game, saying, "The football game this afternoon between Harvard and Stagg's team was one of the cleanest games of the year resulting in a victory for Harvard by the score of 34 to 0.... Stagg's men put up a beautiful team game."[6]

Neither now nor later, Stagg never feared scheduling games against big-time opponents which his team was likely to lose. Besides Harvard and Yale, Stagg scheduled games against some best-known schools including Amherst, Brown, Dartmouth, Princeton, Trinity, Wesleyan, and Williams. The Springfield College Digital Archives contain copies of letters to Stagg from athletic managers at these schools agreeing to play the YMCA team and suggesting possible dates.[7]

Besides coaching at the YMCA School, he held a part-time job coaching football and baseball at the Williston Academy. Located in Easthampton, Massachusetts, Williston was a college preparatory school. The job required a twenty-mile train trip from Springfield to Northampton one afternoon a week. In his first year at Williston, the team won seven games and lost three, including a victory over Stagg's own International YMCA School squad. There is no record of how Stagg managed to simultaneously coach two teams playing against each other, but there were no rules at the time. The *Boston Globe* described the game: "The training school has been coached by A.A. Stagg, the famous Yale pitcher, and it was his first game. They came off with much glory, though with many bruises. The score was 15 to 10 in favor of the Willistons." The next week, his YMCA team defeated Williston by a score of 14–9 with Stagg scoring the winning touchdown.

Stagg invented the "ends back formation" while coaching at Springfield that was implemented by many other college teams until 1906 when the Rules Committee started requiring six men on the line. "I broke away from the standard, traditional seven-man line by using only five men on the line. I played the ends back of the line similar to the double wingback formation. This play was particularly effective on end-around-end plays on which we made long runs against Yale and Harvard in 1891," Stagg wrote.[8] Many college and pro teams today use variations of the formation with backfield men split out wide behind the line of scrimmage.

Naismith and Invention of Basketball

James Naismith, the founder of basketball, seemed to have more trouble than Stagg making up his mind about what he wanted to do. At various times during a ten-year period, he studied theology, athletics, and medicine. He played rugby at McGill University, which he graduated from in 1887. For the next three years, he was a physical education director at McGill while studying for the ministry at the Presbyterian College of Montreal. Then he enrolled at the International YMCA School in 1890, the same year as Stagg, where both played football and basketball. After finishing his degree at the YMCA School, Naismith earned the M.D. degree at Gross Medical College (now the University of Colorado College of Medicine) in 1898. Spurning a medical career, he then went to the University of Kansas where he became its first basketball coach.

During his years at the YMCA School, Naismith played center on the football team. In 1891, YMCA physical instructors came from all over the country to Springfield for a summer workshop. They told Naismith and Gulick that they had no indoor, winter game that consistently held the interest of their students. Consequently, Gulick asked Naismith to create an indoor winter game. Naismith later remarked, "The invention of basketball was not an accident. It was developed to meet a need. Those boys simply would not play 'drop the handkerchief.'"[9]

To minimize injuries, Naismith wanted a game that allowed the ball to be thrown, not carried. His original basketball rules did not allow dribbling and only permitted the ball to be moved up or down the court via passes between players. He also wanted a target for the ball that discouraged the use of force. At first, he tried to modify a few existing outdoor games to meet these goals. None worked. Then with the help of Stagg and two classmates, Naismith nailed two half-bushel, vegetable baskets from the elevated running track above the gym floor. They put a student on the track to empty the baskets after a score. Sometimes the ball bounced out, so Stagg suggested to Naismith that he switch to peach baskets because they were deeper. Naismith cut out the bottoms so that they didn't need to be emptied. The game began by tossing the ball up between one player from each team standing in the middle of the court, as it is today.

"There is a great furor among the boys in the school over a new game which Naismith, our center rusher [on the football team], invented, called basket football," Stagg wrote his sister Ruth, who was teaching at a girls' school in Connecticut. "It is played indoor in the gymnasium or some good-sized room. Any number of persons on a side. A basket with a large enough opening to take the ball easily is hung at each end about eight feet from the floor.... I think the game could easily be adapted to girls."[10]

Naismith invited Stagg to play in the first public basketball game. On March 12, 1892, the YMCA school's faculty, which included Dr. Gulick, competed against its students. Stagg scored the faculty's only basket in a five-to-one loss. The *Springfield Republican* reported on the game: "Over 200 spectators crammed their necks over the gallery railing of the Christian Workers gymnasium while they watched the game of 'basket ball' yesterday afternoon between the teachers ... and the students. The most conspicuous figure on the floor was Stagg in the blue Yale uniform who managed to have a hand in every scrimmage. His football training hampered him, and he was continually making fouls by shoving his opponents. He managed, however, to score the only goal that the instructors made."[11]

Naismith wrote the original thirteen rules of basketball, which were first published on January 15, 1892, in the YMCA's school newspaper, *The Triangle*. For example, rule three read: "A player cannot run with the ball. The player must throw it from the spot on which he catches it, allowance to be made for a man who catches the ball when running at a good speed if he tries to stop." Number five read: "No shouldering, holding, pushing, tripping, or striking in any way the person of an opponent shall be allowed; the first infringement of this rule by any player shall count as a foul, the second shall disqualify him until the next goal is made, or, if there was evident intent to injure the person, for the whole of the game." His rules contained fewer than 500 words; today's basketball rules contain more than 30,000 words.

When Stagg was coaching at Chicago in 1898, the University of Kansas chancellor visited the campus and was introduced to Stagg. The chancellor told Stagg he was looking for a basketball coach and athletic director and asked for any recommendations. Stagg recommended his friend James Naismith, who was in Denver finishing medical school. Naismith was offered and accepted the job. He organized the Kansas basketball program, coached its team until 1907, and remained athletic director until he died in 1939. Today the Kansas team plays basketball in the Allen Fieldhouse, and the playing surface is named the "James Naismith Court" in his honor.

Naismith, Gulick, and Stagg were among the seven inaugural members of the 1959 class of the Naismith Memorial Basketball Hall of Fame in Springfield. Edward J. Hickox, executive secretary of the Hall of Fame, wrote Stagg on April 21, 1959, saying, "We were very happy to award you a life membership in the Naismith Memorial Basketball Hall of Fame. We feel you had a real share in the origin of the game called basketball." Stagg's official Hall of Fame citation recognizes that he brought basketball from Springfield to Chicago, where he popularized five-man basketball. He coached the Chicago basketball team against Iowa in the first college game played with five men on a side on January 16, 1896. The citation also recognizes Stagg for organizing the Chicago National Interscholastic Basketball Tournament from 1917 to 1931, which helped "improve and standardize the rules and interpretation of those rules for high school play."[12]

The "Muscular Christianity" Movement

Stagg, Naismith, and Gulick were among the pioneers of the "Muscular Christianity" movement in America. Originating in Britain in the mid-nineteenth century, the movement emphasized the role sports played in developing moral and spiritual character. It had no formal organization, conventions, or memberships. "Muscular Christianity" was more of a philosophy taught by coaches and Christian leaders who emphasized how sports participation developed fair play, persistence, endurance, physical fitness, and teamwork. Athletes were encouraged to apply these values in other areas of their personal and professional lives.

John Miller wrote, "The genius of Muscular Christianity was in how it appealed to the spiritual value of athletics, answered Calvinist reservations about sports, and addressed Darwinist concerns about survival of the fittest."[13] Lawrence Doggett wrote in *Man and a School*, "They [Stagg and Naismith] wished to use physical education as a means of building character in young men and believed that the course of training at Springfield would better fit them for this purpose." Movement leaders drew upon metaphors from the Bible, which compared the Christian life to running a race, such as "Let us also lay aside every weight and sin which clings so closely, and let us run with endurance the race that is set before us" (Hebrews 12:1) and "I have fought the good fight, I have finished the race, I have kept the faith" (I Timothy 4:7).

With the national reputation developed as a Yale athlete, Stagg received frequent speaking invitations. During the fall of 1891, Gulick asked Stagg to develop a lecture to explain "the theory or underlying ideas of the Physical Department work of the School" and help promote the school's work. Stagg presented a lecture titled "The Modern Athlete" in cities as far west as Omaha and south as Washington, D.C. Attracting crowds up to 2,500, his fame as a Yale baseball pitcher was a drawing card. His theme was that of "Muscular Christianity," teamwork, and "the harmonious development of all the organs and parts of the body into a symmetrical whole."[14]

In January 1892, he gave speeches in New York, Massachusetts, Vermont, Iowa, and Nebraska. In September 1892, just prior to moving to Chicago, he spoke to YMCA groups at the University of Minnesota, Carleton College, and at the Minneapolis YMCA.[15] The honorariums he received from these engagements supplemented the small salaries he received from the YMCA School and Williston Academy. The *Minneapolis Tribune* reported on Stagg's visit to that city. "The most widely known athlete in America will spend the next few days in Minneapolis. He is the man who pitched for Yale and carried the football team through opposing rush lines to victory on many a hard-fought field. A. Alonzo Stagg is the man and his name is talismanic in college athletics."[16]

While Stagg was working at the YMCA School, his father died of apoplexy in January 1892. In a letter written during a train trip on January 29, 1892, he expressed deep regret that he could not be with his mother and sisters during his father's illness and death. "While oppressed with a feeling of sadness, by far the larger part of it is because I am far away from little mother and sisters in this hour of affliction.... But dear me, when I think of how powerless I am to help or comfort at this distance, I want to speed with electric quickness to little mother and sisters." He expressed a strong admiration for his father saying he had lived a "heroic life for years battling with poverty of the severest kind and while the depressions of sickness overshadowed our home."[17]

Chautauqua Institution

Between 1888 and 1892, Stagg directed the summer athletics program at Chautauqua Institution, a large Christian conference center in western New York that combined classes, lectures, athletics, and recreational activities. In addition to baseball and tennis, it held track and field events in running, jumping, shot-putting, and hammer throwing. Stagg worked closely with his Yale professor, William Rainey Harper, who was chosen as Chautauqua's principal in 1883. Harper gained considerable administrative experience here that prepared him to become a university president. Gould wrote in *The Chautauqua Movement* that Harper was responsible "for securing fifteen department heads, a hundred or more teachers, preparing sections for over two thousand students, planning a curriculum that was to include language and literature, art, physical culture, and practical art."[18] Although Chautauqua does not have this broad of a program today, it continues to offer a wide variety of summer lectures, music, and recreational activities.

Stagg received a small honorarium with room and board from Chautauqua, which did little to relieve the financial pressures he faced after the YMCA School fell behind in his salary. "My last year's salary is behind $400, and I never ask for any for I know how hard it is for them [the YMCA School] to get money together.... Just at this moment I am what you might term dead broke. I had to borrow $5 the other day to buy a pair of shoes."[19]

Despite the financial strain, however, the summer offered some lighter moments.

His days were filled with Bible study classes, baseball, and gymnasium work. During the evenings, he met some of the young ladies attending the summer conference. In one of his letters, he wrote, "This has been a sweet evening. Its sweetness started out with close environment with the highest type of personified sweetness, namely, five lovely maidens. We went out for a row on the lake. We were among the privileged witnesses of one of the most beautiful sunsets I have ever seen.... We had a lovely row. Two of the girls insisted on rowing ... so I sat in the bottom of the boat and tried to be good. We sang and chatted and laughed a great deal. When we came in, I took the girls up and treated them to ice cream."[20]

Stagg and Grace Livingston met again while he was working at Chautauqua. She was the young woman from West Orange who first encouraged him to consider the ministry. He wrote to a friend, "Tonight I attended the Christian Endeavor meeting. My old schoolmate, Grace Livingston, has charge of the movement here. She is one of the loveliest and most zealous Christian girls that it has been my very good fortune to meet. Last night at the meeting in the Amphitheatre, she gave the sweetest, prettiest, and most graceful report of the Convention in New York."[21] She later published more than 100 Christian romance novels during her lifetime and taught college classes. Did she and Stagg have a romantic relationship? Daana Crill, curator of the Gravelivingstonhill.com website, said, "To the best of my knowledge, their relationship was purely friendship and not romantic. Grace had a penchant for encouraging friends who were interested in ministry. In later years, she helped to send several young men to school for this purpose."[22]

Stagg's star was rising after two seasons coaching the YMCA football team against nationally recognized opponents. He began receiving offers or inquiries about coaching jobs from Dartmouth, Syracuse, Harvard, Bowdoin, Haverford, and the University of North Carolina.[23] But he had not forgotten the breakfast meeting with William Rainey Harper in New York City in 1890, which changed his life forever.

5

Finding Football's Place at Chicago, 1890–1892

A school without football is in danger of deteriorating into a medieval study hall.—Vince Lombardi

While teaching at Yale Divinity School, William Rainey Harper wrote a letter to Stagg on October 21, 1890, when he was at the YMCA School in Springfield. "My dear friend, I have an important matter about which I wish to talk with you at an early moment." He asked Stagg if he could meet for breakfast with him at the Murray Hill Hotel in New York.[1] When Harper wrote Stagg, he had been offered but not yet accepted the position of founding president of the University of Chicago. The board of trustees elected the thirty-five-year-old Harper as president at their second meeting in September 1890.[2] Harper, however, asked the board for six months to make his decision.

He invited Stagg to meet with him four months before he officially accepted the presidency on February 16, 1891.[3] Harper might have hesitated because he wanted time to determine the interest of prospective faculty members and especially from the football coach he had in mind. As a Yale faculty member, he had witnessed its great sports heritage and wanted football to become an integral part of the new university's student culture. In a story frequently repeated in Stagg biographies, Stagg recalled, "We met in the breakfast room of the Murray Hill Hotel in New York. Dr. Harper then unfolded his plans for the university and broached the subject of my heading up the athletic department, first offering me the salary of $1,500. The whole idea was new to me, and I kept still and just thought." Harper interpreted Stagg's silence as a feeling that the salary was too low, so he said, "I'll offer you $2,000 and an assistant professorship." Stagg still sat silently thinking, so Harper said, "I'll give you $2,500 and an associate professorship, which means an appointment for life."

"I suppose Dr. Harper thought it was money. It wasn't that at all.

Money was never an object with me. I had studied for the ministry and believed I could perform as great a service in athletics as I could in the pulpit. While Dr. Harper was talking during that breakfast, I was wondering if Chicago would be a better 'field to till' than the East," Stagg recalled.[4]

Harper's goal was to create a major research university modeled after the European research universities. But he also wanted "a vital undergraduate institution with high academic standards and a vigorous student culture, whose graduates would serve the economy of the city of Chicago and provide a pipeline into the graduate programs that he envisioned."[5]

Stagg was crucial to his plan. Harper remembered him as a student "at the height of his athletic achievement at Yale," and said, "An attachment formed between us that, so far as I am concerned, has grown closer every year since that time."[6] In hiring Stagg as the nation's first full-time professional football coach, he envisioned a successful football program that would publicize the university and contribute to a "vigorous student culture."

Rockefeller and Harper

The University of Chicago was originally founded by Baptists. When the American Baptist Education Society decided to create a new university in the Midwest, they found a sympathetic donor in John D. Rockefeller, who was also a Baptist and the wealthiest man in America at the time. He offered an initial $600,000 for the endowment if the American Baptist Education Society could raise another $400,000. About three months after the Baptists met that condition, he gave an additional $1 million and another $1 million in 1892. By 1910, Rockefeller's gifts to the university totaled $34,702,375 or about a billion dollars in today's currency.[7] Although established by Baptists, the university was nonsectarian from the beginning and welcomed women and minority students in an era when many universities did not.[8]

Although he was a Baptist, another reason for Harper's delay in accepting the position was uncertainty over how well his progressive views would be accepted. He believed in the critical approach to Biblical interpretation and once told a newspaper reporter, "I believe in applying to the Bible the principles of literary criticism to determine when its books were written and the particular purpose for which they were written.... Inquiry does not imply a doubt in the divine origin of the Bible."[9] He told Rockefeller in a letter, "I do not wish to enter into the position and thereby bring upon the institution the distrust of the denomination."[10] Rockefeller replied and urged Harper to accept the job: "I agree with the Board of Trustees of the Chicago University that you are the man for president, and if you will take it, I shall expect great results. I cannot conceive of a position where you can do the world more good."[11]

By any measure, Harper was a brilliant scholar who possessed a genius-level IQ. He learned to read at age three, entered Muskingum College in Ohio at age ten and graduated at age fourteen. After working in his father's store for four years, he entered Yale graduate school at age seventeen and received the Ph.D. in Semitic languages and literature at age nineteen in 1875. His dissertation was titled "A Comparative Study of the Prepositions in Latin, Greek, Sanskrit, and Gothic." After teaching at Denison College in Ohio, he was appointed as an instructor in Bible and

Hebrew at Morgan Park Seminary on Chicago's south side. While teaching at the seminary, he became acquainted with John D. Rockefeller, who was a benefactor of the seminary. Rockefeller was impressed with this rising academic star. Harper, however, could not resist the offer of a prestigious endowed professorship at Yale and left the seminary in 1886. At Yale, he taught courses in Hebrew and Biblical interpretation. Everywhere he taught, students described him as an "electrifying" or "charismatic" teacher.[12] One historian described him as a man with "enthusiasm, originality and practical skill.... Open and friendly to all, he never forgot names. No one was too high or too low to gain Harper's interest and attention."[13]

John D. Rockefeller (left) with William Rainey Harper at the 1901 Decennial Celebration of the University of Chicago. University of Chicago Photographic Archive, apf1-02512, Special Collections Research Center, University of Chicago Library.

Stagg Sort of Accepts Harper's Offer

Stagg replied to Harper on November 25, 1890. "After much thought and prayer, I feel decided that my life can best be used for my Master's service in the position which you have offered. I am therefore willing and desirous to sign a contract, subject of course to the conditions agreed upon by you in our talks," he wrote.[14] Harper understood the relationship between football and public support better than most of his contemporaries and "saw it as a way to advertise the raw institution," wrote Ingrassia in *The Rise of Gridiron University*.[15] When Stagg asked Harper about his attitude towards football, he replied, "I want you to develop teams which we can send around the country and knock out all the colleges. We will give them a palace car and a vacation, too."[16]

What really happened was more complicated. After making the decision, Stagg was still enticed with inquiries and offers from Yale, Johns Hopkins, Pennsylvania, and Harvard. The *Boston Globe* reported on November 28, 1891, "Stagg … said that he had received a letter from Yale authorities offering him a similar position at his alma mater and that he will probably accept…. Stagg stands in the highest favor with the faculty, graduates, and undergraduates of the university…. Old Yale coaches and the players of this year's team lay all their laurels at Stagg's feet and to his ingenuity attribute the victories of this year."[17] The *Globe* reported a week later: "Stagg, the well-known Yale athlete, who is taking a course in the School of Christian Workers, is in receipt of an offer from Johns Hopkins University to fill a vacancy occasioned by the resignation of Dr. Hartwell."[18]

Harper wrote Stagg on December 6, "I see in today's paper that the Johns Hopkins directors are trying to get you for the athletic work at Baltimore. You must stand firm for Chicago. They will give you no such position as you will have in Chicago. There can never be the number of students there that there will be in Chicago."[19] Stagg wrote back

> I was startled by seeing a dispatch in the papers stating that I was going to give up going to Chicago University [and] I was going to accept a similar position at Yale. Thinking that you may have seen this dispatch also, which by the way did not spring from me, I hasten to write you this letter.
>
> Proposals in truth were made to me this week to fill the position at Yale. Day before yesterday I also received a committee from the University of Pennsylvania urging upon me the department of Physical Culture in that university. A few weeks ago, one of the Harvard professors told me that Harvard had a proposal to make to me, though it was not put in definite form then. A position at Harvard or at the University of Pennsylvania has appealed to me chiefly from the financial side as I was given to understand I would receive at least $1,000 and probably $1,500 more than you are to give me. The Yale proposal has appealed to me the most.

Trying to leverage his offers, he asked Harper, "I want to ask your advice as a good friend what you would do under a similar situation, provided of course that a release from my pledge were [sic] granted? The position would be as head of the Physical Culture Department and a member of the faculty. I would have at least one and probably two assistants at the start…. As one interested in my making the most of my life, does not your unbiased judgment concur with that of all with whom I have spoken that my opportunities are greater and the arrangements more satisfactory at either Yale or the University of Pennsylvania?"[20]

Harper persisted with his aggressive recruitment, and Stagg finally agreed to come to Chicago. His appointment as "Associate Professor and Director of the Department of Physical Culture and Athletics" with tenure was a precedent in American higher education. Stagg was the first athletic coach to hold a faculty position with tenure. Among the original eighty-seven Chicago faculty members, thirty-one received the rank of full professor and sixteen received an associate professor rank. Stagg was the not only the first full-time coach in America, but also the first to receive a tenured faculty appointment as director of an athletic department. He was a faculty member, athletic director, and department chair. Hitherto, athletics in colleges had been under the control of student athletic associations. In the years that followed, Stagg coached football, baseball, track, and field, and even the basketball team a few years. He developed team schedules, taught courses, hired, and supervised faculty members. In its first year, the Physical Culture department had three other faculty members besides Stagg.[21]

Stagg's Demands

Despite his feelings of inadequacy, Stagg could be demanding in telling Harper what he needed to staff the Department of Athletics and Physical Culture.

> You will readily see that it will be impossible for me to do what I desire to do with one assistant. I expect on account of the nature of the work in my department to be compelled to give a larger number of hours of actual leadership in the gymnasium and on the field, but I demand the right to certain privileges as set forth in the bulletins and as promised by you; time for study, sufficient capable help, proper equipment. You will remember that I accepted the position once for all after talking over the matter and having these conditions met by your promise.
>
> Time for study—that is necessary to keep abreast with the advances in the department of science and practice in Physical Culture. I am to be more than a "trainer of teams."
>
> Sufficient capable help. On the basis of actual work laid out for classes and athletic teams, there would be too much physical work to be done by two men.

Now I expect you to back me up and get a larger appropriation for salaries in the department. There ought to be $2,500 set aside for this purpose instead of $2,000 as you suggested.[22]

The paradoxical Stagg could be humble and unassuming, yet also possessed with a relentless ambition to succeed. In another letter he wrote to a friend, he said, "I mean business. My ambition is fired. I will become a leader in physical morality in my own life and preaching it to the broad earth! I will be a scholar in all lines of physical culture."[23] Before and after he was hired, Stagg began to assert his brashness and independence. He told Harper, "I understand that I am not to be hampered in my work in any way…. I am not compelled to explain for what purpose money is to be used."[24] Stagg would learn many lessons in humility in future years.

Because a prominent and successful football team was a high priority for Harper, he eventually gave Stagg most everything he wanted. Harper said at a spring convocation, "The athletic work of the students is a vital part of the student life…. It is a real and essential part of the college education. The athletic field like the gymnasium is one of the university's laboratories…. The director was not a professional coach, who must manage to win games in order to hold his place, but a permanent member of the teaching staff of professorial rank."[25]

In a speech he gave at Carnegie Institute of Technology years later, Stagg said the Department of Physical Culture at Chicago was a "pioneer" among colleges in three respects: "First—It combined all of the physical activities of the students including the athletics as well as the required work into a single department. Second—The members of the department were to be members of the faculty. Third—All athletics were to be managed and coached by members of the department."[26]

"Physical culture" (today known as physical education) was a previously unknown course requirement that Stagg initiated with Harper's support. All students were required to take physical culture courses in their freshman, sophomore, and junior years. The curriculum included an elective course in the "Theory and Practice of Football," which Stagg taught for several years. In 1906, the *Chicago Tribune* reported that current students in the class included six Chicago players and fifteen high school instructors who enrolled "in search of ideas to impart to school pupils when they return to their pedagogical duties next fall."[27]

Harper's Vision

The city of Chicago was on the move, and Harper was poised to make the University of Chicago a significant part of its growth. Since the famous fire of 1871 that destroyed large parts of the city, it had experienced remarkable growth and almost tripled its population to one million. The city's size grew from thirty-five to 178 square miles.[28]

The fledgling university would have never survived without the donations from John D. Rockefeller. "Harper often struggled to recruit faculty away from more established and familiar campuses and only succeeded by overpaying them," said John W. Boyer, author of *The University of Chicago: A History*.[29] A year after it opened, the Panic of 1893 struck the nation, creating unemployment that reached nearly 20 percent during its four-year run. Stock prices plunged, 600 banks or savings and loan associations closed, and 15,000 businesses failed.[30] Harper's sizeable budget gave him the resources to attract ten professors who had previously served as presidents at other universities. Inspired by a visit to Cambridge University, he planned an undergraduate college and graduate school that freed senior professors from heavy teaching loads so they could pursue research. He wanted to focus the graduate school on discovering new knowledge through research rather than transmitting established information. No university, including Harvard, Yale, and Princeton, had ever invested so heavily in developing a strong athletic program with rigorous academic programs. Harper was the first university president to envision the athletic program as a way to achieve public visibility and support. His recruitment of Amos Alonzo Stagg was the primary element in achieving that goal.

Harper planned every detail of the university including its year-round quarter system, academic calendar, faculty course loads and vacations, and departments and divisions. He also created extension programs and a university press as key elements to extend the university's public outreach. The adult education programs received full status in the curriculum. The summer quarter attracted hundreds of teachers working for certification and advanced degrees. After the university opened, Harper continued to develop new departments and added professional schools for medicine, education, and law.[31]

Stagg described Harper as an "unusual combination of a sound scholar and a born organizer, promoter and advertiser."[32] He also said Harper "was doing a revolutionary thing…. Chicago was to be a great experiment divided into the colleges, the academies, the graduate schools, the divinity school, the university-extension division, and the university press, all to operate twelve months in a year…. And Chicago was to be co-educational, a further heresy possibly the most scandalous of all."[33] By 1900, Chicago, Stanford, Harvard, Columbia, Johns Hopkins, and California-Berkeley accounted for 55 percent of faculty members with earned doctorates in the U.S.[34]

The University of Chicago became a trailblazer in using its football program to bridge the gap between academic and popular culture. Michigan had already built a successful football program, but Chicago's model was followed by other Big Ten universities that built huge stadiums in the 1920s and used football to attract public support, donors, and students. Football made universities appear meaningful to the public because it was "a popular activity intended to make highbrow intellectual culture legible, or palatable, to the public," Ingrassia wrote in *The Rise of Gridiron University*.[35] With the university's esoteric academic disciplines, sports was one part that the public could see and support.

The University of Chicago opened for its first day of classes on October 1, 1892, with eighty-seven faculty members and a freshmen class of 520 from thirty-three states and fifteen countries.[36] Stagg described his arrival this way: "The land was all pasture surrounded by barbed wire.... When I reported for duty in September 1892, no building had been completed, and the carpenters were still at work in Cobb Hall, the one structure near completion. We entered the building over bare planks, and in lieu of knobs on the doors, the teachers carried square pieces of wood to insert in the doors to turn the latches."[37] With faculty and staff in place and strong support from an innovative president, Chicago, Stagg, and a few players prepared for their first football season.

6

The Early Years of Chicago
Football, 1892–1894

*I want you to develop teams which we can send around the
country and knock out all the colleges.*—William Rainey
Harper, University of Chicago Founding President

When Stagg put a poster on the Cobb Hall bulletin board announcing the first football practice in early October, only eleven men turned out. "Some had never played, most of them very little ... and all the other colleges in the Chicago territory had been practicing for nearly a month," he wrote. He told the players he would teach them how to throw, kick, pass, and run with a football. The team had only a bare field on which to practice, no dressing room, stadium or even seats for fans and spectators. He had to schedule away games or rent a nearby high school field for home games. After a week with only three practice sessions, the inaugural eleven went out and won their first game 11–0 on October 8 against nearby Hyde Park High School.

Table 4: University of Chicago Football 1892–1894

(does not include high school and YMCA opponents)			
Year	Wins	Losses	Ties
1892	4	4	1
1893	6	4	2
1894	10	7	1
Totals	20	15	4
Source: UChicago Department of Athletics and Recreation.			

The team played thirteen games in 1892 and won the first six against high school and YMCA opponents. After the Hyde Park game, the team played three games the following week, first beating Englewood High School 12–6 on Monday. Stagg later wrote, "I made the last touchdown by running around the end for one half the length of the field. The crowd was wildly excited."[1] The team played Hyde Park High School again on Tuesday, the Englewood YMCA on Wednesday, and Hyde Park a third time on Monday, October 17. It played the Englewood YMCA a second time two days later. Stagg's teams continued to schedule games against high school teams as late as 1897 when the team twice defeated Hyde Park High School. However, the team managed only four wins, four losses, and one tie against collegiate opponents that first season. It defeated Lake Forest 18–16 on November 5 and Illinois 10–4 on November 16. Stagg scored his team's only touchdown in the Illinois game. In his first season, no rules prohibited coaches from playing on their teams. That first season he played both offensive halfback and defensive linebacker. Other losses came against Northwestern, Michigan, and Purdue. The team played Illinois a second time later in the season and also lost. After the first Illinois game, Stagg sprained his ankle during practice when one of the players ran into him. He couldn't play in the

University of Chicago's first football team in 1892. Stagg is sitting in center holding football. University of Chicago Photographic Archive, apf5-03209, Special Collections Research Center, University of Chicago Library.

second Illinois game in Urbana, so the Illinois coach asked him to referee it. Stagg explained why he was asked to referee: "The game was not well-known then, and it was a regular thing to ask those of us who knew about the game to referee it. They ran through us and beat us."[2] Illinois won the game 28–12.

The first Michigan game occurred by accident. A Lehigh-Michigan game was scheduled for November 12 in Toledo, Ohio, but Lehigh University (in Pennsylvania) sent a last-minute telegram saying the team could not make the trip. Michigan, therefore, sent a telegram to Stagg inviting Chicago to play. "We caught the last train that would put us into Toledo in time for the game," Stagg wrote. The game was heavily advertised and attracted a large crowd who did not realize that "Lehigh was being represented by eleven imposters from Chicago until the second half," he said.[3] Although Chicago lost the game 18–10, it was the beginning of the great Chicago-Michigan rivalry that lasted more than forty years.

Chicago ended the season with a 7–4–2 record, including the high school and YMCA opponents.[4] The lack of a home playing field hampered first season attendance. Stagg kept meticulous records and newspaper clippings about all his games. His records show that the first season barely broke even with $732.92 in gate receipts and $633.33 in team expenses. Keeping detailed records of everything was characteristic of Stagg. Amos Alonzo Stagg, Jr., once said of his father, "He was a very unusual man in that he was exceedingly meticulous, a perfectionist. Everything he did, he finished, he dated and filed it away."[5]

The first year's team faced huge competition for fans because the Chicago World Columbian Exposition was held at the same time just a few blocks south of the campus. Created on a 600-acre park now known as the Midway Plaisance, the fair attracted 200 exhibitors and twenty-seven million visitors from forty-six countries during its six-month run.[6] The white material covering of the buildings gave them a marble-like look, which gave Chicago its nickname "The White City." Stagg stayed four hours to watch the dedication of the buildings and hear musical performances on October 21, 1892.[7]

At the season's end, Stagg invited the team to his apartment: "My football eleven have been over to see me tonight at my invitation. We had a jolly good time together. I set the boys up for a little spread of ice cream with three kinds of cake, grapes, bananas, oranges, and nuts." The team elected Andy Wyant as its first captain at the meeting, and Stagg told them he would no longer play in games.[8] Wyant had already played four years of football at Bucknell University and enrolled in the Divinity School to study for the ministry.

Surviving the Panic of 1893

The Panic of 1893 during Grover Cleveland's administration marked the worst economic depression to hit the U.S. until that time. Historians say the poor economy helped William McKinley defeat Cleveland in his 1896 re-election bid. One cause of the panic was a "railroad bubble" due to overbuilt railroads with 70,000 miles of poorly financed track. Half the railroad companies filed for bankruptcy and went into receivership.[9] Unemployment climbed from 3 percent in 1892 to more than 18 percent in 1893 and never dropped to less than 10 percent until 1899. One historian described the period this way: "All around were breadlines of hungry men without a nickel in their pockets.... Prices fell. Banks closed. Farm mortgages were foreclosed. Ready cash was not to be had. The government itself was dangerously short of funds, and its credit was not good."[10]

The poor economy added to the difficulty of launching a football team and attracting fans. "The panic of '93 tackled us low and accurately, and every dollar in the land hid out in bombproof dugouts," Stagg recalled. Since a permanent football field would attract more fans and more revenue, Stagg asked for Harper's help. Harper sent a telegram to Marshall Field, the Chicago department store magnate, asking for his permission to use a square block of vacant land he owned near the university. Marshall Field cabled back on April 3 from Europe allowing the university to lease it for a dollar a year.[11] "This land between fifty-sixth and fifty-seventh avenues was appropriately named 'Marshall Field' ... in honor of the generous donor. The faculty and offices of the university contributed $490; the students added $281.... Two lumber companies donated boards. I hired one carpenter to put in the posts and stringers while the students ... nailed home the boards and made a lark of it. We graded the uneven pasture, sodded in the infield, and I never labored harder on the Newark salt meadows," Stagg wrote in Touchdown![12]

The football team began its 1893 season playing on this field, but without seats for fans until Thanksgiving. Stagg wrote, "Some wooden horses and planks that were being used in the construction of the new university buildings were utilized as a temporary stand" for the Thanksgiving game.[13] The dressing room was what he described as a "contractor's shanty" used by construction personnel. The football and baseball teams ended the 1893–1894 season with a $238.93 deficit.[14] Nevertheless, while building and field construction was being completed, Chicago finished its first two seasons with a respectable 10–8–3 record against collegiate opponents.

West Coast Trip Highlights 21-Game Season

The 1894 season was the most unusual in Stagg's forty-one years at the university. Chicago played twenty-one games—seventeen regular season games and four post-season games—the most of any season in its history. Following the regular season, Stagg scheduled four West Coast teams, which were the first cross-country games before the Rose Bowl originated eight years later. When Stagg arrived in San Francisco, he told a reporter, "This is the first extended tour of any football team, but I think it will be the setting of a fashion that will be widespread."[15]

Stagg's new wife, Stella, accompanied her husband and seventeen members of the team on a 3,100-mile trip to play three California teams and one Nevada team. "Stagg must have loved the boys on that team because he took ... them with him on his honeymoon," said team captain Andy Wyant.[16] President Harper saw the trip as a wonderful opportunity to promote the university and give it West Coast visibility. Stagg said Harper favored "anything legitimate that put the university's name in print."[17] Walter Camp left Yale for a couple of years to coach Stanford in 1894 and 1895 before returning to Yale. He offered to play two games against Chicago and give 75 percent of the gate receipts. Stagg happily accepted the terms and scheduled a game with Stanford in San Francisco on Christmas day and another in Los Angeles on December 29. He also scheduled games with the Reliance Athletic Club of Oakland on New Year's Day and the Salt Lake City YMCA team on January 4, 1895, during their return trip to Chicago.

"The news that the Chicago team would spend the Christmas holidays in California created all the stir we had hoped," Stagg wrote. One of the first letters he received after he made the announcement came from a Chicago woman named Mary McMahon offering to let the team use her private railway car called "the McMahon" for the unbelievable price of $220.[18] This seemed like great news to Stagg, but it turned out to be an old Pullman car in such poor condition that it made for a disastrous trip. Stagg and his team never saw the car until they boarded it at Chicago's Union Station. Failing to inspect the car prior to accepting the woman's offer was poor judgment.

"The car looked as if Sherman had just marched through it. It was ... a condemned Pullman that had been down the river in its old age to limp from siding to siding on the kerosene circuit, housing this carnival troupe and that minstrel company. The wheels were flat, the paint scabrous, the body humped at one spot and sagged at another. Vestiges only remained of the upholstery," he wrote.[19]

The train departed Chicago at 5:00 p.m. on December 19. "The time was mid–December, and the weather bitter cold crossing the mountains,"

Stagg wrote. "In the middle of the night on top of the Rockies, I woke to hear that the car was afire. The coal stove at the forward end, becoming red hot, had ignited the woodwork. We had no way of signaling the train crew. While the train toiled upgrade, we fought the fire with axes and water and beat it after a blistering fight." After this episode, Stagg wired ahead and arranged to rent a standard sleeper car in Sacramento, which enabled the team to arrive in style at San Francisco.

Stagg was nervous and restless during the trip worrying about game details and finances. He woke his wife up one night after he grabbed her head in his sleep. "I had dreamed I was falling on a fumbled ball on the field. It is not unusual for a football player to take the game to bed," he wrote.[20] The team made several stops along the way for fresh food and exercise. "We have been a little off the regular diet on the way out. But we have played football in about six states, and the team was never in better form," the team captain told a reporter. "Every station when the train took any kind of breathing spell, we piled out and had a run. If the stay was long enough, we took the ball and went through a bit of signal practice."[21]

A *San Francisco Morning Call* advertisement promoted the Stanford-Chicago game on Christmas day. It advertised general admission and reserved seats for $1 and "no charge" for carriages. The ad read, "Great interest is centered in tomorrow's football game between the Palo Alto and Windy City boys, and if the weather permits it is likely that a large portion of the Los Angeles population will spend the afternoon at Athletic Park."[22]

Chicago defeated Stanford 24–4 before 4,000 fans. The *Morning Call* reported, "Stanford encountered its first Waterloo. It was outclassed and outplayed. The home team spurted well, but when pressed on the home stretch, it withered and fell before the invaders, who punched them off the earth, so to speak. Words are inadequate to portray … successfully an idea of the skill the Maroon people displayed to the San Francisco public. Fancy tricks were executed with a haste never before witnessed on the coast. Swiftness in putting the ball in play was the feature in which Chicago stood head and shoulders above Stanford."[23]

The *Los Angeles Times* reported, "The Stanford men were plainly out of condition, while the Chicago boys were hard and active and stood the severe work as if they thrived on it. Chicago won the game by superior teamwork, marvelous interference, and by doing everything connected with the game better than their opponents."[24] In the next game, a rainy day in Los Angeles on December 30, Stanford turned the table and defeated Chicago 12–0 in front of 3,500 fans. "It was Stanford's game when it started, and Stanford's game when it ended, and all through the game the crowd yelled wildly for the boys who wore Stanford colors—the California boys," the *San Francisco Examiner* reported.

The New Year's Day game against the Reliance Athletic Club of Oakland yielded a bruising 6–0 loss for the Maroons. "It was a fierce, uncompromising game in which both sides showed no mercy. It was smash, bang, biff, bing from the kickoff to the end.... Down they went, wriggling, twisting, kicking, and crashing the breath out of one another," reported the *San Francisco Examiner*.[25] The next game, however, was a breeze as the Maroons stymied the Salt Lake City YMCA team by 52–0 on January 4. "The Stalwarts from the Windy City gave Salt Lakers an exhibition of up-to-date football science and defeated the Utah boys by a score of 52 to nothing— Salt Lakers made a plucky fight," the *Salt Lake Tribune* reported.

The West Coast trip resulted in two wins and two losses. It brought gate receipts of $2,920 against expenses of $3,056 for a loss of $136, which was caused by replacing the dilapidated railway car in Sacramento. But it was a public relations victory for the University of Chicago. Fulfilling Harper's goal, the football team received dozens of stories in San Francisco, Los Angeles, and Salt Lake City newspapers. Thousands of West Coast fans who had never heard of the fledgling Chicago university now knew about it. Tully Knoles, a University of Southern California student who rode his bicycle to watch the Stanford game, would rise to become a college president and significant influence on Stagg's career forty years later.

Chicago finished its 1894 season with a 10–7–1 record against collegiate opponents and gate receipts totaling $5,840—eight times as much as $732 during its 1892 season.[26] The team finished its first three seasons with a 20–15–4 record. More than that, the University of Chicago's 1894 team established the precedent of a Big Ten team playing against a Pacific coast team in the Rose Bowl, which was inaugurated in 1902 as America's oldest bowl game.

Stagg Meets Stella

In 1893, Estelle "Stella" Robertson arrived in Chicago as a seventeen-year-old freshman and valedictorian of her graduating class in Albion, New York.[27] She was raised by a single mother who managed a farm and raised four daughters after their father died at an early age. Stagg met his future wife when he was invited to address the women at Drexel Hall and explain the game of football. "In the question period that followed I was asked several questions by Stella Robertson.... Her interest and attraction immediately caught my eye and when football season was over, I made it a point to meet her and seek her friendship."[28] Stagg's son recalled in a 1985 interview, "My mother came up and talked with him. I think she had an IQ of 140. I don't know what my father's IQ was, but I think my mother was even brighter than my father."[29]

Newlyweds Amos and Stella Stagg in 1894. University of Chicago Photographic Archive, apf1-07768, Special Collections Research Center, University of Chicago Library.

Although custom dictated that faculty members should not date students, no university rule prevented it. Stagg described the progress of their relationship in his own words:

> Faculty members for academic reasons carefully avoid dating college girls and for a period of time, I steadfastly supported the tradition. On each occasion that I did meet her, I became more and more attracted by her loveliness and finally before the end of the college year, I asked her for a date. During the summer I was in charge of the athletic program at Camp Lake Chautauqua in New York and corresponded with her by letters. When the camp was over, I took a train to Rochester, N.Y., and finding no connection with Albion, purchased a bicycle and paddled thirty miles to her home to see her.[30]

Stagg had a tender side and frequently wrote poems. His papers contain "A Sonnet" he wrote for Stella while they were dating in 1894:

> I have not seen her face, nor heard her voice,
> nor looked into those mirrored eyes so true
> and soft. And yet I know if I should view
> that face, my heart could but commend by choice.
> I fancy that she had eyes that did rejoice
> to show in roguish mirth their love for you;
> A cheek so fair that veined blood shone through
> like turquoise laid in marble, to re-voice
> the fairness of her soul; a wayward throng
> of half rebellious hair which hung in glee
> around her shapely head. No poet's song,
> no artist's brush, though dipped in imagery
> of soul divine, could stray these charms,
> except to feel them, outward marks of inward purity.[31]

Stella Robertson wrote "Written at Sunset" for Lonnie the same year:

> Dear Lonnie, tis the solemn sunset hour
> when dismal apparitions of my past misdeeds
> flit through the mind. And there is one that speeds
> with mocking smile to see my spirit cower.
> My hopes, my aims, my plans, the very power
> of good I once possessed—the simple creeds
> I learned at mother's knee, my life now needs.
> But all have left me to the shades that lower.
> But yet, remember this, dear friend of mine,
> where'ere I go whatever my life may bring,
> remember that I strove for the Divine.
> I tried to live for right. The years may bring
> thee happier days, but never love like mine
> which came to you unbid and asked—nothing.[32]

Their courtship raised eyebrows among university officials. Lester wrote in *Stagg's University,* "Harper and senior faculty looked uneasily at the open campus courtship of ... Stagg and the teenaged Robertson, the youngest freshman woman on the campus" and said Stagg was troubled by some of the criticisms.[33] Stagg's brother, George, wrote and advised him against such an early marriage with a student. "I do believe that it is not wise. It will take two or three years for both of you to prepare for the event. Your feeling quite sure that you would be very much better off if you were married is no proof that you would be.... All things considered, she is too young." Robertson's sister also advised her against marriage because of their "vast" age difference of thirteen years. She wrote Stella a lengthy letter urging her to finish her degree and then return home for a year to prepare for marriage.

President Harper opposed the marriage. He told Stagg that it would damage his influence among faculty members and students, hurt the university's reputation, and not be in the young lady's best interests. In a letter to Stella, Stagg quoted Harper as saying,

> He also told me that if we get married, as we plan to, that would be a most anomalous position for you—you would be a prof's wife and a student at the same time. At the receptions you would sometimes come in with students and sometimes with the faculty. But I told him we could fix that all right by not coming. He didn't like that because he wants us present....
>
> He told me that if it were anybody else of my rank or lower that did as I proposed, he should ask for their resignation. But he told me he would not do that with me because he valued me so highly and because he believed in me, etc., etc. On four different occasions during the conversation he came to: "but you should do what you think best, and I'll stand by you."[34]

Stagg initially agreed to postpone the wedding until after the 1894 football season. However, Harry Pratt Judson, dean of the faculty, felt they were "perfectly suited" and encouraged them to go ahead with their plans. A few days later, the wedding was back on. The couple married at her mother's New York home on September 10, 1894, just before she began her sophomore year. A newspaper reported, "They were married in their tennis clothes and even practiced on their wedding day."[35] Two years later, she was a member of the university's first graduating class in 1896 with a foreign language major.

Even after two years of full-time coaching, Stagg had not saved enough money for a honeymoon. Stella later recalled: "When I married Lon, I was surprised that he didn't have more money on hand than he did. I don't remember the details, but I remember the feeling of surprise. I knew that he had helped his folks and I knew that he had sent his sister Pauline to Vassar, but ... his bank account was low. We even put off our honeymoon, and that turned out to be a long trip to California with the football team."[36]

Despite Stagg's football success, Chicago was not an easy adjustment after living in the smaller cities of Springfield and New Haven. "I am sick of all this hurly burly—all this rush after money—all of this disbelief in people—all of this criticism whether of work or of character," he wrote to his sister in September 1894. "Such has seemed to me for a long time the way of the Chicago world, and I hate it with all the intensity of my nature.... I am just selfish enough to want to settle down in some peaceful New England town ... and pass the rest of my life."[37] He wavered about his future plans for a couple of years but never left Chicago until he was forced to.

During his first few years in Chicago, Stagg also vacillated between a brash overconfidence and feelings of inferiority to other faculty members. Despite receiving the title of "associate professor," Stagg did not feel comfortable being addressed as "Professor Stagg" because of his lack of an advanced degree. Almost every other professor held a doctorate. Shortly after he arrived on campus, Stagg wrote to a friend. "I have not done anything to warrant a 'Prof.' to be placed in front of my name. I have to be asking people constantly not to call me Professor. I do not deserve all this advancement. I fear greatly that I cannot fill the position I am placed in. I am such a slow brained chap."[38] Six weeks later, however, he said, "I am getting accustomed to seeing 'Professor A.A.S.' and also hearing myself addressed as such that I have got to 'grin and bear it.' But I don't want to one single bit. I am so glad that real professors and instructors of the university have decided to address each other as 'Mister' in order to prevent embarrassment and mistakes," he wrote.[39]

Stagg Publishes Football Textbook

Stagg used the writing ability he developed at Yale to write his first book two years after his arrival in Chicago. Walter Camp wrote *American Football,* the first published book about American football, in 1891. Stagg wrote the second book, *A Scientific and Practical Treatise on American Football for Schools and Colleges,* which he co-authored with his Yale football classmate, Henry L. Williams, who later became the University of Minnesota coach. Self-published in late 1893, the book was picked up by a New York commercial publisher before the 1894 season began. Their book was the first to include diagrammed plays and specific suggestions for teams to follow. Forty-one of the fifty-five plays diagrammed in the book originated with Stagg to show how the game is played. It included chapters on field tactics, rules, signals, and training regimens and a chapter on each position (guards, tackles, ends, quarterback, halfback, fullback). Publishing the book was a significant accomplishment for the thirty-one-year-old coach. Stagg and Williams explained in the book's introduction why they wrote it: "The game of football is fast becoming the national fall sport of American youth [and] there is a widespread want for some source of definite information which will describe the manner of executing … the more difficult and complicated."[40]

The book contained Stagg's axioms for football, which revealed the philosophy that he wanted players to follow:

- Line up quickly the moment the ball is down and play a dashing game from start to finish.
- Never under any circumstances talk about hurts and bruises. If unable to play, tell the captain, he will release you.

- When thrown hard always get up as if not hurt in the slightest—you will be thrown twice as hard the next time.
- When coached upon the field, never under any circumstances talk back or make any excuses.
- Never play a "slugging" game; it interferes with good football playing.
- Don't wait for a runner to meet you; meet the runner.
- Never under any circumstances give up because the other side seems to be superior.
- Let each man encourage the others on a team and keep up a "team enthusiasm."
- Tear up the line, break through, and stop every kick that is made.
- Never converse with an opponent during the game but wait until the game is over for the exchange of civilities.
- Do not contend with a superficial reading on football, but study it carefully if you would master it.[41]

Stagg saw football as a builder of character and preparation course for life. He expressed character-building values in speeches and interviews throughout his life: "I believe in football with all my heart as a developer of men. I know of no game, no other training, which will give the manly vigor and education for meeting life's work and fighting life's battle manfully, as does football. It is a marvelous developer of character in training men to preserve their temper, in self-control under the most aggravating circumstances," he said in a letter written in 1892.[42]

From Yellow to Maroon

Chicago's athletic teams have been called "the Maroons" for more than a century. However, goldenrod—a shade of yellow—was chosen as the original team color during the university's first two years. It was chosen because "the prairie from which the school rose was a mass of goldenrod," according to a university historian. Team members wore yellow stockings and a yellow monogram on their jerseys. At a football reception held in November 1892, yellow was the most common color in the dining room of the Grand Pacific Hotel. "Yellow is the varsity color which will someday be as famous as the crimson of Harvard of the blue of Yale," a *Chicago Herald* article said.[43] But goldenrod didn't work out too well. It ran and soiled the jerseys easily, especially on rainy days. It was also a symbol of cowardice that opponents used to taunt and tease the team.

Opposing fans and players sometimes shouted words like "Hey, yellow, looks like you got a yeller streak." Consequently, Joseph Raycroft, an assistant coach, researched the available team colors in 1894 and recommended maroon at a university-wide meeting in the chapel. It was "one of the few unappropriated shades in the spectrum," Stagg wrote.[44] Therefore, in a conference full of Badgers, Boilermakers, Buckeyes, Golden Gophers, Wolverines, and Hawkeyes, Chicago's athletic teams have been known ever since as "the Maroons."

While developing and promoting school spirit was important to Stagg, he strongly opposed the fraternity and sorority system. When the faculty debated in 1892 whether to allow the Greek organizations on campus, Stagg wrote in a letter to his sister that he believed fraternities were "undemocratic, subordinate college spirit to frat spirit, harm athletics, make factions, produce despicable politics, harm morals, detract from scholarship." He also said they were "largely made up of the sons of rich men and men of social prominence."[45] Nevertheless, ten fraternities and four sororities were eventually organized at the university.

The team's success created considerable local interest in Chicago football; attendance increased every season while Chicago played most of its games at home. Chicago was the largest city west of Philadelphia and could attract the most fans in "the West," as the Midwest was then known. While Michigan had a larger and more prestigious football program, typical attendance in Ann Arbor was no match for Chicago. Stagg had little difficulty in convincing opponents to play at Marshall Field because visiting teams earned more money than they could in their hometowns.

During those first three years, however, there were no conference rules or eligibility requirements. Widespread injuries created the perennial debate over football violence and how to prevent it. Coaches could play on their own teams. Non-student "vagabond" athletes peddled their abilities to the highest bidder. A few athletes played four years at one university, graduated, and another three at Chicago while enrolled in its medical school or divinity school. But the era of unregulated football was about to end, and the conference era was about to begin.

7

Building a Football
Powerhouse, 1895–1905

Football is like war. It's about taking territory.—Condoleezza
Rice

During their first fourteen seasons from 1892 to 1905, Stagg and the Chicago Maroons established their prominence as a national football powerhouse by winning 154 games, losing 38, tying 13, and without any losing seasons. The team's most phenomenal run occurred in 1902–1908 when it compiled a 54-6-2 record and was unscored on in thirty-seven of those games.[1] The university, meanwhile, was establishing its academic prominence as enrollment tripled to 1,868 students by 1901. Graduate and professional schools in medicine and law quickly gained national recognition. The picturesque Gothic-style campus designed to rival Cambridge University was completed.[2]

The team's first undefeated season came in 1899 when it won twelve and tied two. After winning the season finale 17–0 against Wisconsin, the *Chicago Tribune* reported, "In the game yesterday with Wisconsin, Chicago proved it has the right to be ranked among the best elevens in the country, either East or West." Stagg told a *Tribune* reporter, "Our men played the game as they had been taught and played the best they had at any time this year."[3]

Players and students addressed him as "Mr. Stagg," but about the time he was thirty-seven in 1899, they began referring to him as "the old man" when talking with one another. He said at first he resented the term, but eventually accepted it as an expression of their admiration. Consequently, he became widely known as "the Old Man" and was frequently called "the Grand Old Man of Football" by sports writers and columnists.[4]

Conference Organized to Establish Rules

As intercollegiate competition rapidly increased during the 1890s, so did the ruthless nature of the game. Tempers flared, fights erupted, and injuries soared. Between 1880 and 1905, college and high school football players suffered more than 325 deaths and 1,149 serious injuries.[5] With no uniform eligibility rules, non-students played on college teams. In 1890, Michigan's team had eight non-student players. William W. "Pudge" Heffelfinger, the All-America guard who had played with Stagg at Yale in 1889, admitted that while he was still a high school senior, Minnesota recruited him to play lineman for the Gophers in 1887. "It was not unusual for a man to play for eight or so years for the same school. No one thought anything of it. Everyone was doing it," he told author John McCallum.[6] There are even stories of players paid to play football for one college and baseball for another.

Table 5: University of Chicago Football 1895–1905

(does not include high school and non-collegiate opponents)			
Year	Wins	Losses	Ties
1895	8	3	0
1896	10	2	1
1897	8	1	0
1898	9	2	0
1899	12	0	2
1900	7	5	1
1901	5	5	2
1902	11	1	0
1903	10	2	1
1904	8	1	1
1905	10	0	0
TOTAL	98	22	8

Source: UChicago Department of Athletics and Recreation.

To deal with mounting criticism of the game, President James Smart of Purdue University invited presidents from six western universities to a Chicago meeting on January 11, 1895. "Gentlemen," Smart told his fellow presidents, "the problems are awesome." The meeting led to the organization of the Intercollegiate Conference of Faculty Representatives—the original name of today's Big Ten Conference. The seven founding members of the ICFR were Purdue, Michigan, Northwestern, Minnesota, Illinois, Wisconsin, and Chicago. When Indiana University and the University of Iowa joined in 1899, the name of the conference was changed to "The Big Nine." Ohio State University joined in 1912. Michigan withdrew in 1908

over disagreement on conference rules but rejoined in 1917 and made it officially "The Big Ten."[7] Michigan State did not join until 1953. The presidents
discussed and approved these twelve rules (which have been edited for clarity) at the 1895 Chicago meeting:

1. Each college and university shall appoint a committee on
college athletics to supervise all athletic matters and enforce all rules
regarding intercollegiate sports.

2. No students may participate in any sport unless they are
enrolled fulltime doing bona fide classroom work in their respective
universities.

3. Students involved in any athletic competition shall not receive
any gift or payment for their participation.

4. Students pursuing graduate work in any university may not
play sports for more than the minimum number of years required
for securing the graduate or professional degree they are pursuing,
such as three years while in law school if they have not played as an
undergraduate.

5. No person employed in training or coaching a college team
may play in any intercollegiate sport. No one who has been a member of
a professional team shall play at any intercollegiate contest.

6. No student shall play in any game under an assumed name.

7. No student may participate in any intercollegiate contest "who
is found by the faculty to be delinquent in his studies."

8. All games shall be played on grounds owned or managed
by one or both participating schools and not under the patronage or
control of any other corporation or private individual.

9. The election of managers or captains on each team shall be
subject to the approval of the university's committee on athletics.

10. College teams may not engage in games with professional
teams nor those representing "so-called athletic clubs."

11. Before every game, a list of team members who have been
certified by the registrar or university secretary as eligible to play shall
be presented to the other team.

12. Managers and coaches of football teams shall revisit the rules
periodically to reduce the likelihood and risk of injuries.[8]

As a coach and faculty member, Stagg represented the University of
Chicago at the ICFR meetings from 1896 to 1911, but his dual role as a coach
and faculty member began to attract criticism. Some committee representatives felt that coaches more likely focused on their particular sport
instead of the general value of athletics to the university. Although Stagg
was also a faculty member, Chicago was the only school to have a coach

as its representative. Responding to these criticisms, President Harry Pratt Judson (who succeeded Harper) wrote Stagg in 1907 suggesting he add another faculty member to represent the university: "We feel there was a certain amount of feelings among the delegates of the nine [conference teams] on the ground that the University of Chicago alone of the nine was represented … by its coach, the other members being represented by members of the academic staff and not by the coach," he told Stagg.[9]

Stagg was offended and claimed that his dual coach-faculty status legitimized his presence, regardless of criticism. Judson relented, and Stagg continued to represent the university for another four years. Consequently, in 1912 the conference established a policy making coaches and members of athletic departments ineligible to serve as representatives.[10] Stagg grudgingly gave up his position and was replaced by Albion Small, a professor of sociology and dean of the Graduate School of Arts and Sciences.

Southern universities preceded the Big Ten schools by three weeks in organizing a conference that managed athletic competition. The Southern Intercollegiate Athletic Association was organized in Atlanta on December 22, 1894. North Carolina, Virginia, and Duke started their first football teams in 1888 followed by Vanderbilt (1890); Tennessee (1891); Alabama, Auburn, Georgia, Georgia Tech, and North Carolina State (1893); Louisiana State, Texas, and Tulane (1894). Universities in the SIAA evolved and split into what became the Southern Conference in 1921, the Southeastern Conference in 1932, and the Atlantic Coast Conference in 1953.

Legal and Illegal Recruiting

While the NCAA did not officially allow athletic scholarships until 1952, Stagg and all other coaches found ways to offer financial inducements to prospective athletes.[11] Legal and illegal recruitment incentives to high school athletes began in the early 1880s as college football transitioned from an extracurricular activity to a commercialized sport. In the beginning, colleges recruited athletes by offering generous assistance with finding jobs inside the university to help pay for tuition, which was the case at the University of Chicago.[12] Sometimes they weren't even required to work.

A football historian wrote in 1935, "So long as there is pressure for a winning team there is sure to be some activity toward recruiting of players, proselytizing, or whatever the name may be to induce athletes to go to a particular school." He also wrote, "The early rules made the stand of the Conference very clear on these matters. But there were always the undercover activities in recruiting and often little real effort to strictly enforce regulations."[13] The conference passed a resolution in 1912 forbidding coaches and athletic directors "initiating" correspondence with prospective athletes, but it proved difficult to enforce and didn't prohibit them from responding to inquiries.

Stagg's papers contain hundreds of letters to and from high school athletes who inquired about attending the university and playing football. He generally wrote three types of letters, depending on his assessment of their athletic ability: "enthusiastic," "maybe," and "probably not." An example of the "probably not" letter is this one to M.J. Casey written in September 1900: "Your letter of recent date received. We are not permitted by our principles and by our rules to offer inducements to any athlete to come to the University of Chicago. While we shall be glad to have the assistance of yourself and your friend if you come without inducement, we shall not be able to offer any such encouragement."[14]

He wrote a "maybe" letter to Charles Harney in March 1899: "In reply to your letter of recent date, I will say that we do not give scholarships or tuition for work in athletics so we could not accommodate you in that matter. There are no positions under my direction which can be given to university students. Some of the university boys work out two-thirds of their tuition … by doing University service and a good many others find jobs in the city … but there are no positions which can be given to athletic men in return for their services."[15]

Finally, Stagg wrote this letter to encourage a highly desirable athlete to enroll: "The University provides university service to help students who are not able to pay full tuition. By this means a man is able to work out two thirds of his tuition…. A large number of our students help pay part of their tuition in this way. The service which they render to the University is in the way of clerical work, library work of various kinds, post-office, and messenger service and such work as a student could readily do at the same time not interfering with his studies."[16]

Stagg sometimes told highly desirable athletes that Chicago newspapers could give them better promotion than those in smaller cities. He told one prospect, "One advantage to our athletes over any of the other Western universities is the fact that the Chicago papers are greedy for athletic news, and in consequence our athletes are far more widely advertised than those of the other universities. This certainly does the athlete no harm. On the other hand, it is an asset to him in a social and business way."[17]

"Quietly securing a menial job on campus for top athletes was standard recruiting procedure everywhere," Kryk wrote in *Stagg vs. Yost: The Birth of Cut-Throat Football.* "That is, find them a barely legit, menial job somewhere on campus to defray some, most, or all of their school-year costs. There was no rule against it, even if it might have outraged some faculty," he said.[18] Stagg wrote Harper before the 1904 football season asking for help in finding jobs for some new players. "Provision should be made so that eighteen students can work out their tuition free." Harper replied, "We will of course do what is necessary to be done."[19] He also found other ways to help athletes pay their expenses. Although classes didn't begin until October under Chicago's quarter system, he asked new recruits to arrive a month early and promised that the athletic department would pay for their living expenses during the September practices.[20]

Prior to 1901, Stagg and the athletic department made little organized effort to recruit football players. Relying on the university's reputation, Stagg responded to hundreds of letters in the ways illustrated above. At the 1901 annual dinner of the Chicago Alumni Club, some alumni argued that Michigan and Wisconsin used aggressive recruiting tactics and Chicago "took a back seat when the scramble for freshmen began, and it ought to wake up and see that prominent freshmen should have just as good an opportunity to become acquainted with Chicago." Stagg admitted for the first time "that the former policy of aloofness which Chicago had maintained would be abandoned and that Chicago would hereafter use all legitimate means to secure promising 'prep' school athletes."[21]

At the next year's alumni meeting, Stagg said, "You made clear to me that we could honorably work to get good athletes here. We have changed our plan. We have endeavored to secure these students and already the beneficial effect is apparent. But I want to say in all these efforts we have put forth there has not been a single thing done which we would wish to cover up. In all the hundreds of letters we have written, there is not one which I would not be willing to have anyone read."[22]

In May 1902 President Harper initiated seven resolutions to the athletic board intended to improve player recruitment. They included using selected preparatory and public schools in Indiana and Illinois as "feeder schools" for Chicago athletes. One resolution asked "that a system be devised for obtaining information in regard to athletics in secondary schools." This led to the development of a comprehensive card file on high school athletes who received letters inviting their applications. Board member Joseph Raycroft provided the rationale: "The university, to protect itself, must actively engage in a canvass for new students. Others did it, and we must do it, too."[23]

However, the invitation to alumni to get involved in recruiting led to widespread abuses at Chicago and other universities. Without the knowledge of coaches or university officials, it was possible for alumni to offer gifts, loans, and other inducements to encourage prospective athletes to enroll at the universities they supported. Chicago officials discovered in 1908 that several athletes were receiving full tuition remission and not doing any work in exchange. Harry Pratt Judson, who succeeded Harper in 1906, wrote Stagg to inform him, "Men who are engaged in athletics may not be excused from the service requirement." Stagg replied to say he understood "student service" meant that athletes were exempt from jobs because their athletic participation was a service to the university. Stagg's assistant Joseph Raycroft investigated the matter and assured Stagg that the athletes in question were assigned jobs "immediately."[24]

Not until 1927 did the conference adopt strict recruiting regulations, which prohibited:

1. Scholarships, loans, and tuition remission on the basis of athletic skill.

2. Financial aid awarded by individuals or organizations for the purpose of subsidizing athletes.

3. Correspondence initiated by coaches or athletic directors for the purpose of recruiting athletes.

4. Secretaries used for contacting athletes.

5. Employment promised to athletes before registration or excessive pay for services rendered.[25]

Starting in 1903, Stagg and the university sponsored high school track and basketball competitions, which became one of his most effective (and controversial) means of recruitment. These competitions attracted hundreds of high school athletes and fans to the Chicago campus ever year. From these meets Stagg identified the most promising athletes and arranged for them to receive a free one-year subscription to the *Daily Maroon*, which was approved by President Judson. Stagg hoped its daily coverage of athletics would influence them to apply and enroll at Chicago.[26]

Stagg's Leadership Style

Stagg didn't like to be told what to do by anyone except for President Harper, and then he sometimes resisted Harper's requests. Erin McCarthy wrote, "Harper struggled to make clear to Stagg that the Department of Physical Culture and Athletics was accountable not only to his office, but also to the Faculty Senate and the trustees. The task proved difficult and never entirely successful."[27] For example, Harper had to ask Stagg for a report on the cost of improvements to the athletic field and reprimanded him for not seeking trustee approval before work began.[28] Stagg didn't always feel obliged to use proper channels for making decisions, and his approach drew considerable criticism. He resented going through the requisition process before he could disburse funds because he felt requisitions placed his actions "under the immediate scrutiny of ignorant and unsympathetic people."[29]

Students protested in 1896 after Stagg put a poster on the gymnasium door stipulating that students could not participate in gym classes unless they purchased a "prescribed" $4 gymnasium suit. This incident made it into the *Chicago Tribune* when it reported, "A.A. Stagg … is fast making a reputation as a composer of ultimatums and the students call him 'Luther' because of his penchant for nailing his productions to the door. The latest thing in the gymnasium suit controversy is a poster on the gymnasium door announcing after Thursday that no person will be allowed to take part in the regular gymnasium classes unless attired in the regulation suit. They are now asked to pay $4 for each prescribed gymnasium suit." Stagg did not give in to the students.[30]

Henry Gale, the captain of the 1896 football team, resigned at the end of the season due to a dispute with Stagg. When he resigned, he cited "lack of time" and "other responsibilities" as main reasons. "Those who are on the inside, however, say that personal reasons are involved," the *Chicago Tribune* reported. "For a long time, it has been known that strained relations have existed between Gale and Stagg. Gale has his own ideas about football and is not backward in expressing them, while Stagg is equally as insistent in preserving the dignity of his position as coach. It is to this incompatibility of temperature that Gale's resignation is attributed."[31] Gale, however, was as strong-willed as Stagg. Chicago's *Inter Ocean* newspaper reported, "Shortly after his election, Gale expressed the sentiment that he should either run the team himself without interference or not run it at all. Since that time, he has looked over the ground and has decided that he would not run the team at all."[32] Such an attitude on the part of a football player, however, is unrealistic, and probably no coach would yield to it.

Graham Kernwein, who played Chicago football from 1922 to 1926, wrote in a letter: "Mr. Stagg ran the show, and everyone knew who was the boss—he ran it superbly. He was an extrovert and autocratic.… He did not want a good loser on his team, but if we did lose, 'You must lose like a gentleman.' There was no doubt that we were out to win, but in an exemplary manner."[33]

As athletic director, Stagg closely managed the other coaches. When the basketball team traveled to Champaign to play Illinois in 1913, Stagg telegrammed Coach Pat Page, saying, "Would like to see Chicago show some fight. Seems as if the men let up as soon as they feel tired and don't force themselves. Chicago must keep up our record at Champaign and not disgrace us. I want to receive telegram that Chicago won. Fight like thunder at every minute."[34] He also directed his coaches to never speak to the press without his authorization.

Dispute with Michigan, Illinois and Wisconsin

Stagg's leadership style also brought controversies with other universities. A dispute arose in 1899 with universities of Michigan, Illinois, and Wisconsin over the division of gate receipts and game locations. Since Chicago attracted higher attendance and gate receipts than any other conference city, the Maroons played about 90 percent of their games at home between 1895 and 1905.[35]

Chicago's population tripled from half a million to more than one and a half million between 1880 and 1900. Ann Arbor, Urbana-Champaign, and Madison were small towns compared with Chicago's vast metropolitan area. The university presidents at Michigan, Illinois, and Wisconsin insisted that Stagg play a home-and-home series and split the gate receipts fifty-fifty at each location. Stagg was willing to play alternating away games but insisted on a guaranteed amount to cover travel expenses for his out-of-town trips. He made this statement:

> Chicago has never denied the right or the justice of visiting teams to demand and to receive return games. The whole controversy is based on the division of gate receipts. The combination [three universities] strenuously insists that "perfect equality" means for each team to take half the receipts, wherever the game is played.... They say that for Chicago to play Michigan at Detroit and receive $1,500 and Michigan to play at Chicago and receive $4,000 is "perfect equality." Chicago contends that for Michigan to give her a guarantee of $2,500 when she plays in Detroit and for Chicago to give Michigan the same sum when the game is played in Chicago is "perfect equality."[36]

The Michigan and Wisconsin presidents issued a statement demanding an equal division of gate receipts: "We mutually agree not to hold athletic relations with any university which shall insist upon an inequality of rights and privileges with any of our number in any class of athletic sports. This agreement shall be interpreted to mean equal rights in determining where games are to be played and an equal division of the net income from all games."[37] When Stagg refused to meet their terms, the three universities announced a boycott of Chicago games until he did.

The feisty Stagg ignored their demands, dropped the three universities from his schedule and scheduled games against Cornell, Pennsylvania, and Brown in their place. "The college athletic pot is boiling over with excitement as the result of a squabble between the Universities of Chicago and Michigan, Illinois, and Wisconsin. The announcement of the University of Chicago's football schedule yesterday came like a bombshell in the camp of the enemy and added confusion to the chaotic state of affairs which already existed," the *Inter Ocean* reported.[38]

Stagg turned the squabble into a victory, however. The 1899 home games with Pennsylvania, Cornell, and Brown gave the University of Chicago its first big eastern media exposure. The Maroons defeated Brown, 17–6; Cornell, 17–6; and tied Pennsylvania, 5–5. The team went undefeated with a 12–0–2 record and achieved a combined score against opponents of 407–23. Stagg's management in securing three games on home ground with Eastern teams of national reputation was a victory and turned 1899 into one of Chicago's best seasons.[39]

Michigan and Wisconsin gave up on their demands and returned to play Chicago in 1900, and Illinois returned in 1901. Because games played in Chicago earned more revenue for both teams, Chicago continued to play most games at home. The *Inter Ocean* reported on November 15, 1901: "Coach Stagg and members of the University of Chicago football team will say farewell to their friends at the Midway institution and start for Michigan territory where the Maroons will play the only game of the season on foreign grounds."[40] After this dispute, Chicago continued to play an average of less than one away game per season for the next eight seasons.[41]

Player Eligibility Issues

While Stagg was meticulous in adhering to a personal code of ethics (no smoking, drinking, or profanity) he was often criticized for bending and stretching player eligibility rules. Harry Pratt Judson, who was dean of the faculty in 1899 (before he became president), wrote Stagg and questioned the eligibility of three football players. "The three graduates on the list of football men received by me from you this morning are J.J. Lewis, R.C. Hamill, and J.G. Webb. … Webb and Hamill are undoubtedly qualified. Mr. Lewis is registered for only a single course. As I understand the regulation in order to be qualified, he must take at least two courses."[42]

Lester said in *Stagg's University* that Stagg sometimes "conspired" to have football players withdraw from school for one or two quarters to prolong their football eligibility. He gave the examples of team captains Milton Romney in 1922 and Franklin Gowdy in 1924.[43] He also said that Stagg kept a careful watch on his players and "was not above using an informal conversation with an instructor as an appeal for a player's eligibility." When a professor flunked a player after the professor told him the player would pass, Stagg wrote a protest to President Harper questioning whether it was "fair treatment" and "according to rule" for the professor to change his mind.[44] At one point, President Harper wrote Stagg, "Please explain to me how [Mr.] Sincere was permitted to play in the Autumn Quarter with three demerits in previous quarters uncancelled on the Examiner's books? Please let me know to-day [sic] how this happened?"[45] Two years later, Harper wrote Stagg to inquire if football captain Walter Kennedy could play in the last game "in view of the fact that he has not been doing his [academic] work since Christmas?"[46]

Stagg's cutting of corners on eligibility rules for players cannot be explained away. Other authors provide examples of his keeping players with marginal grades on the team. It was documented not only in Robin Lester's *Stagg's University: The Rise and Fall of Big-Time Football at the University of Chicago*, but also in John Kryk's book, *Stagg vs. Yost: The Birth of Cut-Throat Football*. Doctoral dissertations about Stagg's coaching career by Erin McCarthy at Loyola University of Chicago and John Berg at Michigan State University provide more examples.

Stagg's pushing the boundaries of eligibility rules could be rationalized by saying these practices were common among coaches of that era and still are. Ray Robinson wrote in *Rockne of Notre Dame*: "It has always been known that Rockne, as well as other formidable coaches of his era such as Warner of Stanford, Stagg of Chicago, Wallace Wade of Alabama … and others, could be 'trimmers' when it came to obeying the strict letter of the football law. They didn't want anybody else to gain an edge on them, so they often marginalized their adherence to the gridiron codes; evasive recruiting tactics were the order of the day, and most of them ran their shops in violation of normal academic and scholastic standards," he wrote.[47] However, the "everybody's doing it" argument has never been an acceptable justification for moral compromise.

The Chicago-Michigan Rivalry

On November 13, 1892, Chicago and Michigan met for their first game, which Michigan won, 18–10. This game began the legendary rivalry between the West's two most formidable teams at the time. In 1893, Michigan and Chicago played twice. The Maroons won the first game by a 10–6 score and Michigan won the second game 28–10. The Chicago-Michigan football game on Thanksgiving Day became a major sporting and social event between 1893 and 1905 with Michigan winning eight of those games and Chicago winning five. This game always attracted the largest number of fans of the season. During the years that Stagg coached, Michigan won fourteen conference championships, while Chicago won seven.[48]

After Michigan won the 1894 game by a 6–4 score, a controversy developed when Michigan's team captain, Jimmie Baird, told the press that the only reason Michigan didn't score more than six points was because Chicago knew their signals ahead of time. "Stagg saw our game with Cornell at Detroit, and I believe he coached his men on our signals. Certainly, they seemed to know them. Every time we started on a play they knew just where the ball was going and how to meet it. One good evidence of that is … that when we scored our touchdown, we did it on reversed signals," he said.[49]

Stagg responded to his criticism the next day: "I did not know a single signal," and Baird's charges were "wholly unfounded," he told a reporter. "I have personally inquired of the men whether they knew the Michigan signals, and they deny the statement. Some of the other players, however, say they were able to tell by the actions of the Michigan men behind the line quite definitely on certain plays where the ball would be carried." He admitted that he scouted the Michigan-Cornell game the week before, and "I picked up a number of valuable points … and I was able to tell the Chicago team some unmistakable points which preceded certain plays."[50] After Stagg's convincing response, nothing more about the controversy appeared in the Chicago newspapers.

In 1896, Michigan and Chicago played again on Thanksgiving Day, which the Maroons won, 7–6. Chicago's scoring came on a blocked punt resulting in a two-point safety and then a drop kick, which was worth five points under the rules of the time. The most unusual feature of the game was that it was played indoors at night at the Chicago Coliseum, which was also the site of the 1896 Democratic Convention that had nominated William Jennings Bryan just a few months earlier.

Michigan's last-minute 12–11 win over Chicago in 1898 earned the Wolverines their first conference championship. Louis Elbel, a Michigan music student, wrote "The Victors," which was later adopted as the university's fight song. He reportedly composed the song at his sister's house in Chicago shortly after the game and finished it during his return train ride to Ann Arbor. John Philip's Sousa's band played the song's first public performance in 1899, and Sousa called it the "best college march ever written."[51]

Fielding H. "Hurry Up" Yost became Michigan's head coach in 1901 and soon rivaled Stagg for his prominence and success. Yost earned the nickname because he often exhorted his players by shouting, "Hurry up! Hurry up! If you can't hurry up, make way for someone who can." The *New York Times* said of Yost in an editorial: "No other coach and no other series of football teams ever so dominated their era as Yost and the Michigan teams of 1901–1905 dominated the Western conference." Grantland Rice wrote after Yost's death: "Yost was a relentless driver and a killing taskmaster. Football was his religion. But he was the smartest football coach of his time, one of the smartest football has ever known, one of the most colorful characters in the history of the game."[52]

The Stagg-Yost rivalry was so intense and prominent that a book was written about it: *Stagg vs. Yost: The Birth of Cutthroat Football* by John

Kryk.[53] Michigan played Chicago for the first time on its home field in 1901 in Ann Arbor. After winning 22–0, Yost said, "I knew long before I came to Michigan of the great rivalry existing between this university and the University of Chicago. It was my desire to win this game above all others."[54] In the second meeting between Stagg and Yost in 1902, Michigan won 21–0 before 14,000 fans at Marshall Field.

The *Chicago Tribune* reported on the considerable controversy preceding the 1902 game over the eligibility of Michigan's All-America guard Dan McGugin. The newspaper initiated an investigation of McGugin's eligibility and reported:

> Rumors concerning McGugin's eligibility have been rife for weeks. Before the Michigan-Wisconsin game, it is known Wisconsin coaches had discussed the matter informally, but no action was taken as Michigan's athletic committee last year twice questioned McGugin concerning his course at Drake and reached the decision he was eligible. These reports reached Coach Stagg of Chicago and when he was questioned on the subject, he said he would not protest McGugin.[55]

McGugin graduated from Drake University in Des Moines in 1901 and was playing his second season of football at Michigan while studying at the law school. At Drake he played football for either two years or three years—depending on which source one believes. If he played three years of football at Drake, he was now playing an illegal fifth year of college football at Michigan. The *Tribune* sent a reporter to Des Moines to investigate the number of years McGugin played for Drake. The reporter found five *Des Moines Leader* articles reporting that McGugin played in five games during his sophomore year, which would have made him ineligible for two more years for Michigan. A Michigan investigation concluded that despite playing for the Drake varsity team during the 1898 season, he was enrolled in Drake's "preparatory school," not the university itself, and was eligible for an additional two years. John Kryk claimed in his book, *Stagg vs. Yost,* that Stagg "lied" about his involvement in protesting McGugin's eligibility, but there is no evidence that he informed the *Chicago Tribune* or was involved in the protest.[56] McGugin, the brother-in-law of Yost, went on to become head football coach at Vanderbilt for almost thirty years.

In Stagg's third meeting with Yost's team in 1903, Michigan again won 28–0. A blizzard and heavy snowfall threatened to cancel the game, but the heavy wind and snow died down shortly before it began. "The Chicago eleven had a decided handicap in the illness of Coach Stagg," reported the *New York Times*. Stagg coached the game from a closed carriage where he lay "bundled up in blankets."[57] The *Detroit Free Press* called the game "the most severe drubbing ever administered to the Maroons in the history of football of that institution."

In Yost's first five years as head coach, his teams compiled a 55–1–1 record, defeating opponents by a combined 2,821 to 42 points. In 1901, Michigan defeated Buffalo, 128–0, and Iowa, 107–0.[58] The teams became known as Yost's "point-a-minute" teams because they averaged at least one point during every minute they played over three seasons. During the twenty-eight years of the Yost era, Michigan's football team earned six national championships and an overall record of 180–37–11.

The pinnacle of the rivalry came in 1905 when both teams were undefeated going into the Thanksgiving Day game in Chicago. The game occurred just before President Roosevelt held a White House conference with coaches to discuss the national uproar over football violence. Chicago had defeated eight teams averaging twenty-six points and allowed its opponents a total of five points. Michigan had defeated nine opponents by scores of 65–0, 44–0, 36–0, 23–0, 18–0, 31–0, 70–0, 48–0, and 33–0.[59] Since Yost was hired as Michigan's coach in 1901, his teams had won fifty-eight consecutive games. In the previous four years, Michigan had defeated Chicago teams by the scores of 22–0, 21–0, 28–0, and 22–12 after its last loss in 1900 against Chicago.

The championship of the West was at stake as more than 50,000 fans requested tickets, twice the capacity of Marshall Field. The official attendance was 25,791 on a day when the temperature hovered around ten degrees. The game was played under the old rules at the time: the field was 110 yards long with no end zone, and goal posts were on the goal line. The forward pass was illegal, and the length of the game was seventy minutes with two thirty-five-minute halves. Touchdowns were worth five points and safeties (when the offensive runner is tackled behind the goal line) were worth two.

William Rainey Harper, Chicago's forty-nine-year-old president, was dying of stomach cancer at home in bed. A telephone earpiece on his pillow allowed him to hear play-by-play reports from a press agent stationed on the field. Mrs. Harper and Professor Elizabeth Wallace took turns sitting with him. Harper could barely speak but sent Wallace with a halftime message to deliver to Stagg and the team: "Tell Mr. Stagg and the team that you must win for me."[60]

After the score was tied 0–0 at halftime, it became a punting duel between Chicago and Michigan and remained scoreless until the third quarter. Chicago's offensive drive stalled, causing the Maroons to punt on fourth down. Walter Eckersall's sixty-yard punt went into the end zone where it was caught by Michigan's Dennis Clark. If he had immediately taken a knee, it would have been ruled a touchback and Michigan would have ball possession on its twenty-five-yard line. Instead, Clark tried to run with the ball. He ran forward to the one-yard-line but was hit hard and pushed back inside his own end zone for a two-point safety. The rest of the game continued as a defensive stalemate. Chicago's 2–0 victory snapped Yost's "point a minute" teams and a fifty-six-game unbeaten streak, giving Chicago the 1905 national championship. Clark, an Episcopal priest's son, received most of the blame for the loss with some newspapers describing his play as a "wretched blunder" and "lapse of brain work."[61] He transferred to M.I.T. the following year.

A huge Chicago celebration erupted immediately after the victory. The university band and an estimated 2,500 students formed a parade and marched to Harper's house singing the alma mater followed by cheers for the ailing president. Harper's son read a statement of thanks and appreciation to the students. Students started a huge bonfire near Ryerson Hall that night while cheering and singing more songs. The celebration did not end until Monday night with a "Monster Football Mass Meeting" in Mandel Hall attended by hundreds of students and alumni.[62] Chicago finished the 1905 season undefeated and was named national champion.

Michigan was a founding member of the Western conference but withdrew in 1906 because Yost considered new conference rules too restrictive for his team. They prohibited the training table (living and eating quarters for players), reduced the season to five games, gave faculty control of athletics, and limited player eligibility to three years. Yost felt the new rules helped small schools the most and limited Michigan's ability to attract top players and increase its gate revenue.[63]

After a twelve-year hiatus, the two teams resumed their series on November 9, 1918, in Chicago. In a pre-game ceremony, members of the 1905 Wolverines football team presented Stagg with a silver pitcher and ten silver glasses. The game was played near the end of World War I while President Wilson negotiated with German leaders for an armistice that was signed two days later. The *Chicago Tribune* wrote, "While the nations of the world are hoping for an armistice, the resumption of hostilities between forces guided by Gens. Yost and Stagg brought joy to thousands of football fans, and the opening battle attracted approximately 7,000 of them." Michigan defeated Chicago, 13–0.

This series lasted only three years before another hiatus from 1921 to 1927. After that, Chicago lost every game to Michigan between 1928 and 1932. In 1930, Michigan defeated Chicago 16–0 in Ann Arbor, which was the first of several charity games arranged by the Big Ten universities to aid victims of the Great Depression. The game sold 70,000 seats and created a charity fund of $120,000 with $80,000 to help unemployed Michigan workers and $40,000 to help those in Illinois.[64]

Opposition to All-America Teams and Pro Sports

Although chosen for Walter Camp's first All-America team in 1889, Stagg became opposed to the concept of All-America teams. He felt no one, including himself, was adequately informed to evaluate every player in the nation. John W. Heisman (1869–1936) asked Stagg to serve on a committee to select an All-America team, and he replied in a telegram: "Regret impossible to accept membership on committee. Have persistently refused Walter Camp and many others to make selections because I feel incompetent to select even the best out of the men I have personally coached, and I could not give an honest opinion about many others."[65]

When he arrived at a New Orleans NCAA meeting in 1928, a reporter asked Stagg why he opposed All-America teams. "How can anyone do it?" he replied. "Why, it takes a football coach in intimate contact with his men two or three weeks and sometimes longer to know which is the best player on his own team for a certain position. So how can a so-called football expert, who has to pick from the entire United States, know which man is the best in the country for a particular position? It can't be done."[66]

He wrote to a sister: "Years ago in the Rules Committee meetings, I raised the question and fought against Walter Camp's All-America selections being put in the *Football Guide*. Walter was secretary of the committee and a long and close friend of mine, but in his presence I fought for three years against the publishing of his All-America selections in the Guide, and finally won the fight, but it took some battling."[67]

Although he opposed All-America teams, Stagg did not prevent his players from being recognized. Stagg's teams produced eight consensus All-America players during his forty-one years of coaching: Clarence Herschberger (fullback, 1898); Fred Speik (end, 1904); Walter Eckersall (quarterback, 1904–1906); Mark Catlin (end, 1905); Walter Steffen (quarterback, 1908); Paul Des Jardien (center, 1913); John Thomas (fullback, 1922); and Joe Pondelik (guard, 1924). Six of these players are also recognized in the College Football Hall of Fame.[68]

He eschewed professionalism and discouraged his players from playing pro football. "I believe in amateur athletics. I believe in playing the game for the game's sake. And I believe profoundly that if such ideas disappear from our playing fields, America will have lost something precious," he once said.[69] He felt that "professionalism" had ruined the character-building qualities of intercollegiate sports by making money the primary incentive. In 1907, he wrote Walter Eckersall, Chicago's All-America quarterback from 1904 to 1906, and said, "As one interested in your personal welfare, I sincerely hope that you will not connect your name with professional football in any way."[70] Eckersall did not play professional football and spent his career as a sports editor for the *Chicago Tribune*. Amos Stagg, Jr., said in an interview, "My father stated many years ago that there was nothing dishonorable about a player becoming a professional, but he felt a young man who has earned a college degree ... ought to have equipment of character, knowledge, and fight worthy of a man's size job instead of snatching at the first roll of soft and easy money."[71] Despite Stagg's admonitions, eighteen of his former players played for professional teams between 1921 and 1930.[72]

Three years after the professional teams were founded in 1920, Stagg sent a letter to Chicago's alumni and supporters speaking out against pro football, especially Sunday games. Addressed to "All Friends of College Football," he wrote: "To patronize Sunday professional football games is to cooperate with forces which are destructive of the finest elements of interscholastic and intercollegiate football.... If you believe in preserving interscholastic and intercollegiate football ... you will not lend your assistance to any of the forces which are helping to destroy it."[73]

One alumnus replied to defend pro football, and Stagg wrote back, "I regret that your point of view and mine can never coincide.... Since all forms of professional athletics are based on personal gain in a monetary way, there can be no satisfactory development of character in the practice of professional athletics.... There are only a few sports left which have not been seriously professionalized and one of these, football, is the most valuable in its character-producing elements."[74]

During its early years, Stagg characterized pro football as "purely a parasitical growth on intercollegiate football, an attempt to commercialize the enormously increased popularity of the college game.... Personally, I shall be a bit surprised if it succeeds," he wrote in *Touchdown!* "Once the college game becomes a nursery for professional gladiators, we shall have to plough up our football fields," he said.[75]

The "Jackass Club"

Stagg never used profanity—except for calling a player a "jackass"—a habit for which he became famous. He even called his two sons "jackasses" while they played on Chicago teams. The first time a player didn't measure up in practice, Stagg called him a "jackass." The second time he made a mistake, he became a "double jackass" and the third time a "triple jackass." It became such a distinction that many of Stagg's players felt ignored if they didn't make the "Jackass Club." Illinois's coach Bob Zuppke agreed that Stagg never swore at his men "because he doesn't have any men. He calls this man a jackass, then that man a jackass, then another, a jackass. By the end of the workout, there are no human beings left playing on the field."[76]

"I have observed that, like all forms of over-statement, that cursing is an opiate and progressively increasing doses are necessary for effect, soon defeating its own purpose," Stagg wrote in *Touchdown!* "When cursing really does get under the skins of the player, it is likely to leave a permanent wound. Many men have left college with an abiding hatred for a coach who probably bore them no malice whatever and who had cursed them quite impersonally," he said.[77]

At an "Order of the C" alumni dinner near the end of his forty-one years in Chicago, he apologized to players he might have offended by calling them a jackass. "Undoubtedly I had sometimes made mistakes in criticizing too sharply," he said, "but my motive was simply to bring out and develop the best.... I said that I wished to ask the forgiveness ... of those whose feelings I might have hurt, and I particularly wanted to ask the forgiveness of the boys that I had forced into the famous 'Jackass Club' by calling them jackasses, double jackasses, and triple jackasses." He told the audience that he never spoke harshly to a player with little talent or room for improvement. "When I seem to bear down on a player, it is because I see football possibilities in him which I am trying to develop."[78]

Despite his use of "jackass," Stagg usually displayed a mild-mannered temperament during games. Colonel John Long, who played football from 1923 to 1926, said in an interview, "He was not flamboyant. He never threw his towel down or waved his arms in a dispute. He was more stoical."[79] Long also said, "He had flashes of humor, but his stern character precluded warmth.... He was a sturdy, handsome figure, grey hair, erect, snapping eyes, vibrant, hatless, and he usually wore grey tweeds."[80] Frank W. Thomson, who played offensive end from 1930 to 1932, said, "He was always calm. It's possible he was inwardly intense, but he didn't show it. He was definitely not excited. He would sit on the bench and do his directing from there. He definitely wasn't one to pace up and down the sidelines."[81]

"I keep a tight rein on my own emotions, the result of years of self-control," Stagg wrote in *Touchdown!* "A coach must keep his mind on the strategy, not the immediate score. To be carried away by either despair or joy would be fatal to his performance. There will be time enough after the game to mope or exult, if he feels like it."[82]

Amos A. Stagg, Jr., said his father did not brood or fret about losing a game. When Chicago lost a game, he said his father moved on to planning for the next game. When Stagg Jr. was an assistant coach at Chicago, he said he always felt upset and angry after a big loss, but his father was always calm. "He would say to me, 'Alonzo, I worked hard all week. I've done all the planning I could possibly do; we've trained the boys; we worked hard; and a better team has won. So, relax. I don't fight the game over and over again. It's better to relax and say I'm going to do my best next time.'"[83]

Order of the C

In 1904 Stagg organized the "Order of the C," which was the first athletic-letter club at any university. The "Award of the C" membership was formally approved by the Board of Physical Culture and Athletics based on Stagg's recommendation. The new member's pledge read: "We hereby denote ourselves as members of the Order of the University of Chicago C Men, avow our steadfast loyalty to our alma mater and pledge our enduring support to her athletic honor and tradition," he wrote in *Touchdown!* "Occasionally I have denied it to men who played full time in every game and given it to others who served much less. With the 'C' goes a code. A man must be an amateur in spirit and in act, disdainful of subterfuge and dishonesty and ashamed to sell his athletic skills. A man who subscribes to that creed is not likely to turn professional and scarcely more than half a dozen C men have travelled that road in the university's history."[84] The Order of the C, still an active organization at the University of Chicago, awards the annual "Stagg Medal" to the student "with the best all-around record for athletics, scholarship, and character."

Coaching with Chimes

Stagg tried to extend his coaching duties over players twenty-four hours a day. He and his wife donated $1,000 to the university in 1904 to purchase and install a set of campus chimes. They made the gift after two players had quit under fire for breaking training rules. Stagg wanted an audible curfew reminder for his players. Recalling his years at Yale, he wrote to President Harper about the reason he and Stella made the donation. "The sweet chimes of Battell Chapel [at Yale] had always been an inspiration to me ... many times during the period of my training that that cheery, hopeful ten o'clock chime had led me to fall asleep with a quiet determination for a greater devotion to duty and to my ideals." Stagg and his wife stipulated the gift condition that the chimes be played every night at 10:05 p.m. "It was our hope that the bells might have for the student body of Chicago the emotional value I had taken from the Battell chimes at Yale ... as they sounded a nightly curfew to me in training."[85]

Stagg was promoted from associate to full professor at the end of the 1899–1900 academic year. This rank is typically given to professors who publish a sufficient number of scholarly articles or books in their fields. In a university convocation on April 3, 1900, President Harper announced several faculty promotions and appointments to fellowships. "None of these announcements elicited more applause than did that of Amos Alonzo

Stagg's elevation to a full professorship in physical culture and athletics," according to the *Inter Ocean*.[86]

Stagg and Harper's Relationship

During the thirteen years of their professional relationship, Stagg and Harper grew increasingly close, and Harper supported the football program in every possible way. He attended every football and baseball game. "It was a good marriage because they knew what to expect from each other, and both endeavored not to let the other down," Lester wrote in *Stagg's University*.[87] Harper was always thinking about new ways to market the university through its football team. For example, he suggested to Stagg adding a scoreboard on the field so that "all can see and understand" the progress of the game. "Should there not be a band at the Michigan game on Thanksgiving Day?" he suggested at another time.[88]

In 1895 Harper appeared unexpectedly during halftime in the dressing room in a Wisconsin game when Chicago was losing 12–0. "Boys, Mr. Rockefeller has just announced a gift of $3 million to the university," Harper told the team. "He believes that the university is to be great. The way you played in the first half leads me to wonder whether we really have the spirit of greatness in ambition. I wish you would make up your minds to win this game and show that we do have it." Wisconsin never scored again, and Chicago won the game, 22–12.[89]

Harper supported football, not only because it attracted favorable publicity to the university, but because, like Stagg, he believed athletics played a significant role in character development. In 1904, he said in a public address, "College athletics during the last twenty-five years have done more to promote honesty and morality among the young men of our country than almost any other power you can name. Young men need such outdoor, vigorous sport as is afforded by college athletics of the present day. Honor and honesty are cultivated on the athletic field. A young man's strength of character is seen there quickly."[90]

Because he received so many letters, Stagg was frequently behind in replying to correspondence. Harper wrote him on November 12, 1900, enclosing a letter from an athletic official at another university who complained to Harper that Stagg did not answer his letter. Harper told Stagg, "I think it is a little unfortunate that the correspondence between our athletic department and that of other universities is not attended to more promptly. This is the fourth or fifth serious complaint that has been presented to me. Will you not kindly answer it at once?"

Once Stagg became annoyed because he felt that the university's treasurer was asking too many questions about athletic expenditures and questioning his work. He wrote to Harper:

> I understand that I am not to be hampered in any way in my work regarding the arrangement of finances, that Major Rust is not to request reasons for this or that expenditure, that I am not compelled to explain for what purpose certain money is to be used, that I am to put my own interpretation on "extraordinary bills" and am not to be called to task by him for the same, so far as Major Rust is concerned my presentation of statements vouches for money received and spent by me is sufficient.[91]

Harper, however, disagreed: "It is Mr. Rust's business to ask questions and things must be made reasonable to him.... Great care must be taken not to enter upon any large expenditure in the way of improvements without the approval of University officers who are held responsible by the trustees for everything of this kind."[92]

Harper also exercised close supervision over game details. He once wrote Stagg asking him to make sure the bleachers were kept clean: "Has anyone looked into the question whether from week to week the bleachers are kept clean? Is it true, as has been suggested to me by some town people, that they are very dirty and in fact utterly unfit to ask ladies and gentlemen to sit upon? Would it be possible to see that they are swept clean before the large games?"[93] Stagg replied, "I feel quite sure the seats have been swept off before each game. I ordered that done early in the season and have on two or three occasions seen men at work."

After his undefeated 1905 season, Stagg wrote President Harper requesting a $1,500 raise from his current salary of $4,500. "My home obligations supported by my recent physical condition have led me to reflect upon the exactions of my work and the financial return, and I feel that I am justified in asking the University for a salary of $6,000." Stagg made six points in the letter about the demanding, stressful nature of his work:

1. The character of my work is of itself extremely wearing nervously and physically.
2. The special dealings and relations with the players, the students, the public, and the other universities are often complex and delicate, quite trying.
3. The worry of carrying on satisfying intercollegiate contests with limited material and the strictest of scholarship eligibility rules is burdensome.
4. The struggle to secure a fair proportion of athletic material from the high and preparatory schools is continuous moral as well as nervous strain.

5. The athletic part of my work is always in the scales and being tested and woe betide one if he does not preserve a good balance.

6. The nature of my work is such that I cannot get away from it because there is a constant University and public pressure bearing down on me.[94]

Stagg received a positive reply three weeks later from President Harper, telling him that the board of trustees granted his request for a $1,500 raise. With a $6,000 salary, he was making considerably more than most faculty members.

William Rainey Harper died on January 10, 1906, at the age of forty-nine. Diagnosed ten months earlier with incurable stomach cancer, Harper carried on his duties knowing that his death was inevitable. "During the many months in which he suffered terrible pain, when he knew that his days were numbered … he remained ever cheerful and until the last moment possible carried on the duties of his position with all of his usual keenness and vigor," the *New York Times* reported. He left written instructions that no university functions should be suspended except during the hours of his funeral services.[95]

Despite occasional friction, letters between Stagg and Harper shortly before his death revealed their close relationship. When Harper was bedridden at home in November, he wrote Stagg, "I should very much like for you to come over some morning and talk with me a little while. I am not able to talk much, but I should be exceedingly glad to see you."[96] Stagg wrote Harper, "The memories of your many helpful suggestions and your invaluable support and your words of commendation so generously given to me at various times, I shall always treasure as among the sweetest things of my life."[97]

Harry Pratt Judson, president of the University of Chicago from 1907 until 1923. University of Chicago Photographic Archive, apf1-03105, Special Collections Research Center, University of Chicago Library.

After Harper's death, Harry Pratt Judson, dean of faculties, succeeded him as interim president and became permanent president a year later. Judson presided over sixteen years of steady growth as the university's budget tripled and enrollment increased from 5,070 to 12,429 between 1907 and 1923. While Judson was not as enthusiastic of a football supporter as Harper, he recognized the program as a great source of publicity and revenue. He also personally liked Stagg and had encouraged him and Stella to marry in 1894 when Harper opposed it. He would prove to be a capable mediator between Stagg's expansive ambitions for the football program and the faculty critics who sought to abolish it.

Notable Players, 1894–1905

This and the next few chapters will offer profiles of the most "notable players" Stagg coached during the years each chapter covers. While not all were chosen for All-America teams, many distinguished themselves in other ways, especially coaching. His annual reports to the president between 1897 and 1932 contained lists of former Chicago players serving as coaches and the names of the schools where they coached. These reports listed former players coaching at sixty-seven colleges or universities and dozens of high schools.[98] In one report, he wrote, "The demand for Chicago men to fill such positions is considerably greater than the supply." Some coached at top-ranked universities such as Alabama, Arkansas, Clemson, Georgia, Indiana, Iowa, Iowa State, Kentucky, Michigan, Minnesota, Mississippi, Notre Dame, Oklahoma State, Oregon, Penn State, Princeton, Purdue, and the U.S. Naval Academy. Two of these coaches—Hugo Bezdek of Arkansas and Fritz Crisler of Michigan—were profiled in *Great College Coaches of the Twenties and Thirties.*

Andrew Robert Wyant, a center and guard, had already played four years of varsity football at Bucknell when he entered the Divinity School to study for the ministry. No rules at the time prevented Stagg from playing on his own team or limiting player eligibility to four years. Wyant played seven seasons in seventy-three consecutive games from 1887 to 1894. He played sixty minutes every game, both offense and defense, and never missed a minute of action. In 1895 Wyant graduated from the Divinity School and started his career as a Baptist minister. He eventually earned an M.A., Bachelor of Divinity, Ph.D., and M.D. He worked as a teacher, minister, author, physician, lecturer, and financier. During World War I and World War II, he worked as a Red Cross physician. He was posthumously elected to the College Football Hall of Fame in 1962.[99]

Hugo Bezdek, an immigrant from the Czech Republic, attended high school on Chicago's south side and played fullback for the Maroons from 1902 to 1905. During his four years, Chicago compiled a 38–4–2 record, and he was chosen as a third team All-American in 1905. He was one of Stagg's two former players profiled in *Great College Football Coaches of the Twenties and Thirties*. He is best known as head coach at the University of Arkansas where he serendipitously came up the team's nickname, "Razorbacks." He stepped off the train platform in Fayetteville after returning from Baton Rouge in 1909 where the team had defeated L.S.U., 16–0. He told the crowd who came to greet the players that "the team played like a wild band of Razorback hogs." Known until then as the "Cardinals," Arkansas teams after that adopted the "Razorback" nickname, which is a breed of wild hog common in the South.[100]

The next year Bezdek asked for Stagg's help in teaching the forward pass to his team. As a result, Stagg and quarterback Walter Eckersall spent two weeks in Fayetteville in the spring of 1910 teaching fundamental pass techniques to Razorback receivers and quarterbacks.[101] Eckersall worked with Arkansas quarterback Steve Creekmore teaching him to throw accurately and successfully.[102]

One biographer described Bezdek as "rough cut, belligerent, autonomous" but also possessing a "sharp and imaginative football mind." He began a successful coaching career soon after graduation. In 1906, he coached the University of Oregon team to an undefeated season and from 1908 to 1912, he coached Arkansas to a 29–13–1 record. After Arkansas, he returned to Oregon between 1913 and 1917 to achieve a 25–10–3 record, including a 14–0 Rose Bowl victory in 1917. After that he became Penn State's head coach and earned a 65–29–9 record, which included thirty consecutive wins. Besides football, he coached basketball at Oregon and Penn State and baseball at Arkansas and Penn State. His football teams at Penn State won thirty consecutive games from 1919 to 1922, and his Penn State baseball team won twenty-nine consecutive games in 1920 and 1921.

He coached the Cleveland Rams (NFL) between 1937 and 1938 and was general manager of the Pittsburgh Pirates from 1917 to 1919 when he elevated a last-place team to fourth. Bezdek has the distinction as the only person to have been manager of a Major League baseball team and head coach of an NFL football team. He was elected to the College Football Hall of Fame in 1954.[103]

Clarence Herschberger, a 158-pound fullback, placekicker, and punter, was Stagg's first All-America player. Joined by Michigan's center Bill Cunningham, they made history for the Western Conference by cracking the eastern monopoly on All-America voting, which Yale, Harvard, Princeton, and Pennsylvania had dominated. Herschberger played for the Maroons from 1894 to 1898, was chosen an All-American in 1898, and inducted posthumously into the College Football Hall of Fame in 1970. He earned thirteen varsity letters in track, football, and baseball. The Maroons had a 35–8 record during Herschberger's years with the team.

After hearing alarming reports about football injuries around the country, Herschberger's mother had forced him to quit football after the 1895 season. Since he could not play football, Herschberger withdrew from the university and took a vacation. On a hunting trip that fall, he shot himself in the hand by accident. After the accident, his mother relented and allowed her son to return to the university and play football in 1896, 1897, and 1898.[104]

The recently invented X-ray machine was used for the first time on a football player after Herschberger injured his left foot in the 1897 game against Illinois. Because of Herschberger's lingering pain, Stagg assumed he had a broken bone. Four days later when no swelling or usual symptoms had developed, Stagg sent him to Professor Straton at the university's Ryerson Physical Laboratory, who supervised an X-ray. The X-ray determined that Herschberger had not broken any bones, and he was able to play in the next game against Wisconsin. German physicist Wilhelm Röntgen invented the X-ray technology in 1895 and received the first Nobel prize in physics for the invention. The *Chicago Tribune* reported "the X-ray has entered the football field" citing it as "the inaugural use of the Röentgen ray."[105]

In 1896, Herschberger picked up a fumbled ball against Michigan and ran it back for a touchdown to enable Chicago's win by a 7–6 score. Stagg credits him as the first player to use the Statue of Liberty play in the 1898 game against Michigan. Herschberger received the ball, faked a kick, and turned around to give the ball to his quarterback, Walter Kennedy, who circled around the end for a thirty-five-yard run.[106]

Stagg, however, also credits Herschberger with causing Chicago to lose one game. He required his players to adhere to strict training rules the week before a game, including a modest diet. Ignoring the rules, Herschberger challenged quarterback Walter S. Kennedy to an eating contest the night before the Wisconsin game. After the Friday night binge, both players gained seven pounds. Determined to win anyway, Herschberger ate thirteen eggs on the morning of the game and couldn't play due to nausea and vomiting. Chicago lost the game, 23–8, leading Stagg to say, "I am still convinced that we were beaten 8 to 23 by thirteen eggs rather than eleven Badgers."[107]

Walter Eckersall grew up in south Chicago and began as a waterboy for the Maroons in 1897. He played quarterback at Hyde Park High School near the campus. In 1903, he led the Hyde Park team to an undefeated season, trouncing Brooklyn Polytechnic 105–0 in its final game of the season.

The high school named its stadium after Eckersall in 1949, and he was elected to the inaugural class of the College Football Hall of Fame in 1951. The Chicago team's record when he played from 1904 to 1906 was 32–4–2.

One of the fans who watched the slaughter against Brooklyn Polytechnic was fifteen-year-old Knute Rockne, whose family had emigrated from Norway about ten years earlier. Rockne later wrote, "I sat spellbound before the brilliant, heady play of a lad named Walter Eckersall." After the game was over, "I tried to get close to the hero of the day. But two or three thousand other youngsters were trying to do the same thing, so I had to go home without a handshake, yet for the first time in a young and fairly crowded life, I went home with a hero. Dreams of how, someday, I might shine as Eckersall had shone that afternoon were my lonesome luxury."[108]

One of Eckersall's two most famous plays was a 106-yard touchdown run against Wisconsin when the playing field was 110 yards long. The other was his sixty-yard punt into the end zone, setting up the two-point safety and historic 2–0 victory over Michigan in 1905. Stagg always had effusive praise for Eckersall: "He was a ten-second sprinter who was quick as a flash…. He was a beautiful punter, an accurate drop kicker, a deadly tackler, a sure punt catcher, a perfect ball handler at quarterback, a splendid tactician, an inspiring signal caller and a dynamic leader." Stagg also said Eckersall was never injured. "He was so quick that at the last second he could throw himself to avoid injury."[109]

Eckersall was one of the first quarterbacks to introduce forward pass plays after they were legalized by the Rules Committee in 1906. Stagg planned for Eckersall to use the pass for the first time in the 1906 game against Minnesota. Due to rainy, muddy conditions, Eckersall didn't use it until the next week against Illinois, which Chicago won, 63–0. He threw the first pass of his college career—a 75-yard touchdown play to Wally Steffen, who later became another Chicago All-American.

Eckersall attracted considerable publicity for the Chicago Maroons, but not all was favorable. The *Chicago Record-Herald* reported that Stagg had arranged admission for Eckersall because he didn't meet the university's requirements. Stagg denied the charges, saying that the admissions dean handled admissions. Eckersall led the team in failing grades and total absences during his freshman year. His academic eligibility was frequently called into question by university officials. But Stagg defended him. By the middle of his senior year, Eckersall earned only fourteen of thirty-six required courses and never graduated. A notation dated January 25, 1907, on his official transcript read, "Mr. Eckersall is not permitted to register to the Univ. again—for cause. By order of Acting President Judson." After his dismissal, Eckersall wrote an angry letter to Judson, which accused the university of being fully aware of his "loose morals" but continuing "to use him for advertising purposes until he had completed his college career."[110]

Eckersall went on to a career as sportswriter for the *Chicago Tribune*. He wrote hundreds of stories about Chicago football for twenty years. Eckersall's alcohol addiction, however, brought him an early death in 1930 at age forty-three due to cirrhosis of the liver and pneumonia. Although Stagg maintained a good relationship with Eckersall for several years, he gradually distanced himself after Eckersall reneged on a $20 debt and was featured in a national ad campaign for cigarettes—a habit Stagg regarded as sinful.[111]

Jesse Harper (1883–1961). After graduating from Chicago in 1906, Harper went on to a successful coaching career at Alma College (1906–07), Wabash College (1909–12), and Notre Dame (1913–17). As Notre Dame's first full-time football coach, he led the team to an undefeated season his first year and initiated its rise to national prominence by scheduling and defeating some top-ranked teams.

Harper's 1913 football squad (starring Knute Rockne as a pass receiver) posted a 35–13 upset win over Army, which was featured in the movie *Knute Rockne, All American*. Harper's five-year record at Notre Dame was 34–5–1 and set the stage for Rockne's future success as a coach. After a close relative died, Harper resigned as coach at the age of thirty-three and returned to Kansas to manage his family's 20,000-acre cattle ranch. He recommended his assistant coach, Knute Rockne, as his successor.

The *New York Times* said of Harper: "Mr. Harper learned football at the University of Chicago…. Under Stagg, he got his first glimpse of the backfield shift. The shift was a very new idea then, but Stagg recognized its possibilities." At Notre Dame, "he proceeded to lay the groundwork for use of the shift and … [Rockne] proceeded to make the shift one of the key plays."[112]

Since Harper's ranch was near the site of Rockne's plane crash in 1931, Harper accompanied his body on the train back to South Bend for the funeral. Notre Dame immediately re-hired him as athletic director where he remained for three years until he returned to Kansas. He was named as a coach to the College Football Hall of Fame in 1971 and the "Hall of Great Westerners" at the National Cowboy and Western Heritage Museum in Oklahoma City.[113]

Conclusion

During Stagg's first fourteen years, the University of Chicago won 118 games, lost 37, and tied 12. By 1905 Chicago was both a conference and national football power. President Theodore Roosevelt took a personal interest in the increasing popularity of college football after his son joined the Harvard team. But it was also the era of muckraking journalism led by writers such as Ida M. Tarbell and Lincoln Steffens, who sought to expose corruption in America's institutions. With its increasing violence, injuries, and deaths, college football could not escape public scrutiny. The next two years were among the toughest of Stagg's career as vocal faculty critics sought to abolish football at the University of Chicago.

8

Continuing the Winning Tradition, 1906–1924

If wanting to win is a fault, as some of my critics seem to insist, then I plead guilty. I like to win. I know no other way. It's in my blood. —Bear Bryant

From 1906 to 1924, the Maroons continued their winning tradition and dominated the Big Ten conference in both victories and gate revenue. In 1913, Stagg wrote the university treasurer asking him not to publish football revenues. "Some of our rival institutions have considerable jealousy and am rather inclined to think that such a statement of our prosperity might tend to intensify it," he said.[1] During this period, Stagg was the undisputed leader of football in the conference. His winning teams at a prestigious private university in the region's largest city enabled him to wield significant power and influence among peer coaches.

Within the university, however, Stagg's influence wasn't as great. Despite his team's success, Stagg began the early twentieth century facing two big setbacks. First, he lost his strongest supporter when President Harper died of cancer in January 1906, and second, the University Senate threatened to abolish football in February. Chicago's football debate mirrored the debates occurring around the country due to the rising number of football injuries and deaths.

Table 6: UChicago Football, 1906–1924

Year	Wins	Losses	Ties
1906	4	1	0
1907	4	1	0
1908	5	0	1
1909	4	1	2

Year	Wins	Losses	Ties
1910	2	5	0
1911	6	1	0
1912	6	1	0
1913	7	0	0
1914	4	2	1
1915	5	2	0
1916	3	4	0
1917	3	2	1
1918	1	5	0
1919	5	2	0
1920	3	4	0
1921	6	1	0
1922	5	1	1
1923	7	1	0
1924	4	1	3
TOTAL	**84**	**35**	**9**

Source: UChicago Department of Athletics and Recreation.

Football Deaths Lead to Reform

The debate over what to do about football violence began in the late 1800s. Ten players were killed and more than 200 seriously injured in the 1897 season. One victim was Richard Vonabalde "Von" Gammon, a University of Georgia fullback who died the day after falling on his head and sustaining a concussion during a game against Virginia. Georgia immediately suspended the rest of the season, and the state legislature passed a bill banning high school and college football. Governor William Atkinson, however, vetoed the bill after receiving a letter from Rosalind Gammon, the player's mother. "It would be the greatest favor to the family of Von if your influence could prevent his death being used for an argument detrimental to the athletic cause and its advancement at the University," she wrote. "His love for his college and his interest in all manly sports, without which he deemed the highest type of manhood impossible, is well known by his classmates and friends, and it would be inexpressibly sad to have the cause he held so dear injured by his sacrifice. Grant me the right to request that my boy's death should not be used to defeat the most cherished object of his life." Rosalind Gammon became known as "the woman who saved Georgia football."[2]

Von Gammon's death was just one of many occurring in college football in the late nineteenth and early twentieth centuries. The *New York Times* wrote, "Every time a youth steps on the field to uphold the reputation of his college he assumes nearly the same risk that a solder does on the battlefield. Every day one hears of broken heads, fractured skulls, broken necks, wrenched legs, dislocated shoulders, and many other accidents."[3] President Charles Elliott of Harvard, the era's best-known educator, issued his 1894 annual report saying that football should be abolished because it leads to "a large number of broken bones, sprains, and wrenches" and helps players "with reckless violence or with shrewd violations of the rules to gain thereby great advantages."[4] He called football "more brutalizing than prizefighting, cockfighting or bullfighting." Columbia's team surgeon said, "The players go on the field expecting to be hurt and are glad if they come off with nothing worse than a broken bone."[5]

President Roosevelt Gets Involved

The controversy over football violence intensified after eighteen deaths and 159 serious injuries during the 1905 season. Columbia, Northwestern, and Union abolished their football teams, although Northwestern reinstated its team two years later.[6] These deaths occurred among three college, eleven high school, and four club teams. President Theodore Roosevelt injected himself into the growing debate in an address at Harvard earlier that year: "Brutality in playing a game should awaken the heartiest and most plainly shown contempt for the player guilty of it; especially if this brutality is coupled with a low cunning," he said.[7] In October, he invited Harvard, Yale, and Princeton athletic officials to the White House to confer about the problem. They included: Walter Camp, Yale athletic director; John Owsley, Yale football coach; John Fine, Princeton's athletic committee chairman; Arthur Hillebrand, Princeton football coach; Bill Reid, Harvard football coach; and Dr. Walter Nichols, Harvard team physician.[8]

Roosevelt had recently won a Nobel Peace Prize for negotiating an end to the Russo-Japanese war. He also fought the railroad industry to stop widespread rate increases. Now he was ready to tackle football reform. He began the meeting at the White House on October 9, 1905, saying, "Football is on trial. Because I believe in the game, I want to do all I can to save it. And so I have called you all down here to see whether you won't all agree to abide by both the letter and spirit of the rules [and] to inaugurate a movement having as its object absolutely clean sport and the eradication of professionalism, money-making, and brutality from college games."[9]

Roosevelt asked the men to publicly avoid disclosing details of their conversation. But he did ask them to write a brief statement on their train ride home, which they could release to the press. "At a meeting with the President of the United States, it was agreed that we consider an honorable obligation exists to carry out in letter and in spirit the rules of the game of football relating to roughness, holding and foul play, and the active coaches of our Universities being present with us pledge themselves to so regard it and to do their utmost to carry out the obligations."[10] In his diary, Harvard coach Bill Reid later wrote this account of what the President told the assembled men:

> The President discussed the question of foot ball [sic] in general and made a few remarks on unfair play, giving an example of what he had remembered of each college's unfair play from several things that had happened in previous years. He spoke of Lewis coaching the Groton team [about] how to break the rules in the rush line without being seen; also one man's being padded up because of a supposed injury when as a matter of fact the man that was playing in the corresponding position on the same team was the man that was hurt. This was simply to see if they could not get the opposing side to attack the well man rather than the injured man. After sighting [sic] points against each of the colleges, Mr. Roosevelt said he thought the position was one to be deplored and he wanted to see if there was not some way in which the feeling between the colleges could not be improved and the training of the players made more effective in the right way.[11]

Although Stagg was not invited to the meeting, he said he was "heartily in accord" with Roosevelt's action. "Brutality and unwarranted roughness in the game should be frowned upon. There is as much of this brutality apparent at times in the West as well as in the East," he said.[12] Roosevelt's meeting rippled throughout the country and stimulated the debate between proponents and opponents of college football. Proponents wanted to reform the game, and opponents wanted to abolish it.

University Senate: Abolish Football

At the University of Chicago, football's biggest critics were Shailer Mathews, dean of the Divinity School, and economics professor Thorsten Veblen. In an article in *The Nation* in December 1905, Mathews wrote: "Football today is a social obsession—a boy-killing, education-prostituting, gladiatorial sport. It teaches virility and courage, but so does war. I do not know what should take its place, but the new game should not require the services of a physician, the maintenance of a hospital, and the celebration of funerals."[13] Veblen did not believe football was a builder of character, but an incubator of "fraud" and "chicanery." He believed it taught the "predatory

spirit pandemic in American business practice" and characterized participation in sports as an "arrested spiritual development."[14]

The University Senate began to debate whether football should be
abolished in November 1905, two days after Chicago's legendary 2–0 victory over Michigan, which ended the Wolverines' five-year winning
streak. Professor William Hale introduced a resolution in the University
Senate: "In the opinion of the Senate, the game of football under rules
permitting either mass-play or tackling should be abolished." Although
defeated, an alternate resolution passed, which read: "In the opinion of
this body, it will be the duty of the university to refuse to sanction participation by its students in intercollegiate football contests unless changes be
made which will eliminate the flagrant moral and physical evils at present
connected with the game."[15] The Senate passed the recommendation, but
President Harper, the ardent football fan, vetoed it a month before he died
in January.

On February 1, 1906, the united faculties of arts, literature, and science
unanimously passed a resolution urging the university and the conference
to abolish football for two years. If the conference decided against abolition, the resolution recommended abolishing training quarters and short-
ening the season. Two days later in a meeting attended by more than 100
professors, the University Senate again concurred with the recommendation. "The sentiment of the body was overwhelmingly against football, and
the vote in favor of suspension went through without the least delay," the
Chicago Record-Herald reported. The resolution stated: "The senate of the
University of Chicago in confirmation of the action taken by the united faculties ... expresses to the Intercollegiate College Conference its preference
for the suspension of intercollegiate football for two years by agreement of
the conference; but this agreement failing it accepts the recommendations
presented to it by the conference."[16]

"I am greatly in favor of dropping the game for two years," said Albion
W. Small, dean of the Graduate School. "The game as it is played presents
the appearance and has all the earmarks of a professional sport, and the
amateurs have no right in such a sport." Dean George E. Vincent said, "The
remedy of rest is the best way in which to eradicate the evils and abuses of
the present game of intercollegiate football. In case the suspension fails, I
am sure that certain beneficial results can be accomplished by putting the
recommendations of the conference into place."[17]

Stagg was outraged that he was not consulted during these debates but
was helpless to do anything since he was in Florida recovering from his
chronic sciatica. Going above the head of Harry Pratt Judson, who was now
interim president, he protested the senate's action in a letter to the board of
trustees:

Last Friday, the University Senate, I am informed, took action which might seriously affect the work of the Department of Physical Culture and Athletics.... I feel it is not fair nor just that the department of Physical Culture and Athletics ... can have no vote on certain questions of great moment concerning itself. This is so manifestly unfair and un–American that I appeal to the Board of Trustees to see that justice is done to the Department of Physical Culture and Athletics.... I feel that justice demands that we have the opportunity for having a voice on matters which concern its own welfare.[18]

Judson replied to Stagg's letter saying he personally supported the football program but also reminded Stagg that the University Senate "has the right to take up any question within the university that it regards as having an educational character." He concluded, "The whole athletic situation is in a critical condition, and we cannot deal with it at arm's length. If you had been here or within reach, of course you would have had a voice in the whole matter. I am sorry you feel hurt about the way in which the faculty have acted, but I am bound to say that the action would have been much more drastic if I had not brought a strong influence to bear."[19]

Conference Adopts New Rules

Meanwhile, the conference began discussing possible reforms. President James B. Angell of the University of Michigan wrote university presidents inviting them to a special meeting of the Intercollegiate Conference of Faculty Representatives (today the "Big Ten") to discuss possible reforms. In his letter, he made the point, which remains a constant criticism of collegiate athletics: "The university is necessarily viewed in a wrong perspective. It is looked on as training men for a public spectacle, to which people come by the thousands, instead of quietly training men for useful intellectual and moral service while securing ample opportunity for reasonable athletic sports. Indeed, the intellectual trainers are made to appear as of small consequence compared with the football coach and trainer."[20]

While the meeting did not abolish or suspend football, its representatives adopted several strict regulations and policies for its member universities. They included:

1. One year of residence for athletic eligibility.
2. Three-year competition limit for players.
3. Five-game limit per season, which cut the season in half. (limited increased to seven games in 1908 and eight in 1923).
4. Training table and training quarters abolished (which led to Michigan's withdrawal from the conference two years later).
5. Fifty-cent limit on student and faculty tickets.

6. No outside games for freshman or second teams.
7. "University bodies" must hire coaches at moderate salaries.
8. Reduction of receipts and expenses of athletic events.[21]

Stagg's worst fears had come true. The reduced schedule meant the loss of revenues and Chicago's most profitable game—the annual Thanksgiving game against Michigan. The conference's actions reduced the number of games by 50 percent, which reduced the department's revenue by approximately $12,000. The "training table" was really a misnomer because they were basically athletic dormitories in which players lived, ate, and slept. Up until then, universities were asked to charge athletes for room and board in training quarters, but many did not.

Stagg was discouraged and angry. He wrote his brother George two weeks later: "I have thought very strongly of resigning my position since President Harper's death. The faculty have taken things in their hands during my absence and have done a lot of damage to my department.... Harper never allowed any matter concerning my department to come up without first discussing it with me.... I am both sore ... because they have damaged my work so much and hurt because they have not even asked my opinion before taking action [on] a vital interest to my department."[22]

Stagg almost resigned. He wrote a letter to President Judson saying, "The time has come, I feel, when conditions in the University prevent my fulfilling my duties with whole hearted devotion, and therefore respectfully tender my resignation as Professor and Director of the Division of Physical Culture and Athletics, the same to take effect at the close of the present quarter." Although this letter remains in his papers at the University of Chicago Archives, he never mailed it.[23]

NCAA Organized

The same debate was occurring at eastern schools. A Union College halfback died from injuries that occurred in a game against New York University on November 25, 1905. Confronted with the tragedy, NYU Chancellor Henry M. McCracken called for a meeting to discuss whether football should be abolished or reformed. He invited two representatives from each of nineteen institutions that NYU had played in the past two decades. McCracken presented three questions for them to discuss: First should the present game of football be abolished? Second, if not abolished, what can be done to reform it? Third, if the game is abolished, what game or games should take its place? Thirteen schools sent representatives to the

December meeting at the Murray Hill Hotel in New York. While four universities favored abolishing the game, nine voted to continue it. The majority, led by West Point's Superintendent Palmer E. Pierce, voted in favor of reforming it.[24]

At a second meeting organized by McCracken on December 28, 1905, sixty-two schools participated. They proposed a newly organized rules committee of seven members that merged with the old rules committee, which consisted primarily of eastern schools. At this meeting, they created the American Intercollegiate Football Rules Committee (now known as the NCAA) and elected Pierce of West Point as its first president. Beside Pierce, the original members included Stagg, Louis M. Dennis from Cornell, Bob Wrenn from Harvard, Paul Dashiell from the U.S. Naval Academy, John C. Bell from Pennsylvania, John B. Fine from Princeton, and Walter Camp from Yale. Stagg was invited to become a member of the original Rules Committee in 1904 and continued on the new committee. In 1932 he was given an honorary lifetime membership and attended the committee's annual meetings until he was in his nineties.

American football now had a centralized national organization to meet annually, respond to problems and issues, and make necessary changes to the regulations. At a meeting on January 12, 1906, it passed three major reforms: (1) increasing the number of yards necessary for a first down from five to ten; (2) raising the number of attempts necessary for a first down from three to four; and (3) legalizing the forward pass. All three measures were intended to increase the safety of the game. Walter Camp advocated increasing the number of yards for a first down from five to ten to force wider runs and prevent mass plays in the line of scrimmage. The main reason to legalize the forward pass was to spread the distance between players and avoid pileups in the center of the line of scrimmage.

Georgia Tech coach John Heisman had been pushing the old Rules Committee for three years to legalize the forward pass. Heisman wrote, "In 1903 I wrote Walter Camp, suggesting the forward pass be permitted in the game as a means of opening up both the attack and the defense. Nothing came of the letter. I wrote him again in 1904."[25] Two years later, he obtained the new committee's sympathetic attention when it legalized the forward pass.

Nobody could anticipate how dramatically the forward pass would change the game. Football historian Allison Danzig wrote, "Out of the meeting in New York of January 12, 1906, came the legalization of the forward pass, the biggest single development since the introduction of scrimmage and the system of downs in giving shape to the American game of football. This was the big turning point; the turning away from heavy-handed, unimaginative mass attack of brute force and labored progress toward the open, quick-striking offense that was so much more attractive for both player and spectator."[26]

The American Intercollegiate Football Rules Committee changed its name to the National Collegiate Athletic Association on December 29, 1910. The NCAA, therefore, grew out of the need for rules reform. The objective of the NCAA, according to its original constitution was the "regulation and supervision of college athletics throughout the United States" so that athletics was "maintained on an ethical plane in keeping with the dignity and high purpose of education."[27] The NCAA, however, was slow to gain credibility and recognition. Many large universities delayed joining for several years because they felt it would reduce their autonomy and control over their teams. The new Rules Committee became only one function of the NCAA as it grew in the scope of its responsibilities.

Forward Pass Legalized

Until 1906 football was a running game only. When forward passes occasionally occurred, some referees allowed them to stand, while others ruled them illegal. The Rules Committee intended for the forward pass to reduce injuries caused by the "mass play" and pileups of running games and create a more "open style" of play. Questions remained, however. Which players were allowed to catch the ball? Where could it be thrown from? Where could it be caught? Who was given possession if the ball wasn't caught—the defense or offense?[28] The committee originally ruled that the defensive team received possession if the offensive player failed to catch it. Two years later the Rules Committee decreased the restrictions and risks on forward passes when it adopted these rules:

- An incomplete pass where the receiver failed to touch the ball meant a turnover to the other team.
- Only one pass could be used in a series of downs, and it could not be thrown more than twenty yards beyond the line of scrimmage.
- The pass had to be thrown from at least five yards behind the line of scrimmage.
- If a receiver touched but did not catch the ball, it was a fumble and could be recovered by either team.[29]

The five-yard rule, which also allowed only one pass per series of downs, was in effect from 1906 to 1909. The Rules Committee did not eliminate the twenty-yard limit for forward passes until 1912. At the meeting that year, it also shortened the length of a field from 110 to 100 yards and used the extra ten yards to create the end zone. For the first time, touchdowns were allowed with a completed pass in the end zone.

These reforms did not damage the Chicago team as much as Stagg feared. The forward pass proved to be a big advantage with his star quarterback Walter Steffen's passing skill in 1906. Although only about twenty men turned out for football from 1906 to 1908, the team continued to win conference championships in 1907 and 1908. Chicago played five games in 1906 and 1907, winning four by large margins and losing only one each season.[30] The conference restored the game limit to seven in 1909 and eight in 1923.

"The revolution in athletics, and in football in particular, which for over two years has stirred the country and especially the Middle West, has proved itself to be a definite benefit to the athletic world." Stagg wrote in his annual report to the president. The only negative consequence of the reforms was Michigan's withdrawal from the conference "because she would not accept certain changes in the conference rules which were passed during the winter of 1906," he wrote.[31]

Who Invented the Forward Pass?

The forward pass has a complicated history, and no single coach or player is credited with "inventing" it. The 1940 movie *Knute Rockne, All American* gave the fictitious impression that Rockne and quarterback Gus Dorais invented it in Notre Dame's upset victory over Army in 1913 (more on that later). The first recorded use of the forward pass, however, came in 1876 during the Yale-Princeton game. The book *Athletics at Princeton—A History* states that when Yale runner Walter Camp was tackled, he threw the ball forward to Oliver Thompson, who ran for a touchdown. Princeton protested and claimed a foul. The referee tossed a coin to make his decision and allowed the touchdown to stand.[32]

Eddie Cochems (1877–1953), Saint Louis University coach, was the first to have his team use it frequently after it was legalized in 1906. "Eddie Cochems at St. Louis University was the first coach to get real mileage from the forward pass in 1906," the legendary sportswriter Grantland Rice wrote. Prior to the season, Cochems took his team to a Jesuit retreat center in southern Wisconsin for "the sole purpose of studying and developing the pass," according to a 1944 *Esquire* article.[33] The Saint Louis team compiled a perfect 11–0 record in 1906, outscoring opponents by a combined score of 407–11.[34]

Although Stagg claimed he was the first to use it "extensively," he did not unveil his passing attack in a game until November 17 when the Maroons defeated Illinois, 63–0. Stagg wrote, "I have seen statements giving credit to certain people originating the forward pass. The fact is that all coaches were working on it, but I was the first to use it extensively.... The schools in the east were slow and overly conservative in getting much use out of the forward pass."[35]

Before the 1906 season began, Stagg created sixty-four different pass plays, which he taught his team how to implement. He kept his plans secret and planned to introduce forward passes in the Minnesota game on November 10. "I believed Chicago could win all her games up to the Minnesota game without recourse to the use of the forward pass," he wrote. Due to rainy and wet field conditions, however, Chicago saved the passing strategy until the next week against Illinois. Chicago romped over Illinois by a 63–0 margin, scoring twenty-two points in the first half and forty-one in the second.[36]

"All the surprise formations we had prepared for Minnesota, we sprung on Illinois the following week. Illinois was completely nonplussed and mystified," Stagg told the *Chicago Tribune*.[37] The *Chicago Record Herald* reported on the game: "Chicago's gridiron warriors yesterday ground the University of Illinois underfoot at Marshall Field by the crushing score of 63 to 0. In Chicago's victory, the 1906 rules triumphed grandly.... The forward pass and the onside kick were in the spotlight, and the intricate formations and novelties were reeled off with amazing finesse and cleverness by the men trained in the Midway's traditionally speedy, open-field style of play."[38]

Danzig described Stagg's nine variations of a forward pass that Chicago used in this and future games:

1. The quarterback running out from his position and making a running pass to the end or wingback.
2. The quarterback feinting [making a deceptive or distracting movement] to give the ball to ... one of the backs and then running back and throwing a forward pass to the end.
3. A running pass made to the end or wingback by the halfback.
4. A line shift in which everybody [moves] over excepting the guard and the pass was thrown to him.
5. A crisscross pass in which the ball is passed by the rear back to one of the halfbacks behind the end (wingback) who runs back and throws a forward pass.
6. Throwing a forward pass to a shoe-string man or a sleeper far out near the sideline.
7. A forward pass to a single flanker.
8. A forward pass to a double flanker, that is, one man 20 or 25 yards out on either side.
9. A forward pass to one of two flankers several yards out on one side.[39]

These changes opened up the game and the number of deaths temporarily declined. From 1905 to 1906 deaths at all levels declined from eighteen to eleven and only three on college teams. The number of deaths at all levels declined to eleven by 1907 with only two on college teams. "The season has been a success, and I feel the rules should be kept intact," Stagg said after the 1906 season. "Not a single member of the squad has been laid up sufficiently to keep him out of one game. Not a man has been taken from a game on account of injury. With the exception of a few scratches, bumps and slaps on the wrist, the list of injuries is nil," he told a newspaper reporter.

After eighteen deaths in 1905, the number declined for the next three years. But suddenly the number spiked to twenty-six at all levels and ten on college teams in 1909.[40] The reasons were not clear. On November 6, 1909, three players were killed on one day including a West Point cadet in an Army-Harvard game. Both Harvard and Army canceled the remaining games of their season.

Chicago's President Judson remained sanguine and supportive of football. "The death of the West Point player is unfortunate and will give football a black eye with some persons [but] it has not changed my attitude. Accidents may occur in any sport, but I think they are less frequent and less dangerous in college football than in any other branch," he told a reporter.[41] Captain Palmer Pierce, West Point superintendent and president of the Rules Committee, told the *New York Times,* "The recent serious accidents resulting in the deaths of several players have again focused public attention on the game and started a new agitation for either the abrogation of the American game of football or such changes in the rules that will make fatal accidents unheard of."[42] The Rules Committee held a series of meetings for six months in 1910 debating changes to make the game safer.

Table 7: Football Casualties, 1905–1916

Year	College	All Levels
1905	3	18
1906	3	11
1907	2	11
1908	6	13
1909	10	26
1910	5	14
1911	3	14
1912	1	11

Year	College	All Levels
1913	3	14
1914	2	12
1915	NA	NA
1916	3	16

Source: John Sayle Waterson, College Football: History, Spectacle, Controversy (Johns Hopkins University Press, 2000).

Considerable debate and division among committee members occurred in the 1910 meetings about whether they should repeal the legalization of the forward pass. "To forward pass or not to forward pass—that was the question which occupied the Intercollegiate Football Rules Committee sitting in its second session of the year" the *New York Times* reported on March 25, 1910. The story cited Stagg as the "leading exponent in the committee of the retention of the forward pass." His blackboard presentation about the advantages and safety of the forward pass was mentioned several times by other committee members who argued in favor of retaining it. But at the end of the day, the divided committee made no recommendations.

At its next meeting on April 30, the committee wrestled all day and "found too many problems still unsolved when evening came" and again took no definite action. It did accept a report from Stagg's subcommittee about ways to increase the game's safety. Its report made some recommendations that included, among others, that games should be limited to one per week, that teams must practice at least two weeks before their first game, ages and weights of competing teams should be approximately equal, and no games should be allowed between college and high school teams.

The committee didn't adopt significant rules changes until the August 17 meeting just before the football season began. Although it retained the forward pass, the quarter structure of the game was changed into what it remains today. Instead of two halves of thirty-five minute each, the committee divided the game into four quarters of fifteen minutes each. A fifteen-minute intermission was allowed between the second and third quarter, and a three-minute intermission between the first and second and third and fourth quarters. At the beginning of the second and fourth quarters, the teams changed goals, but the team possession and distance remaining for the first down remained the same.[43] Although it isn't clear exactly what caused the 1909 spike in deaths, the number of deaths and injuries in football began a steady decline in 1910 season and succeeding years. Reducing the game's length by ten minutes gave less time for serious injuries to occur and adding three-minute breaks between quarters gave coaches time to assess and remove injured players from the game.

Stagg's Football Innovations

Stagg is widely credited with originating the huddle in 1896. A huddle gave the quarterback time to explain the next play and signal when to hike the ball. During the first thirty years of college football, however, huddles were unknown. In a 1941 letter, Stagg said that Robert Zuppke, Illinois coach from 1913 to 1941, was probably the first coach to use the huddle "regularly in game after game." But Stagg said he was the first to ever use it in a game. In an indoor game at the Chicago Coliseum, he said the crowd noise was so loud that players couldn't hear the signals.

"In the Chicago-Michigan game played on November 26, 1896, I had the Chicago players trained to group themselves a few yards back of the scrimmage line in what now is termed as a 'huddle' to get the signal, and I also used series plays. My reason for doing both [of] these was that I feared the cheering would reverberate so loudly in the Coliseum that our boys would have difficulty in hearing the signals. In that game, Chicago played much faster than Michigan whose play was slowed down by their difficulty in hearing the signals," he said.[44]

"The advantage of the huddle system is that, first, the signals can be given without the opponents being able to hear them and interpret them," he wrote to a friend. "Second, everybody being able to understand them; third, in case one or two of the players do not understand the signal, it can be made plain to them before they leave the huddle; fourth, in some games when there is a good deal of noise from cheering through megaphones, the signal is sometimes not clearly heard under the quarterback system of calling," Stagg wrote.[45]

In the 1894 Michigan game, which Chicago lost, 6–4, Stagg used the "onside kick" on a kickoff for the first time. The onside kick is popular today in the closing minutes of a game when the team losing by a few points wants to get the ball back quickly and go for the winning touchdown. John Heisman credited Stagg as the first to use it in his book *Intercollegiate Football.* "The fake kick-off—a dribble kick which travels slowly and gives the kicker's own side time to overtake and recover the ball—was invented by Stagg," Heisman wrote.[46]

In 1896 Stagg was also the first coach to use his offensive center to hike the football directly to the punter instead of the quarterback. He wrote, "So far as I know, I originated the quick kick in football; for in 1896, I had Herschberger, my punter, drop back quickly from his position at left half and receive a direct pass five or six yards from the center. Previously the ball had always been passed back by the quarterback."[47] What a quick kick meant was that Herschberger kicked the ball sooner than the other team expected and it wasn't properly positioned to catch it. "Quick kicks" are still used today by professional and college teams.

Until 1913 reporters and fans had trouble distinguishing between players because they did not have numbers or names on their jerseys. Stagg was the first coach to use numbered jerseys when Chicago played Wisconsin on November 22, 1913. The twelve Chicago team members wore jerseys with white numbers beginning with "1" and ending with "12." Little more than a week later, the conference adopted his proposal to require all teams to put numbers on their players' jerseys. A year later the national Rules Committee recommended it. "In 1915 the Rules Committee had for the first time recommended that players be numbered. It had urged this policy at subsequent meetings and, during this period, practically all colleges complied with the request," Weyand wrote in *American Football: Its History and Development*. Not until 1937 did the Rules Committee start requiring numerals on the front and back of jerseys of all college teams.[48]

Stagg invented the lineman's charging sled. Still used today for linemen practice, a charging machine is a steel sled about twelve-feet wide with six or seven padded, erect dummies. Coaches could stand on the sled and give instructions to offensive linemen to practice their charging and blocking. The *Chicago Record-Herald* wrote on September 23, 1904: "A new feature was added to the practice of the Maroons yesterday. In addition to the usual punting, going down the field for the ball, signal drill and scrimmage, Stagg brought into use for the first time his new charging machine."

Stagg also innovated the use of protective knee pads. Bill Reid, Harvard's football coach in the early 1900s, wrote, "Stagg uses sponge put into the men's stockings for knee pads and has found them thoroughly successful, owing to the great amount of resilience in the porous sponge. He says that if the stockings are pretty fairly tight, there is no danger that the sponge will shift, and that the sponge is not only light but fairly cool. To prevent injury in falling on the ball, Stagg practices a pretty good scheme."[49] Knute Rockne also credits Stagg with creating the backfield shift, an offensive formation he used successfully while Notre Dame coach (more about the backfield shift in Chapter 12).

According to Danzig's *History of American Football,* Stagg made four contributions to the principles of the T-formation, which is when the backfield lines up in the approximate shape of a "T." First, he changed the low position of the quarterback to a stand-up position in 1894. Second, he originated in 1899–1901 the split buck plays preceded by feints and pivots. Feints, pivots, and bucks are deceptive plays where the quarterback fakes a pass or a handoff and gives it to a halfback coming around from behind or in another direction. The third was the quarterback "keeper" play in 1905 where he pivots, fakes a handoff, and runs around the end. The fourth was the "man-in-motion" play that Stagg called a "Pedinger," Danzig wrote.[50]

Cohane's *Great College Football Coaches of the Twenties and Thirties,* Danzig's *The History of American Football,* and other football histories credit Stagg with originating twenty-nine "firsts" that included[51]:

1899—Tackling dummy
1890—Ends-back formation
1890—Reverse play
1890—Hidden ball play
1891—Indoor game under lights
1891—7–2–2 defense (seven linemen, two linebackers, one safety)
1893—Football technique book with play diagrams (co-authored, 1893)
1894—Intersectional game (Chicago vs. Stanford)
1894—Quarterback in upright position instead of kneeling
1894—Onside kickoff
1896—Quick punt (unexpected by opposing team)
1896—Huddle
1896—Direct hike to the punter
1896—Wind sprints (for practices)
1897—Line shifts
1891—7–3–1 defense (seven linemen, three linebackers, and one safety)
1898—Quarterback lateral pass
1899—Halfback in motion
1900—Unbalanced offensive line
1900—Lights on practice field
1904—Backfield shift (later known as Notre Dame shift)
1904—Linemen's charging sled
1905—Quarterback keeper play
1906—Awarding letters to players
1908—Statue of Liberty play
1913—Numbers on jerseys
1918—Cross-blocking (in offensive line)
1927—Knit pants
1932—6–2–1–2 defense (six linemen, two linebackers, one safety, two deep safeties)

This list compiled from several sources is not definitive since there are no official record books on football inventions and innovations. However,

Lester wrote in *Stagg's University*, "Stagg was the most prolific creator of game strategies and play tactics during the last decade of the nineteenth century and the first twenty-five years of the twentieth." He added, "Stagg's most significant contributions occurred in two major areas of the development of intercollegiate football: the 'open game' and the forward pass. These proved to be lasting features of the twentieth-century game and became irrevocably tied in the American mind with the nature of the game."[52]

Stagg also became known for creating trick plays that deceived the opposing team. Chicago was losing when it played Iowa in 1913 and needed a big gain for a first down. Just before the ball was hiked, the Chicago fullback pointed into the Iowa backfield and shouted, "Hey, what's that?" When Iowa players turned around to look, Chicago hiked the ball, and the quarterback passed it for a twenty-yard gain. Stagg said, "It was a perfectly legitimate play. In football, the game is to outwit your opponents. The Iowa players hadn't learned that they should keep their minds on the game, even if a boy burst behind them."[53] At another time, he asked a pass receiver to limp to the sideline and pretend he was injured. Defensive players shifted their coverage. Just as the quarterback started calling signals, the receiver lined up and ran to catch a pass with no defensive players anywhere around.

Other trick plays Stagg developed were the "sleeper" and "shoestring" plays. On the sleeper, a player strays away from the scrimmage and plants himself on the sideline so the opposing side won't notice him. From here, "he can be tossed a wide lateral pass with a clear field for a long run." The shoestring is similar in that the player strays away from the scrimmage and then, "He kneels down to tie his shoestring." From here, he can receive a lateral pass and have a clear field ahead of him toward the goal line, according to a description in a 1929 *Christian Science Monitor* article.[54]

The "Statue of Liberty" play used by Stagg for the first time in 1908 was another trick play. Although many variations are used today, it originated as a result of the legalization of the forward pass. The quarterback drops back and pretends to throw a pass. As he raises his arm holding the football, a split-end or wingback comes around from behind and takes the ball out of his hand and runs around the other end. When properly executed, the quarterback has one hand in the air and the other at his side, resembling the pose of the Statue of Liberty.[55]

Chicago Athletics Expand to Other Sports

By 1908, Chicago's intercollegiate athletics had expanded beyond football, baseball, and track. "The division has made a strong effort to broaden the athletic work of the university so that it would touch a larger number of the student body," Stagg wrote in his 1908–1909 annual report. The university now sponsored intercollegiate athletic teams in swimming, water polo, gymnastics, fencing, wrestling, cross-country running, and basketball. "There has been so much interest in the last sport, namely basketball, during the past two years that it has practically taken its place among the major sports," he wrote. Both the basketball and swimming teams won conference championships in 1908, 1909, and 1910. The baseball team won conference championships in 1909 and 1913.[56]

Women's athletics had also expanded to include many teams. "It has now become the great ambition of women students to make one of the several teams sponsored by the [women's] department, namely the baseball, basketball, or hockey teams. There is intense interest among the women in these sponsors and keen competition to secure places on the teams." There were also opportunities for women to participate in rowing, tennis, golf, swimming, and ring hockey. "Under the instruction of Mr. Knudson, eighty-one women students have learned to swim during the past year," Stagg reported.[57]

A 1913 editorial in the *University of Chicago Magazine* stated: "Mr. Stagg is now fifty years old. He has given twenty of the best years of his life to the incessant service of the University. His accomplishments in athletics speak for themselves. For all the slenderness of our material and the strictness of our scholastic requirements, Chicago is usually the team which must be beaten if the championship is to be won. The West is unanimous in the opinion that as a football coach Mr. Stagg is the best ever. As a moral force he is extraordinary. The moral evils of which we hear so much ... simply do not exist under his leadership."[58]

Marshall Field to Stagg Field

The gridiron where Chicago football teams played was known as "Marshall Field" from 1893 until 1913 when it was expanded and renamed "The Athletic Field of the University of Chicago." That name didn't last long. *Chicago Tribune* sports editor Harvey T. Woodruff wrote a column urging the university to rename it "Stagg Field." He wrote: "Marshall Field, a punning misnomer which became attached to the athletic grounds of the University of Chicago as a supposed honor to the late Marshall Field has given way to the official title of 'the Athletic Field of the University of Chicago.' The new handle is cumbersome. It is too long for colloquial or newspaper use ... but WHY NOT CALL IT STAGG FIELD?"[59]

The idea caught on quickly. More than 500 members of the Chicago Alumni Club endorsed Woodruff's idea a month later at a dinner and petitioned the faculty and trustees to adopt it. Stagg, who was the guest of honor, protested. "It is not my idea that any memory of myself be left to the university. I ask that the old name be not changed," he said. But the measure "passed over his objection and was approved by the board of trustees."[60] With ticket demand exceeding seating capacity for many years, Stagg continually lobbied the president and trustees to build a new stadium. He never got the new stadium, but in the last of its expansions, Stagg Field was expanded to 56,000 seats in 1925.[61]

After the university abandoned its football program in 1939, the federal government secretly built the world's first nuclear reactor in the former squash courts underneath the west stands of Stagg Field. Beginning in October 1942, scientists, students, and laborers worked side by side as many as ninety hours a week to build a lattice of graphite bricks and uranium into a twenty-foot-tall, beehive-shaped structure. This structure known as "Chicago Pile-1" created a chain reaction from the splitting of a single uranium nucleus on December 2. Led by Italian scientist Enrico Fermi (1901–1954), the Manhattan Project's achievement led to the atomic bombs dropped over Hiroshima and Nagasaki, Japan.[62] The 577,000 square-feet Joseph Regenstein Library now stands on the twelve-acre site of the original Stagg Field. The university built a new Stagg Field on the northwest corner of the campus and included the gate from the original facility.[63]

World War I Forces Restrictions

The federal government forced Stagg to relinquish control of physical education and athletics during World War I. In the summer of 1918, the U.S. War Department created the Student Army Training Corps (SATC) to train soldiers for the war. Every male student became "a private in the U.S. Army under military discipline and orders and subject to military duty in the field at any time." Male students were required to enlist in SATC and train for the military while taking courses. SATC regulations also superseded conference rules, and the conference relinquished control over intercollegiate athletics at its member schools.[64] "The regular physical culture requirement was in the hands of the military department. The gymnasium and athletic field [were] taken over for drill; the room under the grandstand was changed into barracks, and military discipline was the dominant feature of the Fall Quarter," Stagg wrote in his 1918–19 annual report.[65]

The War Department initially asked all universities to suspend intercollegiate athletics for the war's duration and, without Stagg's leadership, that almost occurred. Stagg was the first western athletic director to publicly oppose this onerous requirement because it would lead to financial devastation for most programs. Wisconsin and Minnesota discontinued their programs, but Stagg appealed to other universities to continue theirs. He argued that the physical conditioning of intercollegiate athletics would prepare men to become successful soldiers. He told the *Christian Science Monitor* that a hundred men "holding themselves with the highest ideals of training and undergoing the practice of athletics will be in far better physical condition to stand the hardships of actual military campaigning than men who take military drill with its minimum of physical exercise."[66] He argued that three hours of drill and two hours of classroom lectures in military tactics still allow plenty of time to participate in athletic practices and games.

Though it didn't require the suspension of all games, the War Department required universities to limit their games to November and two away games. These restrictions severely hurt Chicago's football revenue. "All of the western universities suffered a great loss of receipts from athletic sources and in as much as the income from the football game is the great source of capital, financially the fall of 1918 was disastrous," Stagg wrote in his annual report.

Stagg's worst season came in 1918 when Chicago lost all five conference games and won only one against a nonconference opponent. The team was also limited by restrictions imposed by the SATC and the Spanish flu pandemic. Eighteen schools did not play football in 1918 and many more played only three or four games because of the war and the flu. At the nearby Great Lakes Naval Air Station, 100 sailors died from the flu and 50,000 were given daily nose and throat sprays.[67]

Stagg wrote in *Touchdown!,* "The success of these S.A.T.C. elevens depended very largely on whether the local commandant happened to be a football fan or not. Those who were saw to it that no bugle calls interfered with practice, and first-rate teams resulted. Elsewhere the squad's life was not a happy one."[68] With a 1–5 season, the University of Chicago's SATC commandant, Major Henry S. Wygant, was probably not a fan.[69]

The United War Work Campaign was organized by international YMCA leader John R. Mott to raise funds for the war-related work of several religious organizations, including the YMCA, Knights of Columbus, Jewish Welfare Board, and the Salvation Army. Mott was ironically the same YMCA leader whom Stagg overheard at the 1888 conference saying to a friend, "Too bad Stagg can't make a talk," which helped convince him to give up his desire to become a minister. The United War Work Campaign planned to raise funds by sponsoring athletic games across the country. A staff member wrote Stagg asking for his approval and assistance in organizing several games to benefit the drive. Stagg replied that their funds had already been depleted by SATC game restrictions. He said he and other athletic leaders with whom he had spoken, including Knute Rockne, strongly opposed donating proceeds from any future games. "To assume further burdens such as you suggest would be suicidal to many athletic departments."[70]

Stagg praised college athletes for their response to the war effort. "No finer testimony of the worth of intercollegiate athletics could be given than in the response of college athletes throughout the U.S. when the call for volunteers for the war was made. Football men, track men, baseball men, basketball men and athletes of all sports answered the summons in enormous numbers," he wrote in his 1916–17 annual report. In an article for *National Defense* magazine, he wrote, "The record of Chicago athletes in the service of their country is one of which the university and Athletic Department are justly proud." He cited 5,155 Chicago students or alumni who served in the war and 1,016 who were commissioned officers. Among those who served, he said 176 including seventy-four commissioned officers were athletes and members of the "Order of the C." Stagg concluded by saying, "God knows I am unalterably opposed to war and believe in governmental use of all just measures for its prevention, but I am unalterably opposed to any theory of unpreparedness."[71]

If the winless 1918 season was Chicago's worst, the Maroons bounced back quickly in 1919 and beat the Great Lakes Naval Station team 123–0 in the season opener. While it was the highest-scoring game in Chicago's football history, the highest-scoring game in college football history occurred in 1916 when Georgia Tech coached by John Heisman beat Cumberland College 222–0.

Chicago finished its 1919 season with a respectable 5–2 record. After the war, the 1920s brought a great expansion in the public's appetite for college football, especially after radio broadcasting of games began in 1922. Football historian Alison Danzig wrote, "The Golden Twenties were truly the golden age of intercollegiate football. It was the period of greatest growth and followed the return of thousands of athletes from the armed forces. It was the decade in which interest mounted to dizzying heights, and new stadiums were opened in all parts of the country."[72] Seventy-four universities constructed concrete stadiums during the 1920s with seven that seated more than seventy thousand.

Meanwhile, Chicago continued to win most of its games and was forced to turn away thousands who couldn't obtain tickets at Stagg Field. "As never before the limitation of the seating capacity of the athletic field was felt during the football season of 1921. At the Ohio State and Wisconsin games, thousands of people failed to obtain tickets. At the [Wisconsin] game the number of those turned away being estimated at 30,000," Stagg wrote in his annual report.

Second Game on National Radio

Eastern football teams, especially Harvard, Yale, and Princeton, dominated college football for its first fifty years. Most Big Ten schools did not become national football powers until the 1920s. The Chicago-Princeton game in 1921 was the first time Chicago traveled to play an eastern team, and Chicago was a three-to-one underdog. New Jersey's two U.S. senators joined President Judson, his wife, and 30,000 other fans for the game. Chicago won, 9–0, in a huge upset. The *Boston Globe* called it "Western football's greatest triumph," saying it marked the first time one of the East's "Big Three" (Harvard, Yale, Princeton) was defeated by a Western team: "This defeat by the Westerners must stand forever in Princeton's football history."[73]

The 1922 Chicago-Princeton game played in Chicago was the second college game broadcast on national radio, which helped stimulate college football in becoming a national pastime. It was also the first time an eastern team traveled to play in the Midwest.[74] The broadcast originated at Chicago's KYW radio station, was re-broadcast on New York's WEAF and then to the rest of the country. Stagg Field was sold out weeks in advance. The Chicago ticket director said, "I could have sold 200,000 tickets if the stadium had been big enough."

Chicago led 18–7 until the fourth quarter when Princeton scored two touchdowns to win 21–18, giving Chicago its only loss of the season. With thirty seconds to go, Chicago was threatening to score from its one-yard line. Chicago's assistant coach, Fritz Crisler, urged Stagg to send his son Paul, a substitute quarterback, into the game with instructions to pass. Crisler believed that Princeton was preparing for a run that would leave the end zone wide open. Stagg refused to send his son into the game. Many Stagg biographies report that he refused because it violated the rule that made it illegal for a substitute player to take instructions into the game. Stagg himself had sponsored that legislation to the Rules Committee in 1917. Years later, however, Amos Stagg, Jr., said the myth wasn't true. He said his father didn't send him into the game because he wasn't as large or fast as the first-string quarterback. "I weighed about 145 pounds at the time, and the quarterback weighed 185 and was faster and had more power," he said.[75] Chicago fullback John Thomas took the ball and plunged toward the goal but ended up inches short.[76]

Stagg was asked later in the survey what effect he believed radio had on football attendance. William F. Osburn, who was research director for the government's Committee on Social Trends, wrote Stagg, "I am writing to ask you whether you will give me your impressions of the effect of the radio on sports. I have been told that the broadcasting of certain athletics, like football, has heightened interest in the game and has resulted in a larger attendance at games."[77]

Stagg replied to tell him that Big Ten coaches believed radio hurt college football attendance. "Broadcasting has been discussed by the Big Ten athletic directors and the consensus of opinion is that it has not increased attendance," he said. "The majority of us believe that the broadcasting of the games is having a deteriorating effect on the attendance because the experts in broadcasting are doing the job so well and in such an interesting manner."[78]

Big Ten Opponents

Between 1892 and 1932, the Maroons won more games than they lost against every conference opponent except Michigan, Minnesota, Wisconsin, and Ohio State. Indiana and Purdue were their easiest opponents. After Michigan seceded from the conference in 1906, Minnesota replaced the Wolverines in Chicago's schedule. Minnesota was coached by Stagg's Yale teammate, Henry Williams (1869–1931) with whom he had co-authored *A Scientific and Practical Treatise on American Football for Schools and Colleges* in 1894. Chicago and Minnesota played each other for thirteen consecutive seasons until 1918 with Minnesota winning most of those games. Stagg's overall record was 6–15 against the Wolverines, 5–11–1 against Minnesota, and 14–18–4 against Wisconsin. After Ohio State joined the conference in 1912, Chicago's record was 2–4–2 against the Buckeyes.[79]

Chicago's 2–0 victory over Michigan in 1905 has probably been written about more than any Chicago game during the Stagg years. The 1924 game against Illinois on November 8, however, comes close. It occurred during the years that Red "the Galloping Ghost" Grange, was a three-time All-American. It was the first game played in Illinois's new Memorial Stadium. Heavy rains during its construction caused a bulldozer to sink deeply into the mud, and the construction manager decided it was cheaper to leave it buried than recover it, so that's where it remains today. Access roads to the stadium were still unpaved, and days of steady rains left fans trudging through heavy mud to get there.

"The miracle man of the 1920s" is how the College Hall of Fame website describes Grange. It said he was named the Galloping Ghost because "no one could catch him. He was fast, elusive, football's greatest open-field runner up to his time."[80] Illinois was a heavy favorite in the game, but Chicago shocked the football world when it came away with a 21–21 tie and scored the most points against Illinois all season.

Grange scored all three touchdowns including a third-quarter, eighty-yard run that tied the game. "The Maroons, expected to fall rather as an easy victim to the superior Illinois eleven … unleashed a cyclonic attack at the very start," the Associated Press reported.[81] Stagg called it one of the greatest games of his career. He wrote: "Taken all in all—the expected one-sided victory, the over-shadowing reputation of Grange … the tremendous upset in the first quarter, the seesaw in the second quarter, Grange's magnificent response in which he brought the Illinois score from 0 to 21 virtually single-handed, the breathless dead-lock in the fourth quarter, with both teams narrowly denied the winning touchdown, made it one of the greatest football dramas ever played on any field."[82] With Red Grange leading in scoring, the Illini compiled a 6–1–1 record in 1924 and outscored opponents 204–71.

Table 8: UChicago Big Ten Record, 1892–1932

Opponent	Wins	Losses	Ties	% Wins
Indiana	19	2	0	90%
Purdue	27	10	1	71%
Northwestern	26	8	3	70%
Iowa	9	3	1	69%
Illinois	17	16	3	47%
Wisconsin	14	18	4	39%
Minnesota	5	11	1	29%
Michigan	6	15	0	29%
Ohio State	2	4	2	25%
TOTAL	**125**	**87**	**15**	55%
Source: UChicago Department of Athletics and Recreation.				

Stagg's National Profile

While Stagg struggled to maintain his influence at the University of Chicago, his national profile continued to grow. "A lot of people at the University of Chicago simply refuse to believe that Stagg and his teams were the most famous part of the school almost from the time he arrived in the 1890s to when he left," Robin Lester, author of *Stagg's University*, said in a 2002 interview.[83] Stagg was a founding member of the American Football Coaches Association (AFCA) started by West Point Coach C.D. Daly at a December 27, 1921, meeting in New York. Today the association's membership includes more than 11,000 football coaches at all levels. Its goals are to "maintain the highest possible standards in football and the profession of

coaching football." Daly appointed Stagg as chairman of the Sportsmanship and Ethics Committee and asked him to recruit fourteen member
coaches representing private and public universities throughout the nation.
On October 22, 1922, Stagg sent the first draft of the statement to committee members with this preface: "Below I am setting forth what I feel is of
importance on these matters and would ask you to look them over and criticize them or add to them or make other suggestions in order that we may
send them out with the endorsement of our Committee for the betterment
of football." The committee and AFCA endorsed the principles and mailed
copies to all universities with athletic programs and asked them to print
and distribute them to their coaches and athletes. The eighteen principles
were grouped under headings of "Fair Play," "Good Sportsmanship," and
"Coaching Ethics."[84]

Three years later, Stagg was elected president of the Western
Alumni Association of Exeter Academy. Its principal, Lewis Perry, said
Stagg's presence in Chicago had helped attract more applicants to the
New Hampshire private school. Perry wrote, "It was a great pleasure for
me to learn that you had been elected president of the [Western Alumni
Association]. We are all proud of what you have accomplished in your
life, and although you were but a short time here in Exeter, and we cannot, therefore, claim too much credit, we do feel that you have shown
those qualities which as Exeter men we most admire. One thing that has
pleased me very much in connection with the Western Alumni Association, and that is the fact that of late we have been getting more and
more boys from Chicago. I hope that this will continue to be the case as
we need these western boys with their enthusiasm and their capacity."[85]
The Exeter baseball field is today called the "Amos Alonzo Stagg Baseball Diamond."[86]

Notable Players, 1906–1924

Walter Steffen (1886–1937) was an All-Big Ten quarterback from 1906
to 1908 and an All-America choice in 1907 and 1908. He led the Maroons
to conference titles in 1907 and 1908 and an undefeated season in 1908.
During Steffen's three years, Chicago compiled a 13–2–1 record and made
some of its most crushing wins. The team defeated Illinois by the scores of
63–0 and 42–6; Purdue by 39–0, 56–0, and 39–0; Indiana by 33–8, 27–6 and
29–6; and Minnesota by 29–0. As the 1908 team captain, Steffen ended his
career in a game against Wisconsin on a frigid November afternoon when
he ran the opening kickoff back ninety-three yards for a touchdown, leading the way to an 18–12 victory for the Maroons.[87]

But Steffen was also Stagg's most perplexing high school recruit. In his freshman year of 1905, Steffen had practiced with the football team for three weeks, attended classes for a week then mysteriously left Chicago on October 10 with two University of Wisconsin coaches. They had vigorously recruited Steffen while he was a high school senior and were still trying. Steffen returned to Chicago on a train three days later at 3:00 a.m., attended classes the next morning, and apologized for his temporary departure. "I made the trip to Wisconsin entirely against my will. For a month I endeavored in every way to avoid going to Madison ... but the pressure became so strong that I could not resist. I told them before I went that I could not enter Wisconsin under any circumstances, and an hour after I arrived I told them I would not remain," he told the *Chicago Tribune*.[88]

Between 1909 and 1912, Steffen was an assistant coach for Stagg while attending the University of Chicago Law School. He began his legal career in 1912 working in the Chicago district attorney's office, later becoming a city judge and Superior Court judge. In 1914, he began his eighteen-year part-time job as head coach at Carnegie Institute of Technology (now Carnegie-Mellon) in Pittsburgh. He became known as the "commuting coach." During football season, he presided in the courtroom during the week, while his assistant coaches managed the practices. Steffen rode the train to Pittsburgh on weekends to join the team and direct its games. Steffen's record for eighteen seasons at Carnegie Tech was 88–53–6. His most celebrated victory came November 27, 1926. Notre Dame entered this game with an 8–0 record, while Carnegie was 6–2. Carnegie upset Knute Rockne's Notre Dame team 19–0 for its only season loss. Rockne chose to miss this game so that he could scout a future opponent, which was a decision he later regretted.[89]

Harlan O. "Pat" Page (1887–1965) played football, basketball, and baseball for Chicago teams from 1906 to 1909 and was Chicago's first athlete to star on conference championship teams in three sports. He played end on conference champion football teams in 1907 and 1908, guard on the champion basketball teams in 1908, 1909, and 1910, and pitcher on the champion baseball team in 1909. He returned to Chicago as assistant football and track coach and head basketball and baseball coach from 1910 to 1920. His basketball teams compiled a 161–76 record.[90] He also rejected several offers to play professional baseball. "It was the Old Man's advice [Stagg], and I never regretted the decision," he said.

Stagg told a reporter after Chicago's 29–0 victory against Minnesota in 1908: "It is a difficult task to declare any one man the noblest Maroon of them all.... If the task must be done, then little Pat Page—that 150 pounds of sheer grit and nerve must be declared the greatest man on the gridiron during the game. It was his wonderful defensive work that stopped the

Gophers time after time.... He was in every play. Never did the Gophers fool him for an instant."[91] Page described an incident in another game that illustrated Stagg's character. Stagg protested a referee's decision to give Chicago a touchdown that he felt the team didn't deserve. As a result, the referee reversed his decision. Page later recalled the incident: "We recovered a loose ball near the goal line for a touchdown. At any rate, the officials called it a touchdown, and we kicked the point following. Just as we lined up ready to resume play, out strode the Old Man [Stagg]. He called the officials into a huddle and spoke to them like this: 'Gentleman, I happen to be on the Rules Committee, and I believe you have erred in giving us that touchdown. Chicago is not entitled to that score as the impetus did not come from our team."[92]

As assistant football, baseball, and basketball coach for ten years, Page worked closely with Stagg. In 1910 and 1915, he accompanied the baseball team to Japan and wrote frequent letters to Stagg giving reports on their travels and game performances. When Stagg took his winter vacations for rest and sciatica treatments, Page wrote him reports about the teams. "I have been going to drop you a line but since losing to Minnesota last Monday, 7 to 3, we have been sort of upset," Page wrote to Stagg in Idaho Springs in 1913. "It was a miserable day for a game with the thermometer down to 34 and a strong northeast wind," he wrote.[93]

Harlan O. "Pat" Page (left) pictured with Stagg. Page coached baseball, basketball, and football from 1911 to 1920 and played all three sports as a student. University of Chicago Photographic Archive, apf1-07822, Special Collections Research Center, University of Chicago Library.

While taking the basketball team on a road trip, Page sent a telegram to Stagg in West Palm Beach to give a report: "Still fighting. Chicago nineteen. Illinois twelve. Great victory, nine field goals to three. Baumgartner, Norgren and Shorty did well. Now for Minnesota and Wisconsin."[94] Yet, even with those with whom he had a close working relationship, Stagg exercised strict control. After Stagg was informed that Page had taken the baseball team to Iowa in 1916 without his knowledge, Stagg wrote Page a stern letter: "There must be perfect frankness with the director of the department and perfect coopera- tion throughout the department. It is the director's business to know plans which are originated by all officials of the department, and it is the duty of each member to advise the director concerning proposed plans before actually putting them into operation," he warned Page.[95]

After leaving Chicago, Page coached three sports for Butler University from 1920 to 1925 and the College of Idaho from 1936 to 1938. He was also the head football coach at Indiana University from 1926 to 1930. Page was named to the Naismith Memorial Basketball Hall of Fame in 1962.

Herman Stegeman (1891–1939) played guard for the football team in 1913–1914 and starred in track and field. He graduated in 1915 and went on to a distinguished football coaching career at Beloit College, Monmouth College, and the University of Georgia. After World War I, the Army assigned him to establish a physical training course for the University of Georgia ROTC program. Georgia hired him as assistant football coach in 1919 and promoted him to head coach from 1920 to 1922. His football record at these three schools was 29–17–6. But his Georgia career extended for many more years as head basketball coach (1919–1931), head baseball coach (1919–1920), and head track and field coach (1920–1937). His Geor- gia basketball teams achieved a 170–79 record and baseball teams earned a 31–13–2 record. In 1996 the University of Georgia renamed the basketball and gymnastics arena "the Stegeman Coliseum."[96]

Paul Des Jardien (1893–1956) was a center for the football teams that compiled a 17–3–1 record between 1912 and 1914 and an All-American in 1913 and 1914. He and teammate Nelson Norgren earned twelve athletic letters in four sports—football, baseball, basketball, and track—about the same time.[97] At 6′5″ and 190 pounds, teammates called him "Shorty." Walter Camp wrote about Des Jardien and called him "the best center in the coun- try—steady, reliable, absolutely dependable for his share of line work on attack, and a power on defense."[98] After graduating, he switched to baseball and played one season with the Cleveland Indians of the American League before pursuing a business career. He was inducted into the College Foot- ball Hall of Fame in 1955.

Nelson Norgren (1891–1974) was the second Chicago athlete to win twelve varsity letters in four sports from 1911 to 1914. He was named to Wal- ter Camp's second-team College Football All-America in 1912 and third team in 1913. Stagg wrote in a letter to the sporting editor of *Big Ten Weekly*: "Norgren certainly ranks as one of Chicago's greatest football players of all time" and also "one of the most outstanding basketball players ever competing at Chicago." Stagg said that Norgren ranked with Clarence Herschberger as "one of the two best punters ever at Chicago."[99] Norgren coached football at the University of Utah from 1914 to 1917. He returned to Chicago to serve as head basketball coach from 1921 to 1957. In 1942, he was elected president of the National Association of Basketball Coaches. He was named to the Helms Athletic Foundation Hall of Fame as a basketball player.

Herbert O. "Fritz" Crisler (1899–1982) won nine letters in three sports—football, basketball, and baseball—between 1918 and 1921. He was an All-Big Ten selection in football and basketball and captain of the baseball team.[100] He played end on the Maroons football team from 1919 to 1921, earning All-America honors during his senior year. He was Stagg's assistant coach from 1922 to 1929 before becoming head coach at Minnesota from 1929 to 1930 and Princeton from 1932 to 1937. He was head coach at Michigan from 1938 to 1947 and Michigan athletic director from 1941 to 1968. He became known as "the father of two-platoon football" after persuading the Rules Committee to adopt unlimited player substitutions. Crisler was inducted into the College Football Hall of Fame in 1955 and was one of Stagg's two former players profiled in *Great Football Coaches of the Twenties and Thirties*.[101]

A self-described "skinny kid" who was six feet tall and 150 pounds, Crisler did not play high school football. He told *Sports Illustrated* how Stagg influenced him to play for the first time.

I applied for an academic scholarship at the University of Chicago and … was awarded one on the basis of my scholastic record. I enrolled as a pre-med, and it was during my freshman year that this trifling incident occurred that changed the course of my life. Before the incident … I had stopped one day to watch football practice. A play headed in my direction. Mr. Stagg, back-pedaling away from the play, bumped into me, and we both went down. As we picked ourselves up, he saw, by my cap, that I was a freshman and so he said, "Why aren't you out for freshman football?" I had gained some weight by that time, but I told Mr. Stagg I had never played football. He said, "You ought to be out anyway with the rest of your classmates."

So, I reported next afternoon, got a uniform, and Pat Page, the freshman coach, put me in scrimmage. I took a terrible pounding. That evening I turned in my uniform. About 10 days later I was crossing the quadrangle, and I saw Mr. Stagg coming along on his bicycle. I ducked my head, but he spotted me and stopped. He said, "Weren't you out for football?" I said I had been, but I had quit because I didn't know anything about the game. I'll never forget the look of scorn Mr. Stagg gave me. "Well," he said, "I never thought you'd be a quitter!"

I said to myself, "I'll show you." I went back out the next day, and I was off on an athletic career that brought me nine letters at Chicago. If the Old Man hadn't come riding by on his bike at that precise moment that day, I wouldn't be sitting here now with all these pictures and souvenirs and mementos on the walls.[102]

Crisler was the best known among Chicago players who later became coaches. During his last year as Michigan coach, he was named "Coach of the Year" in 1947. He was a member of the NCAA Rules Committee for forty-one years and chair for nine years when he persuaded the committee to allow unlimited substitution. "By nature, and by training Fritz measures up to the moral and spiritual leadership of a great coach," Stagg said of Crisler. "He possesses splendid human traits in his personality. He has plenty of warmth of heart along with forcefulness and will power."[103]

Paul D. "Tony" Hinkle (1899–1992) was another Chicago athlete to win nine varsity letters in football, basketball, and baseball. Hinkle captained the Chicago Maroons basketball team and was chosen to the All-America teams in 1919 and 1920. After graduating from Chicago, the Indiana native went to Butler University in Indianapolis, where he was head football, basketball, and baseball coach for many years. Hinkle was inducted into the Naismith Memorial Basketball Hall of Fame in 1965. The Butler basketball arena was renamed the Hinkle Fieldhouse in 1966.[104]

The Winning Tradition Ends

The seasons between 1906 and 1924 were Stagg's most successful during his forty-one years at the University of Chicago. Gate receipts for all sports totaled about $1.1 million. Some years produced a surplus and some years a deficit. But football always produced a large surplus, which funded teams in ten intercollegiate sports, the intramural program, women's athletics, and even the Maroon band.[105] During these years, Chicago teams won eighty-four, lost thirty-five, and tied nine games. After his successful 1924 season, the president and trustees recruited him for a nationwide speaking tour that raised $17 million in donations for the university. He and vice president Tufts traveled to fifteen cities in less than a month, appearing before alumni clubs, schools, and business organizations. By this time, Stagg had long since overcome his lack of self-confidence that convinced him he could never become a preacher. At Hollywood High School, Stagg spoke to a crowd of 2,500. "I never had better attention and never such an inspiring audience and I don't think that I ever talked better to high school boys and girls.... After which they broke into rounds of applause," he wrote to Stella.[106]

Stagg's admiration among students and alumni made him the subject of more than one football fight song. The most popular was "Grand Old Stagg," which was sung to the tune of George M. Cohan's "You're a Grand Old Flag."

He's a grand old Stagg tho' we don't like to brag
And his worth we will prove to you soon.
He's the idol of the team we love
That fights for the dear old Maroon (rah, rah, rah)
We will stick for him
Tho' we lose or we win
And our faith in him can't lag
Tho' other coaches be forgot
Take your hat off to grand old Stagg.[107]

Times were good. The 1920s were characterized by a robust economy, the first radio stations, talking movies, and the wide expansion of electricity and telephones into American homes. The elite eastern universities no longer dominated college football as Big Ten universities built big budgets, huge programs, and winning teams. The *Chicago Tribune* reported that national attendance figures for the 1924 season were the greatest in gridiron history and that attendance in the Midwest topped eastern teams for the first time.[108] The "Roaring Twenties" ended with the stock market crash on October 29, 1929, and the beginning of the Great Depression. The depression, however, hit Chicago football in 1925 when it began a string of losing seasons and never again won a conference championship. Stagg was faced with a battle he could not win.

9

The Decline of Chicago Football, 1925–1933

It's not whether you get knocked down; it's whether you get up.—Vince Lombardi

In 1926 at age sixty-four, Stagg was knocked unconscious during a Chicago spring practice when he failed to move out of way of a runner who banged into him. Twenty more players piled on top of them. It took three or four minutes and a bucket of water before Stagg got up. He promptly lectured the defensive players on their failure for not stopping the runner more quickly. Reporting on the incident, the *New York Times* said he got up the next morning "with no aches or pains" and "none the worse to return to practice that afternoon." By the late 1920s, Stagg had been at the University of Chicago for more than thirty-five years—longer than any coach at any university.[1]

Table 9: UChicago Football, 1925–1932

Year	Wins	Losses	Ties
1925	3	4	1
1926	2	6	0
1927	4	4	0
1928	2	8	0
1929	7	3	0
1930	2	5	2
1931	2	6	1
1932	3	4	1
Totals	25	40	5
Source: UChicago Department of Athletics and Recreation.			

One Winning Season in Eight Years

Stagg's resilience, however, could not carry the team to success during the next eight years when it had losing seasons every year except one. The team's overall record from 1925 to 1932 was 25–40–5. Gate receipts declined 50 percent from 1926 to 1929 and continued after the Depression began.[2] During Stagg's final season in 1932, the Maroons won three, lost four, and tied one. Chicago's only winning season during those years came in 1929 when it won seven and lost three.

Nothing illustrates Chicago's decline more than six humiliating losses to Purdue in a seven-year span: 6–0 (1926), 40–0 (1928), 26–0 (1929), 27–6 (1930), 14–6 (1931), and 37–0 (1932). Between 1898 and 1925, Chicago defeated Purdue twenty-six times, lost one and tied one. In twenty of those games, Purdue failed to score a single point. When asked by sportswriters to comment on an upcoming game, Stagg was always cautious and pessimistic. He never predicted a win against Purdue and always said he "feared" Purdue.

"Stagg fears Purdue" became a joke among sportswriters. A *Chicago Tribune* headline shortly before the 1924 game read, "Ho Hum! Coach Stagg fears Purdue again." The first sentence of the story read, "'Stagg fears Purdue' has become a traditional phrase in Big Ten football circles during the last score of years." But two years later, the *Chicago Tribune* headline read, "Stagg's fears come true, Purdue beats Chicago, 6–0." The first sentence read, "It is written that all things come to him who waits. Purdue waited—twenty-nine years to be exact—and yesterday was its day." The sportswriter got the number of years wrong because Purdue defeated Chicago in 1918 during the depleted years of World War I. But the sentiment was correct.

Chicago ended the 1927 season with a mediocre 4–4 record, which could have easily been 5–3 except for a controversial 13–7 loss to Ohio State. Stagg publicly criticized a referee's decision that nullified a touchdown run. The referee ruled that the run resulted from an illegal formation. At the annual football dinner attended by more than 500 alumni a week later, Stagg said, "I saw the play clearly, and it was executed perfectly.... The referee made a mistake. It was an honest mistake, and we don't hold it against him, but it was a mistake just the same." With these words, the *Chicago Tribune* reported, "Stagg for the first time in his career as a coach criticized an official of a conference football game."[3]

In 1930, Chicago's only victories came in the first two games of the season against little-known Ripon, 19–0, and Hillsdale, 7–6. The team lost to every conference opponent by lopsided scores. At the annual dinner sponsored by the Chicago Alumni Club, Stagg praised the team for its fighting spirit. "I have no criticism to make of the spirit of this team. I have criticized them individually, and I have criticized them collectively. But I have no criticism to make of their spirit. They have given all they have, and they have never quit," he said.[4]

Reasons for Decline

The decline in the quality of Chicago's football fortunes can be attributed to multiple causes. Chicago's admissions standards increased, the best athletes could not meet these standards, competition for fans with other universities increased, and consequently, ticket sales and revenue declined. As the frequency of losing seasons increased, recruiting became difficult because no athlete wanted to play for a losing team. Nearby Northwestern University and Notre Dame expanded their stadiums, increased their attendance and their football budgets. Notre Dame, whose campus was 100 miles away, began playing many home games at Chicago's Soldier Field, where it attracted up to 120,000 fans for its biggest games against Southern California and Army. Games at Stagg Field attracted mediocre attendance, at best, and pathetic attendance after the Great Depression began. Wins during these years were primarily against small college teams.

The Great Depression hurt donations and caused budget cutbacks. Private college and university endowments nationwide shrank by 26 percent, and gifts from alumni and wealthy benefactors fell by more than 70 percent.[5] Declining attendance and revenue forced the athletic department to reduce expenses. In February 1928, Stagg wrote a "general letter to all of the coaches" imploring them to reduce the travel expenses of their teams. He asked them to reduce the number of players they took on trips unless the player could "figure in the scoring" or "make a definite contribution to the team." His other suggestions were: (a) do not use parlor cars on short trips such as Lafayette, Champaign, or Madison; (b) use street cars instead of taxies whenever possible; and (c) avoid extravagance of eating on dining cars. He also suggested setting a maximum cost per meal and asking players to reimburse the difference if they exceeded it.[6]

Besides losing seasons, Chicago also faced increased competition for fans, which reduced ticket revenue. During the 1920s, all Big Ten universities built new stadiums or expanded their old ones. The seating capacity of 135 college and university stadiums increased from 929,523 to 2,307,850. College football was becoming more popular in the U.S. at the same time Chicago was increasing its admissions standards and decreasing its pool of qualified football players.

Table 10: New Stadium Construction
and Seating in Big Ten Universities, 1920–1929

University	Year Built	Original Capacity
Ohio State	1922	63,000
Illinois	1923	55,000
Purdue	1924	13,500
Minnesota	1924	53,000
Northwestern	1926	25,000
Michigan	1927	72,000
Iowa	1929	53,000

Source: Walter Tamte, Walter Camp and the Creation of American Football (University of Illinois Press, 2018).

Stagg Field, which began as one of the conference's largest, gradually became its smallest. Stagg worked tirelessly to convince the administration and trustees to build a new 100,000-seat stadium. A new stadium, he argued, would help Chicago maintain athletic supremacy, boost enrollment, enlarge the donor pool, and provide new revenue of up to $400,000 per year. But the university made do by increasing its capacity to 56,000 in 1925.[7] A *Big Ten Weekly* article said, "Football as the big wholesome spectacle of the college year has come to stay. Until Chicago does what practically every other university in the country has done or is planning to do, it cannot expect to have a contented alumni body."[8]

As enrollment at other Big Ten state universities grew, Chicago's remained stable to maintain its academic prestige and selective admission standards. As a result, the university lost its competitive advantage in attracting athletes. In 1900–1901, Chicago was one of the conference's two largest universities with 3,346 students, second only to the University of Michigan. In 1930–1931, it had the smallest male enrollment of any conference school. The 686 male students at Chicago represented a tiny percentage of potential athletes at other schools, where enrollment ranged from 4,447 men at Purdue to 10,225 men at Ohio State.[9] Chicago and Northwestern, the conference's two private universities, also charged the highest tuition.

Since its founding in 1892, the quality and reputation of the University of Chicago's graduate programs exceeded that of its undergraduate college. During its early years, the undergraduate college attracted mostly middle-class students from the greater Chicago area. During the 1920s, however, Dean Chauncey Boucher initiated curriculum reforms that led to sweeping changes to enable the university to compete with prestigious eastern schools in attracting the highest-caliber students. Formally implemented in 1931 under President Robert Hutchins, the "New Plan" eliminated required courses and mandatory class attendance. Courses were replaced by new survey courses that culminated with mandatory exams at the end of the sophomore year. A board of examiners administered the exams so that individual professors no longer gave grades. The "New Plan" had much more in common with a graduate program than the undergraduate curriculum at other universities. As a result, athletes could no longer take an easy major.

After 1925, Stagg found himself more and more on the defensive against faculty critics of football. Not only was the football program under attack, but his Department of Physical Culture and Athletics came under increasing scrutiny as a viable academic department. Chicago required ten quarter hours of physical education courses for graduation until 1921 when the number was reduced to six. In 1932, the physical education requirement was abolished.

Wisconsin was the first conference school to offer the physical education major in 1911, Purdue was the last in 1929, and Chicago never did.[10] Wisconsin's new major was considered odd, if not inappropriate, for a university in 1911. As the first with a physical education major, the *Chicago Tribune* reported, "The University of Wisconsin, leader in the purification crusade … has come to the fore again with … startling athletic propaganda," calling it a "new-fangled bachelor's degree."[11] The lack of a physical education major made it difficult to attract athletes. In priority and funding, Stagg focused on developing intercollegiate sports, neglecting to build intramural programs and a physical education curriculum that could have attracted better athletes.[12]

The academic changes were indeed successful in attracting more highly qualified students, who sought admission in unprecedented numbers. By 1929–1930, enrollment had risen to 4,483 undergraduate and graduate students. "Bright high school seniors were attracted by the prospect of not having to attend classes, of advancing toward a B.A. at their own (perhaps accelerated pace) and enjoying access to the vaunted intellectual resources of the university," wrote Professor William McNeil in *Hutchins' University: A Memoir of the University of Chicago 1929–1950*.[13]

A Perfect Storm

It was the perfect storm of events. If Harper's vision for the university had survived and succeeding presidents had given Stagg the same unqualified support, he might have continued to recruit and retain talented

players. However, steadily increasing admission standards, more competition for the best players, and the Great Depression made it more difficult to
attract good athletes. In responding to an opinion survey sent to Chicago's
alumni, Pat Page, Indiana's head coach, said that many of his players from
the Chicago area had wanted to attend the University of Chicago but could
not meet its high admission standards.[14]

As a result, Chicago did not produce any All-America players between
1925 and 1932. Frank W. Thomson, who played offensive end from 1929 to
1932, said, "At that time, there were no outstanding athletes. It was sort of a
dry period. We used to say if we got beat 33–0, it was a moral victory."[15]

But a Few Successes

Stagg, nevertheless, achieved a few personal successes during these
years. He published *Touchdown!* in 1927, which was an "as-told-to" biography written with co-author Wesley Winans Stout. The book was originally published as a seven-part series in the *Saturday Evening Post* in the
fall of 1926. Stagg spent a month during the summer dictating the material to Stout. He spent the first three chapters describing the history of football. He said the game can be traced back to antiquity when the earliest
explorers found the Eskimos and other aboriginal peoples "who conceived
it independently through the human desire to kick an object."[16]

He didn't go into many details about himself except for his early
years of growing up, going to Exeter, and studying and playing football
at Yale. The British philosopher and social critic Bertrand Russell (1872–
1970) wrote a favorable review of Stagg's book in the *New York Times*. He
wrote, "Mr. Stagg spends a good deal of attention to the history of the
game," "an interestingly written history of American football constantly
interspersed with anecdotes of [his] games and players and illustrative
incidents."[17]

After a 4–4 season in 1927, the Chicago City Council passed a resolution expressing appreciation to the University of Chicago team for its
"Good Sportsmanship." An engraved copy was presented to Stagg and team
captain Ken Rouse that read: "Resolved, that the City Council express its
appreciation of the indomitable 'I will' fighting spirit of the University of
Chicago football team whose splendid record during the season is a tribute
not only to Coach Amos Alonzo Stagg and Captain Ken Rouse but to the
City of Chicago as well."[18]

In 1930 Stagg was chosen the "All-America coach of all time" by a
unanimous vote of fifteen college coaches, but he refused to accept the
honor. He felt it would be hypocritical to accept the honor. He wrote,

"It would not be fitting for me to be given public recognition as the All-America coach because my attitude is well-known toward All-America selections of football players…. It would be inconsistent for me to accept public recognition of the honor conferred by vote of fifteen fellow coaches."[19] Coaches ranking behind him in the top five included Glenn "Pop" Warner of Stanford (second), Knute Rockne of Notre Dame (third), Louis Little of Columbia (fourth), and Walter Steffen of Carnegie Tech (fifth). One of Stagg's recommendation letters said, "During his thirty-nine years in charge of athletics at Chicago, he has developed many great football teams; but more important still, he has developed the highest ideals of sportsmanship in the thousands of young men who have come under his influence."

In 1931, Chicago played Stagg's alma mater, Yale, for the first time. Yale had never scheduled any team in the Midwest before. This historic game was initiated a year earlier by the Yale Club of Chicago, which recommended it to the Yale Athletic Board. Board chair George Nettleton wrote Stagg, saying, "Our board recognizes that your significant services to the best interests of college athletics is national rather than local in its influence, and the college of which you are a graduate is especially glad to share in honoring your name and work." The *New York Times* reported that Yale graduates living in Chicago "were overjoyed with the announcement of the game and plans were launched to make the game one of the greatest of football spectacles." The game, however, did not live up to expectations as Chicago lost to Yale, 27–0.[20]

Stagg managed to win an interstate recruiting battle during the middle of the Depression when Jay Berwanger, an all-state Iowa halfback, chose to attend Chicago. Declining offers from four other Big Ten schools, Berwanger said he picked Chicago because "I wanted to attend a school that would give me a first-rate education in business without special treatment, so that I would be prepared when opportunities were certain to return." To meet his expenses, Berwanger waited tables, cleaned the gymnasium, ran elevators, and fixed leaky toilets. "Times were tough then," he said in a 1986 interview.[21] In 1935 three years after Stagg left, Berwanger became the first recipient of the Downtown Athletic Club Trophy, which was renamed the Heisman Trophy the following year. He was a unanimous All-America selection and the most valuable Big Ten player for a team whose record that year was 5–4–1. He was the team captain and the president of the senior class. He was also the first player drafted in the first-ever NFL draft in 1936 but decided to enter business after failing to reach a salary agreement with Chicago Bears owner George Halas.[22]

The next chapter turns to Stagg's successes and failures in coaching baseball for twenty years, track and field for thirty-five years, and even basketball for a few years. He brought more national publicity to the university with the baseball team's five trips to play in Japan. He organized interscholastic track and basketball events for more than twenty-five years, which attracted high school athletes from all over the nation but also produced the most controversy. Stagg was never idle and never bored.

10

Coaching Baseball, Track and Basketball, 1893–1926

Love is the most important thing in the world, but baseball is pretty good, too.—Yogi Berra

Chicago's baseball and track teams during the Stagg years achieved admirable records, winning seasons, and a few conference championships. While these sports did not attract as much press attention as football, they were an important part of Stagg's legacy in Chicago. He brought basketball to the University of Chicago from the YMCA School where he learned it from James Naismith. He coached Chicago's first basketball teams from 1894 to 1896 and again as an interim coach in 1920. Finally, his Chicago athletics record includes hosting interscholastic meets in track and basketball from 1904 to 1930, which attracted as many as 1,000 high school athletes from thirty-three states in their peak year.

When the University of Chicago opened its doors, baseball was well-established throughout the country. After organizing Chicago's first football team in the fall of 1892, Stagg organized its first baseball team in the spring of 1893. He coached the baseball team for twenty seasons from 1893 through 1913, compiling a team record of 285–168–3. His baseball winning percentage of 63 percent was only slightly less than his winning football percentage of 66 percent. His baseball record included nineteen winning seasons, one losing season, and conference championships in 1895, 1896, 1897, and 1898. From 1913 to 1933, while he was still athletic director, the team was coached by his assistants and former players Pat Page, Fred Merrifield, Nelson Norgren, Fritz Crisler, and J. Kyle Anderson.[1]

Chicago played most of its baseball games against conference opponents and other schools such as Beloit, Amherst, Virginia, Wake Forest, Pennsylvania, Brown, Marquette, and Syracuse. The team overwhelmed some opponents in lopsided wins. In 1895, Chicago defeated Iowa, 40–6. In 1897, it defeated Wisconsin, 18–3, and Michigan, 24–3. In 1901, it played nearby Wheaton College in a game the Maroons won, 36–3. Stagg scheduled only one game against his alma mater, Yale, which proved to be a lopsided loss when Yale won, 31–5, in 1896.

During his first season as coach in 1893, Stagg played both pitcher and catcher since no rules prohibited coaches from playing on their own teams. "I did my best to develop a pitcher for my first baseball team in the spring of 1893, but he was so wild in the first game that I, who had been coaching, reversed positions with him and was forced to pitch for the rest of the season," he wrote.[2] In a May game against Illinois, he pitched a one-hitter and hit a home run. The *Chicago Tribune* reported, "Professor Alonzo Stagg pushed his locks well back from his forehead yesterday afternoon and gave the University of Illinois young men an object lesson on pitching at the South Side City league grounds. Until the ninth inning, not a hit had been made off him, nor anything that could be mistaken for one."[3]

Gate receipts for Chicago's 1893 baseball team were $451, but the team's expenses were $689, resulting in a $238 deficit. By 1927, baseball was still losing money. "It [baseball] continued to lose money, as it does in many colleges. We no longer charge admission," Stagg wrote in his annual report that year.

Table 11: UChicago Baseball Record
Under Stagg, 1893–1913

Year	Wins	Losses	Ties
1893	11	4	0
1894	11	7	0
1895	15	5	0
1896	19	11	0
1897	16	4	0
1898	12	7	0
1899	18	8	0
1900	17	16	1
1901	11	19	0
1902	18	8	0
1903	16	5	0
1904	21	8	1
1905	13	12	0
1906	14	7	0

Year	Wins	Losses	Ties
1907	14	10	1
1908	12	7	0
1909	13	6	0
1910	8	7	0
1911	11	8	0
1912	8	7	0
1913	7	2	0
Total	**285**	**168**	**3**

Source: UChicago Department of Athletics and Recreation.

Table 12: UChicago Baseball, 1914–1932

Year	Wins	Losses	Ties	Coach
1914	7	2	0	Pat Page
1915	7	4	0	Pat Page
1916	5	6	2	Pat Page
1917	8	10	0	Pat Page
1918	10	5	0	Pat Page
1919	5	4	0	Pat Page
1920	*games played in Japan*			Pat Page
1921	5	10	0	Fred Merrifield
1922	1	9	0	Nelson Norgren
1923	2	10	0	Nelson Norgren
1924	1	11	0	Nelson Norgren
1925	12	5	0	Nelson Norgren
1926	3	7	0	Nelson Norgren
1927	5	9	0	Fritz Crisler
1928	11	6	0	Fritz Crisler
1929	6	10	0	Fritz Crisler
1930	4	10	1	Nelson Norgren
1931	8	3	0	Pat Page
1932	6	10	1	J. Kyle Anderson
1933	14	11	0	J. Kyle Anderson
Total	**120**	**142**	**4**	

Source: UChicago Department of Athletics and Recreation.

According to the *Chicago Tribune,* Stagg invented the batting cage in 1896, which is today commonly used by college and professional teams. However, the inventor of the batting cage is disputed in other sources. Although some sources give credit to Wellington Titus, his patent claim wasn't filed until 1907.[4] The U.S. Patent Office awarded a patent for a "Baseball batting cage" to Danny Litwhiler and Murray Grabowsky in 1965.[5] Regardless of the inventor, Stagg's baseball teams were among the first, if not the first, to use it.

The batting cage made batting practice more efficient since it did not require outfielders to chase and return balls to the pitcher. The *Chicago Tribune* reported in 1896, "An innovation in the methods of baseball practice is about to be introduced at the University of Chicago in the shape of an outdoor batting cage.... It will be of wire netting fastened to upright posts set firmly in the ground: 70 feet long and 10 feet wide as to give ample room for the battery [sic] and batter to work." The roof and walls of the batting cage prevented balls from soaring too high, too far, or too wide. "Another good point about the new cage is that it will keep the men from trampling over the outfield until the grass, which is about to be sown, has got a start," said the *Tribune.*[6]

Games in Japan

The most unique baseball tradition Stagg developed at Chicago was the exchange trips he arranged with Japanese universities every five years between 1910 and 1930. The two countries shared a love of baseball. More than thirty-five collegiate, semipro, and professional teams crossed the Pacific to play Japanese teams between 1905 and 1934.[7]

Most University of Chicago games were played against Waseda University and Keio University, two well-known private universities. In exchange, Stagg invited the Waseda University team to the U.S. to play Chicago and other Big Ten teams during the year that followed each of Chicago's visits. The tours generated immense favorable newspaper publicity in both countries and served as a recruiting tool for prospective athletes. A Chicago athletic promotional brochure said: "A unique distinction, much as our eastern games in football, is the international baseball series ... a tour of Japan every five years. What an experience for red-blooded young fellows to travel across the Pacific in a jolly group—all expenses paid—and touring the Orient, where games, sightseeing, banquets, and hobnobbing with Nipponese dignitaries are part of the program." Since many baseball players also played football, Stagg found these tours useful in recruiting athletes in both sports.[8]

Their 1910 agreement stipulated that Chicago and Waseda would guarantee each other $3,500 in travel expenses plus hotel accommodations during their respective visits. Stagg arranged some of Waseda's games against other Big Ten universities, which paid the Japanese teams' travel expenses to their games.[9]

After their steamship journey across the Pacific in 1910, team captain Josiah James Pegues described their first impressions: "When we were hauled thru the streets of Yokohama in 'rickshaws,' we insisted on leaving the tops of our man-drawn carriages down in spite of the steady rain; so that we might have an unobstructed view of the strange sights which surrounded us. Most novel to our eyes were the people themselves, stalking thru the mud of the narrow side-walkless streets on stilt-like wooden clogs and protecting their flapping skirts and kimonos from the rain with oil-paper umbrellas."[10]

Stagg credits the idea for the exchange to two Chicago baseball alumni, Alfred Place (class of 1902), and Fred Merrifield (class of 1890), who were teaching and working in Japan. Stagg described Place, who had the nickname "Stuffy Place," as "a brilliant baseball player who went to Japan as president of a missionary college and helped coach the Waseda University team." Merrifield also went to Japan as a missionary and became the first coach of the Waseda team.[11] The trips were arranged and coordinated with Professor Iso Abé, the superintendent of athletics and a Waseda professor.

Stagg made all the arrangements but did not accompany the teams to Japan in the five visits. "It would be a great pleasure personally to me if I could visit Japan with the boys, but it is out of the question because I have to remain here and coach the football team," he wrote Professor Abé.[12] Assistant coaches accompanied the team. Each trip lasted about two and a half months during the fall quarter. Team members, therefore, enrolled in extra summer classes so they could make the trip during the fall quarter.

Abé wrote Stagg on April 18, 1910, inviting him to bring the Chicago team to Japan that fall: "It is a great pleasure for me to ask you if it is possible for the University of Chicago baseball team to come over to Japan next fall…. If you come here next fall, all the baseball fans here will surely welcome you with open arms." Abé offered to pay travel and hotel expenses for fourteen men for twenty-five days. In exchange, he asked Stagg to invite the Waseda team to Chicago in 1911 and guarantee similar travel and hotel expenses. "We would not expect to be entertained in a first-class hotel at all but be satisfied with a second-class or a third-class hotel, or even a boarding house," he wrote.[13] Abé also said, "You know…. Fred Merrifield and Alfred Place have done a great deal in coaching our teams, and we believe we can give you tolerably good games if you would come here."[14]

During the 1910 trip to Japan, Chicago played nineteen games, winning sixteen and losing three. The trip covered 19,000 miles starting in Chicago on September 2 and returning on December 27. The team took the train to California, making stops to play five games with teams in Montana and Washington before departing by ship for Japan. Chicago dominated the Japanese teams and won most games by large margins. The team played six games with Waseda University, winning all by a combined score of 69–12. Chicago defeated the tougher Keio University teams three times, winning by combined scores of ten to four. On the return trip, the team stopped in Manila to play four games with U.S. Marine teams stationed in the Philippine Islands.

Both Japanese and American players were praised by newspaper writers for their politeness and good behavior. A Japanese columnist wrote:

> In the United States, the East claims almost a monopoly of politeness and refinement. The West is generally considered as rough and unrefined. Yet the 'Western' Chicagoans were gentlemen.
>
> We had the pleasure and satisfaction of welcoming here a baseball team most exemplary not only in the skill of the art, but also in their conduct on the field … entirely beyond reproach even in minor details … [and] not a word of indecent language came out of their lips.

The headlines in a Tokyo English-language paper read:

> "Keio falls before classy Chicagoites; premier Japanese team meets superiors at national game"
>
> "Chicago wins first international game; Midway team defeats Waseda in opening match; friendly and clean contest; superior batting of the American players spells downfall for the local boys"[15]

Merrifield wrote Stagg that Japanese players also possessed admirable qualities: "They may not be good hitters yet and may not know much about curves, but they listen to the umpire and know how to accept decisions without a question…. I have seen ball after ball skim the batter's eyes, and 'strike!' from the umpire would not affect his temperament in the least."[16]

Collier's published an article titled "Japan Invades America" about the Waseda team's Chicago visit in 1911 and made the same observation about Japanese politeness. "Games are considered friendly contests between gentlemen, and nothing but gentlemanly conduct is tolerated…. The umpire is supreme. When his decisions are a matter of judgment, as on balls or strikes, or on whether a man is safe or out on a close play, he is never questioned, no matter how important the bearing of his decision may be on the result of the game. Anger is never shown by a Japanese player on the field and would meet with the instant disapproval of the spectators."[17]

The Waseda University baseball team made its first trip to the U.S. from April to July 1911 and played more than twenty games. After arriving in San

Francisco on April 20, Waseda played Stanford and California-Berkeley before heading east and stopping to play Utah, Colorado, and Nebraska Wesleyan along the way. Waseda played Chicago twice and other games against Northwestern, Grinnell, Iowa, Minnesota, Illinois, Indiana, Purdue, and Wabash. The Waseda team defeated California, Indiana, and Northwestern, but lost twice to Chicago. After the games, the Waseda team visited Niagara Falls, New York City, Washington, D.C., and several other U.S. cities before departing for home in a trip that covered 18,000 miles.[18]

The second trip of the Chicago baseball team to Japan took place in the summer and fall of 1915. Twelve men accompanied by Coach Pat Page and Professor C.W. Wright made the trip. "Five months were consumed in the journey of more than 22,000 miles [with] games being played en route to San Francisco, in Honolulu, Japan, and in the Philippine Islands. The university won all of its games in Japan…. In the spring of 1916 … the baseball team of Waseda University made a return visit to the United States

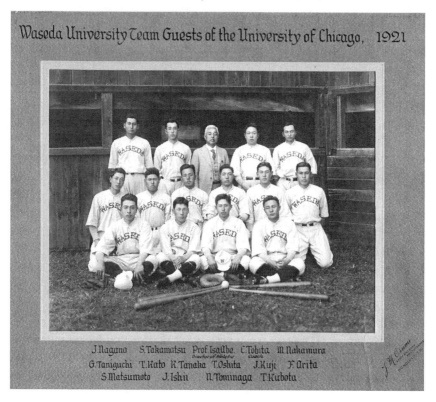

Waseda University baseball team in Chicago, 1921. University of Chicago Photographic Archive, apf4-00148, Special Collections Research Center, University of Chicago Library.

playing three games with Chicago," Stagg wrote in his annual report to the president.[19]

During the 1920 trip to Japan, the Maroons played eighteen games and compiled a 10–6–2 record. They played a Tokyo YMCA team, winning 70–0, and an Osaka YMCA team, winning 40–0. The Keio and Waseda games were more competitive. Against Keio, Chicago won one, lost two, and tied one. Against Waseda, the Maroons won four, lost two, and tied one. The outgoing trip included one U.S. game against California, which defeated Chicago, 6–2. During the 1925 trip to Japan, the Maroons played thirty-two games with a 19–8–5 record. Against Waseda, they compiled a 1–2–2 record on this trip and only played Keio once, winning 3–2. The outgoing trip included six games against U.S. teams in North Dakota, Montana, Washington, and California.

In a written report on the 1920 trip, Chicago pitcher H.O. "Fritz" Crisler, highlighted the favorable publicity the university and its team received in Japanese newspapers. He wrote, "Japanese papers devote almost one-half page a day to the publicity of the University of Chicago team." But he recommended that in future trips Stagg choose the most articulate players to serve as media spokesmen. He urged Stagg to "select at least two speakers from the team to make responses and give talks at banquets and other functions. These men should really be diplomats and be very careful in what they say and the manner in which they give their response. Then it will be necessary to have a publicity man to talk with the various newspaper reporters. Newspaper reporters met the train in practically every city on the way to the coast as well as in Japan. The newspapers seem to be very eager for stories regarding the team and the University of Chicago," he wrote.

Crisler also warned Stagg that players were sometimes mobbed by Japanese students who initiated conversations to help them learn English and ask players to pose for photos and autograph baseballs. "The boys will be asked to autograph baseballs by the thousands and various other articles until it sort of gets on one's nerves, but nevertheless all this must be tolerated in order to retain the good will of the Japanese students. A great many of these requests are made while they are warming up for the game, and you will find it is a bothersome thing."[20]

The Japanese exchange trips were an unusual experiment in international goodwill before the onset of Japanese American hostilities. After the Great Depression began, the expense made them impossible. The Waseda University team adopted Chicago's own maroon and white colors for their uniforms to honor the tradition. To commemorate the historic series, the University of Chicago baseball team traveled to play three games in 2008 against Waseda at Hiroshima City Stadium on March 23, Osaka Dome on

March 24, and Seibu Dome in Tokyo on March 25.[21] Shortly after arriving, more than twenty players, coaches and staff attended services at Noboricho Catholic Church in Hiroshima on Easter Sunday. "The priest acknowledged our presence and asked us to stand, and the congregation of approximately 400 rose, faced us, and applauded," Coach Brian Baldea recalled. "It was a special moment."[22]

The rise and fall of Chicago's football team coincided with the rise and fall of its baseball team. During the twenty years that Stagg coached baseball, his winning record was 63 percent. Between 1913 and 1933 under other Chicago coaches, the baseball team won only 45 percent of its games. Between 1926 and 1933, the baseball team had three winning and four losing seasons. The reasons were similar—higher admission standards, a decreasing pool of qualified athletes, and more competition for players from other Big Ten schools.

Track and Field Teams

Stagg organized and coached Chicago's track and field teams for thirty-five seasons from 1894 to 1928. During those years, the team compiled eighteen winning seasons, ten losing seasons and seven break-even seasons. His thirty-five-year record in track meets was 102–87 for an overall 54 percent wins. This track record against single-team opponents did not include the conference meets with multiple opponents. In multiple-opponent track meets, Stagg coached the team to four Big Ten outdoor track titles and three indoor championships.[23]

By 1902, Chicago's track athletes held conference records in five of sixteen events: (1) 100-yard run (Charles L. Burroughs, ten seconds); (2) 220-yard run (Charles L. Burroughs, twenty-two seconds); (3) 880-yard run (W.A. Moloney, two minutes, two seconds); (4) one-mile run (Byron B. Smith, four minutes, thirty-three seconds); and (5) sixteen-pound hammer throw (T.W. Mortimer, 121 feet, two inches). Chicago's five record-holders equaled Michigan's and surpassed Wisconsin and Iowa, each with three record holders.[24]

Stagg coached the track team by correspondence while he was recuperating from sciatica in Hot Springs, Arkansas, in 1904. Former track star Fred Moloney was coaching the track team in Stagg's absence, but resigned unexpectedly to devote fulltime to his medical studies. Therefore, Stagg informed the university that he planned to coach the team by writing letters with instructions to his captain Hugo Friend until he returned on April 21.

Stagg kept records in his Hot Springs hotel room of the previous

University of Chicago 1897 track team. Stagg, sporting a coat and tie, is sitting in second row, right end. University of Chicago Photographic Archive, apf1-03743, Special Collections Research Center, University of Chicago Library.

performance of all team members. "He figures out carefully what each man can stand from day to day, decides how much running the dash men should do, how far the quarter-milers and the distance runners should go, how strenuously the weight men should exert themselves, and how much the jumpers and vaulters should practice form instead of weight and resistance. Then he writes down orders and sends them by his aide de camp, Uncle Sam's post office, to his lieutenants on Marshall Field," the *Inter Ocean* said.[25]

When he returned on April 21, Chicago students planned a rousing welcome with a celebration that included cheering, a band, and speeches in Mandel Hall. A large group planned to meet him at the railroad station when he was scheduled to arrive at 11:30 a.m. and accompany him back to campus in a carriage. "The demonstration planned will rival that of a commander of a victorious fleet," a student told the *Tribune*.[26] But the train was eleven hours late, and the Stagg family didn't arrive until late that night to be met by a small crowd. Stagg enthusiastically told the small group of students, "I feel fine. Never felt better. My rheumatism is nearly all gone. I am mighty glad to get back again and only stayed … as long as the doctor made me and no longer…. My only trouble now is with the nerve of the leg which I strained a year ago. My rheumatism has left me entirely, but the injured nerve is slow in recovering, and I shall have to humor it for some time."[27]

Between 1910 and 1920, H.O. "Pat" Page was the assistant track coach, besides an assistant coach in football, baseball, and basketball. For some of those years (and it isn't clear from the records which years) Stagg made Page the de facto head track coach. Page also accompanied the baseball team on at least two of its Japan trips. A January 1914 *Inter Ocean* article reported that Stagg announced his intention of "taking personal charge of the Midway track aspirants.… In recent years, it has been Coach Stagg's custom to turn everything over to Coach Page and his other assistants immediately after the close of the football season." Two weeks later, Stagg "personally directed" the Maroon track team to a 57–39 victory over Northwestern in the first conference meet of the season.[28]

Almost all meets were held against Big Ten opponents, which at the time included Michigan, Wisconsin, Illinois, Northwestern, and Minnesota. The only non-conference school that the track team competed against was Notre Dame. As other Big Ten universities began to develop track and field programs, Stagg scheduled games against Indiana, Purdue, Ohio State, and Iowa. Chicago defeated Ohio State 47–39 in a meet on February 14, 1920.[29]

Notable Track Athletes

James Lightbody was one of Chicago's greatest track athletes and competed from 1904 through 1907. He won six Olympic medals, three gold (steeplechase, 800-meter run, 1,500-meter run) and a silver (four-mile relay) at the 1904 St. Louis Olympics. Two of his medals are no longer recognized by the Olympic Committee because of a change in standards. Lightbody also posted a world record in the 1,500-meter run at the 1904 games. At the 1906 Olympics, he won a gold medal in the 1,500-meter run and a silver in the 800-meter run. He was posthumously inducted into the University of Chicago Athletics Hall of Fame in 2004.

Nicknamed "Deerfoot Lightbody," he faced an uncertain future in 1905 when an eye condition forced him to withdraw for surgery. The surgery was successful, however, and he was able to re-enroll wearing glasses for the 1906 spring quarter and train for the Olympics.[30] His gold medal for the 1,500-meter run in the 1906 Athens Olympics was unexpected because runners from Scotland and Sweden were highly favored. In describing the event, the *New York Times* reported, "When the men came to sprint home, the wonderful grit of Lightbody asserted itself. The wonderful runner, who never lost a game from scratch in his career, maintained his reputation in the finest style. His shorter stride seemed to place him at a disadvantage, but he went to the front and refused to be dislodged and finished a half yard before McGough."[31]

Henry Binga Dismond, a Black medical student, was also one of

Chicago's best runners. After graduating from Howard University in 1912, he enrolled at the University of Chicago Medical School and joined the track team. Dismond broke a nineteen-year Central Amateur Athletic Union record and was later chosen for the 1916 U.S. Summer Olympics in Berlin. They were later canceled due to the outbreak of World War I. Dismond, however, received a gold medal for matching the American quarter-mile record time set by national champion Ted Meredith. After later defeating Meredith, he became the western intercollegiate champion and earned his varsity letter.

After finishing medical school, Dismond enlisted in the 370th infantry during World War I. Near the end of the war, he received an honorable mention for courageous leadership. Under heavy air and ground fire, he and Chicago teammate Sam Ranson led a victorious raid on German trenches in the Argonne Forest. During an exemplary medical career that followed, he established the Physical Therapy Department at Harlem's Sydenham Hospital. He later established the Emergency Industrial Service, Harlem's first workmen's compensation clinic. A Haitian native, Dismond founded the Society of the American Friends of Haiti to educate Americans about Haitian history, culture, and socio-political and economic issues.[32]

Olympic Committee

Stagg served on the U.S. Olympic Committee for the games in St. Louis (1904), London (1908), Stockholm (1912), Antwerp (1920), Paris (1924), Amsterdam (1928), and Los Angeles (1932). He coached the 400- and 800-meter runs and 1600-meter relay for the American team at the Paris Olympics in 1924.

Stagg took the U.S. track and field team to the 1900 Paris Olympics, which included athletes from Georgetown, Michigan, Syracuse, Chicago, Pennsylvania, and the New York Athletic Club. "I persuaded President Harper and Secretary Goodspeed [secretary of the Board of Trustees] to join me in borrowing $2,000 from the bank to take the Chicago track team to the Paris Summer Olympics in 1900," he wrote.[33] After arriving, he learned that the finals were scheduled on a Sunday, so he decided that no American athlete could participate. While the Chicago athletes followed his ruling, several New York and Pennsylvania athletes ignored it and competed.[34] He blamed the French for deceiving him and said he would have never made the trip if he had known about the Sunday meet.

"Before we sailed, we learned that all the Olympic finals were to be run on Sunday. The trip was off," Stagg wrote. "A few days later a cable came from Paris to the effect that the French would defer to the peculiar

Sabbatarian sensibilities of America and shift the finals to a weekday. Once in Paris, and with four of my five men qualified for the finals, I discovered that they were to be held on Sunday after all. Chicago, Princeton, Syracuse, and Pennsylvania refused to compete. For years I was bitter over the inconstancy of the French and held them lowly as a people."[35]

Not until twenty-four years later did Stagg discover his misplaced blame against the French. In 1924, a friend who was an Olympics official in 1900, confessed to Stagg that he had sent the cable. "I couldn't stand by and let things go to smash, so I sent that cablegram on my own authority hoping to make the French see the light before the games," he told Stagg. But he was unable to do so, and the Sunday events remained on the schedule. "I publicly apologize to France," Stagg wrote in *Touchdown!*[36]

Stagg also coached the American team at the 1924 Paris Olympics. "The outstanding event of the year 1924 for me was attending the Olympic games at Paris as coach of the thirteen boys who competed in the 800-meter run, the 1,300-meter run, and the 1,800-meter relay. This … added considerable information to what I had gained when I took a University of Chicago team to Paris in the Olympic games of 1900, and also when I accompanied the American Olympic team in London in 1908 as a member of the American Olympic Committee," he wrote to a friend.

Stagg (right) and Stella traveled to the 1908 London Olympics on the ship *Philadelphia*. Accompanying them were Sophonisba Breckinridge, dean of arts, literature and science (left), and Marion Talbot, professor of anthropology (second left). University of Chicago Photographic Archive, apf1-07792, Special Collections Research Center, University of Chicago Library.

Stagg with the American Olympic track team at the 1924 Paris Olympics. University of Chicago Photographic Archive, Special Collections Research Center, University of Chicago Library.

Stagg retired from coaching track in 1928 to focus on football and his work as athletic director. He offered the position to his assistant coach, Ned Merriam, whom he told in a letter, "I have decided to withdraw from coaching track and field athletics this year, and I wish to do it while we have the prospects of a good team, rather than when our prospects might be less good. I am appointing you to take full charge." But then he added, "On all matters involving policies affecting the department and finances, it is understood that I am to be consulted." Merriam had competed in track as a Chicago student in 1906–1908, winning the Big Ten 440-yard run all three years and the 220-yard low hurdles in 1907 and 1908.[37]

Coaching Basketball

After basketball was invented in Springfield, it spread quickly across the country through a network of YMCAs. By February 1893, teams in Chicago-area YMCAs had formed a league. Stagg formed the university's first team, which played in the YMCA league in 1894 and 1895. In 1896, he took the team to play the University of Iowa in Iowa City on January 18, a game that Chicago won, 15–12.[38] Stagg arranged the game with H.F. Kallenberg, Iowa's athletic director, who had also been a student at the International YMCA School five years earlier. Kallenberg had written James Naismith and asked for a copy of his rules so he could introduce the game to Iowa fans. The Chicago-Iowa game was the first collegiate game to be played with five players on a side and a referee, which was Stagg's and Kallenberg's idea. Previously, each team had seven to nine players and the players themselves called the fouls.[39]

After Pat Page left the head basketball coaching position in 1920 to accept the job at Butler University, Stagg coached the team again during the 1921 season. Stagg's year as basketball coach was marked by controversy, and he gave it up at the end of the season. While the team finished with a 14–6 overall record that year, its conference record was a disappointing 6–6. As a result, Stagg became the subject of heavy criticism from students and alumni. Since this team included four returning starters from the previous year's conference champion, fans expected another championship team. But after losing the first three conference games and three later in the season, Chicago was "out of the running" for the conference title and ranked behind several other teams.

Stagg (upper left) with the 1921 Chicago basketball team. University of Chicago Photographic Archive, apf5-02967, Special Collections Research Center, University of Chicago Library.

After these losses, the *Daily Maroon* printed several letters in February criticizing Stagg and his team's poor performance. One letter said, "We think that in Crisler, Birkhoff, Hallday, and Vollmer, Chicago has four of the most skillful as well as most experienced players in the conference, and that if they lose games it is because something is wrong with the coaching. We cannot see why no good man is secured to replace Pat Page. ... We think Mr. Stagg is the best football coach in the country, and we know he is the best influence for manliness in athletics. But we have doubts whether Michael Angelo [sic] would have been a good instructor in sociology or Napoleon a good tennis teacher."[40]

Another letter-writer said, "At Illinois and in the recent Michigan game our failure ... was through inefficient coaching. Faulty judgment, very apparent to Chicago spectators, in putting in decidedly second-class men at wrong times, men against whose insertion into the game the majority of the team objected, was the chief cause.... Let us get rid of the athletic monarchy, get more specialization in our coaching system, and get out and be something." Another letter said, "Chicago should have as a motto, 'A coach for every sport,'" while another stated, "Our basketball team has the personnel, but the men have not been taught a concentrated plan of attack."[41]

Stagg answered his critics in a letter published the next day in the *Daily Maroon*. He argued that "defeat at the hands of Michigan Saturday night was because Vollmer, the best of Chicago's scoring men, could not play because of illness, and that Stahr, who replaced him for part of the game, could not be used for the full forty minutes because he was recovering from an illness." He also pointed out that other nine conference teams have "from three to four times as many available men from which they get their teams as we have at Chicago" and "no amount of explanation could possibly satisfy men who are disposed to criticize."[42]

Stagg's reply to his critics, however, produced another flood of letters criticizing his angry response to the first group of letters. "We complain that the basketball team is not well coached. Mr. Stagg replies that it is for him to decide and no one else. That assumption is rather remarkable, but it is characteristic of Mr. Stagg's method that he takes the position that he is infallible." Another letter-writer said, "In every game that Chicago played, even in those she won, the team has used a hit-or-miss style that showed no understanding of the fundamentals of the game. Chicago has not been taught to control the ball in a passing game.... Some of the moves that he made in substitutions in the Illinois and Michigan games were puzzling to followers of the team, and almost created mutiny on the squad.... Coach Stagg is trying to do too much. He is coaching football, he coaches track and is acting as athletic director, filling positions that nearly every other school in the conference hires three men to do. Now he has taken on basketball [not aware] of his ignorance of the technique of the game. We have lost prestige."[43]

Harvey T. Woodruff, *Chicago Tribune* sports editor, defended Stagg in a long article he wrote two weeks later. He explained that since its inception, the university did not charge any student fees to support athletics, and Stagg paid for many expenses from his own salary. Woodruff said that baseball, basketball, and track did not produce enough revenue to support their coaching salaries and were funded by the surplus revenue from the successful football program. Woodruff explained that other Big Ten teams had substantially higher athletic budgets and that some of their athletic expenses came from the university's general budget in addition to gate receipts.

Woodruff wrote, "On the board at various times were a certain element opposed to the prominence given to collegiate sport. To avoid arousing their hostility, Stagg always tried to be modest in his budget and often the amount he recommended for coaching expenses was entirely inadequate for the needs of the athletic teams." Stagg wrote in his autobiography, "For ten years the university's athletics owed me money, a debt that fluctuated around $1,000, until Mrs. Stagg despaired ever of having a bank account of our own."[44]

Stagg was, indeed, trying to coach too many sports and was limited in financial resources for teams other than football. He probably should have tried to give up baseball and track years before he finally did. But his student critics overreacted to a team with a 14–6 winning season—one that would have been commendable in any other circumstances.

Interscholastic Track Meets

In 1904, the Cook County Athletic League decided to organize a "systematized series" of indoor track meets for Chicago-area high schools. The only obstacle was finding a facility to host and sponsor the meets. Albert A. Clark, chair of the planning committee, wrote Stagg inquiring about a university sponsorship: "The suggestion has been made that it might be possible to induce you to take hold of these meets and run them; i.e. supplying gymnasium, ribbons, officials, medals, etc. The committee is desirous of making this a yearly event." Stagg eagerly accepted the invitation because he saw the track meets as an opportunity to obtain favorable publicity and recruit prospective athletes. Clark's invitation marked the beginning of almost thirty years of Chicago's sponsorship of interscholastic basketball and track tournaments, which in the end turned controversial.

The *Inter Ocean* praised the first event: "A better system of conducting a championship where so many schools are involved does not exist in the country. The main room of Bartlett Gymnasium is spacious, beautiful, and airy … and a seating capacity for 1,500 persons. Besides, every accommodation known to modern athletic science is afforded the athletes in the way of locker rooms, rubbing rooms, baths, etc."[45] After the final meet, the newspaper continued to praise it: "The final meet of the Cook County Athletic League, held at Bartlett Gymnasium Saturday night, brought to a close the most successful indoor season for high school athletes ever known in Chicago."[46]

Chicago's interscholastic tournament was not the first in the conference. The University of Illinois Interscholastic meet was first in 1893. The University of Wisconsin followed with a state tournament in 1895; the University of Michigan launched its tourney in 1898; and Northwestern started its meet in 1902. Stagg's track meets, however, achieved a national reputation that the others did not. They grew from a few dozen participants in 1902 to more than 1,000 in 1930, attracting high school athletes from states as distant as Massachusetts, Florida, and Washington.[47] Stagg continued to host the track tournaments through his final year in Chicago, but participation declined as national criticism of interscholastic meets increased.

Interscholastic Basketball Championships

In 1917, Stagg organized the National Interscholastic Basketball Championships.[48] The first tournament attracted twenty-three schools including eleven out-of-state teams. World War I interrupted the tournament in 1918 and 1919, but it resumed in 1920 and 1921. In 1922, Stagg moved the event to April and branded it as a "national tournament." It attracted 800 athletes from 125 high schools in twenty-eight states.[49] The 1923 event attracted forty teams from thirty-one states. The 1927 event reached an all-time high with participation from forty-three teams in thirty-three states. Stagg's tournaments, however, included only public high schools. Parochial, private, and African American schools were not invited.

In 1923, Loyola Academy asked Stagg to include Catholic and private schools in the tournament, an invitation that he ignored. The Loyola administration believed that Stagg's rejection was based on anti–Catholic sentiment. As a result, Loyola University led in establishing the National Catholic Interscholastic Basketball Tournament, which became very successful. By 1926, *Loyola News* boasted that ticket sales reached more than 35,000.[50]

Stagg publicly promoted the basketball and track tournaments to "improve high school track and field teams," but privately he used them as a recruiting tool. "The original motive which led me to start the … [meets] was that we might profit athletically," he wrote. He sent invitations to top athletes in Illinois and other states to encourage them to participate in the tournament. He kept lists of all participants, a record of their performance and his interviews with them. If an athlete excelled in the tournament, Stagg invited him to attend the University of Chicago.[51]

By the late 1920s, Chicago's basketball and track tournaments started to receive considerable criticism from the National Federation of High School Athletic Associations, which represented public school educators and coaches. They saw little benefit from paying expenses for their athletes to travel hundreds of miles to participate in tournaments. They thought the tournaments commercialized high school sports and created tremendous pressure from press and civic leaders for schools to produce winning teams. These pressures resulted in broken eligibility rules, neglected schoolwork, and exploitation of the players.

After 1930, more state associations started banning their athletes from attending intersectional contests including Stagg's Chicago event. Charles W. Whitten, executive secretary of the National Federation, organized the opposition to national tournaments. He wrote, "The transportation of high school teams to distant sections of the country for athletic contests seems to be a growing evil. Boys are away from their school work for days at a time to what educational end? There is little enough of educational warrant for [local and state championships].… What then should be said of so called 'national' meets and tournaments?"[52] At the 1929 meeting of the National Federation, Whitten proposed a resolution stating that the federation would refuse to sanction "any interstate tournaments," which passed by a twenty to two vote.

The North Central Association of Colleges and Secondary Schools joined the National Federation and passed a resolution prohibiting member schools from holding high school meets. This forced the University of Chicago administration to respond. Vice President Woodward appointed a committee to investigate whether to continue the tournaments. They mailed letters to 269 principals whose schools participated in Chicago's tournaments during the last ten years. Among principals who responded to the survey, more than two-thirds voted against the tournaments and a third favored retaining them. Bowing to the public pressure, Stagg terminated his national tournaments in December 1930, but continued to host tournaments for Chicago-area schools as long as he remained at the university.[53]

During his last five years at Chicago, Stagg didn't coach baseball or track teams but as athletic director, he continued to supervise the coaches, team scheduling, and all other athletic activities. That job ended in 1932 when President Robert Hutchens relieved Stagg of his athletic director duties and replaced him with T. Nelson Metcalf. He came from Iowa State University where he had been its athletic director. In *Stagg's University*, Lester described Metcalf as "comparatively dull and lifeless after the volatile Stagg" and "Metcalf was very much Hutchins' man and in the transition the university lost much of the spirit and verve that had characterized Stagg's administration."[54] Stagg saw the writing on the wall and knew that his days at the University of Chicago were numbered.

Mandatory Retirement, 1933

Are there any conditions under which intercollegiate football can be an asset to a college or university? I think not.... Football has no place in the kind of institution Chicago aspires to be.—Robert Maynard Hutchins

When Stagg was sixty-four in 1926 and near the university's mandatory retirement age of sixty-five, he was beginning to feel uncertain about his job. He wrote President Max Mason saying that he had received a job offer from another university. "Since I am within a year and three months of the university's age for retirement, I feel compelled to give consideration to this offer," he told Mason. But, he added, "I don't wish to go elsewhere unless the university wishes to have me retire." He then asked the president for his opinion on whether he could keep coaching after the mandatory retirement age.[1]

Mason replied, "The University Statutes call for retirement after the age of sixty-five but allow the Trustees to continue any member of the faculty in his position beyond this age, the action for continuing being taken year by year.... There is no thought in our minds except that of hoping for your services for many years to come and to wish for you the long continuance of your marvelous health and vitality which is so apparent.... The athletic history of the university is synonymous with your name."[2] After three years in office, Mason resigned unexpectedly in 1928 to accept a position at the Rockefeller Foundation. The next president would not be as sympathetic to Stagg.

A New President Arrives in Town

Robert Maynard Hutchins (1899–1977) became president in 1929 at the age of thirty. Both Stagg and Hutchins graduated from Yale, but that is where their similarities ended. Hutchins graduated from Yale Law School at age twenty-five, became a faculty member the same year, and dean of

Chicago football coaching staff in 1931. From left (back row): H.O. "Pat" Page, Saul C. Weislow, (front row) Nelson H. Norgren, Lawrence E. Apitz; J. Kyle Anderson, and Stagg. All assistant coaches were former Chicago players. University of Chicago Photographic Archive, apf1-06674, Special Collections Research Center, University of Chicago Library.

the law school at age twenty-seven. He served as president of the University of Chicago until 1951. Hutchins was no friend of football and was frequently quoted as saying, "Whenever the urge to exercise comes upon me, I lie down for a while, and it passes."[3] He was not joking. A biographer said of Hutchins: "He was not violently opposed to exercise; to have been violently opposed would itself have been more exercise than he was impelled to. He was opposed to both violence and exercise. He could not see why people had to hit, kick, or throw things around, why they could not keep in condition by getting up early, going to work, going home, going to work again, and going to bed; and eating and drinking enough to keep going."[4]

Nevertheless, he publicly supported Stagg and the football program for a couple of years. He attended home games because, as he wrote in his memoir, "It was good for a man to do the things he did not want to do." In 1931, he approved a Yale football game at Chicago to celebrate Stagg's fortieth anniversary of coaching. The Yale University Alumni Association of Chicago sponsored a testimonial dinner for Stagg on the weekend of the game. Hutchins spoke at the event and praised Stagg as "the greatest coach in the country."[5]

Privately, however, he resented Stagg's influence and knew it would be hard to get rid of him. "The Old Man was sacred, sacred to a relatively small but ardent segment of the alumni, sacred to some of the old professors who had come with him in 1892, sacred to some of the trustees ... sacred to the students, who had nothing else to hold sacred, sacred to the local barbers and their customers, sacred, above all, to the local sports writers who, with the Cubs and the White Sox where they were, had nothing much else to write about," Hutchins wrote.[6]

Hutchins believed football had no place in a

Robert Maynard Hutchins shortly after he became president of the University of Chicago, 1929. University of Chicago Photographic Archive, apf1-05031, Special Collections Research Center, University of Chicago Library.

research university. In his article "Gate receipts or glory?" published in the *Saturday Evening Post*, he wrote, "Young people who are more interested in their bodies than their minds should not go to college." Years later he wrote in *Sports Illustrated*: "Are there any conditions under which intercollegiate football can be an asset to a college or university? I think not.... Football has no place in the kind of institution Chicago aspires to be."[7] As early as 1930, Stagg saw the writing on the wall and advised his assistant coach, Fritz Crisler, to accept the head coaching job offer at the University of Minnesota. "The game is finished here. This man is going to kill it," he told Crisler.[8]

Stagg Faces Criticism

Stagg's last three seasons at Chicago were difficult because of losing teams, increased criticism from students and faculty, and a new president who wanted to abolish football. Exacerbated by the Depression, football revenue and attendance continued to decline. The team's losing records attracted increased criticism from students and fans. After the 1931 season ended with a 2–8–1 record, *The Daily Maroon* published "An Open Letter to the Old Man" criticizing Stagg, telling him, "you have lost your grip."

> Here are a few of the facts: the football team has not won a conference game since 1929, and the one victory that season was the contest with Indiana. During the same period that Chicago has been apologizing profusely for its football teams, the gymnastic teams have been winning conference championships with admirable persistence, the track team has had several good years, the baseball squad had one of its best seasons, and the tennis teams have monopolized the honors in the … conference meets. So, it can't be the dearth of material that causes the football team to lose so dishearteningly every Saturday. Now, Mr. Stagg, the fact remains that as a coach of football you have lost your grip….[9]

Soon after that, Stagg wrote Hutchins a letter similar to his letter to President Mason asking for assurance he could continue to coach after the age of seventy. Hutchins demurred, but they continued a conversation about Stagg's future. Stagg submitted a plan whereby he would "retire" from the faculty but continue as football coach and maintain control of the athletic budget, schedules, and appointment of assistant coaches until 1936. Hutchins did not immediately respond.

Hutchins Offers Stagg a Non-Coaching Job

Months later in April 1932, Hutchins wrote to tell Stagg he could not continue as football coach but offered him a public relations position. "I suggest that on July 1, 1933, you retire from the faculty and take up special work under direction of the President. The compensation would be $5,000 a year," Hutchins wrote. "The duties I have in mind are those of director of student relations for the Committee on Development of the Board of Trustees, or those of chairman of a new Committee on Intercollegiate Relations." Hutchins explained that he could arrange a combination of both positions. In the first position, Stagg would be working with high schools and alumni; in the second position, he would be Chicago's official representative with outside intercollegiate athletic organizations.[10] A $5,000 salary combined with his $3,000 retirement pension as coach would allow Stagg to continue to receive the same salary. Stagg did not reply to this offer for eight months.

Meanwhile, before Stagg had replied, Hutchins announced on October 14 following a board of trustees meeting that Nelson Metcalf, athletic director at Iowa State, would become the university's athletic director beginning the next academic year. Up until this time, Stagg held the positions of both athletic director and football coach. Hutchinson also told the press two weeks later, "There is no faculty rule as to the age limit of a coach," and that Metcalf "is at liberty to recommend Stagg as football coach if he desires."[11] Metcalf was still working at Iowa State in December when he told the *New York Times*, "Following conferences in Chicago yesterday, I have decided that I shall not recommend Mr. Stagg's reappointment as football coach for next year." He said he had been given a free rein "without pressure or dictation from any outside source."[12]

Two days later on December 6, Hutchins wrote Stagg again. "We are now beginning preparation for the budget of 1933–34. In this connection it is necessary for me to know whether you wish to accept either or both of the positions suggested in my letter of April 4.... I should be glad to know your wishes as soon as possible."[13] In a terse, one-sentence letter, Stagg replied the same day: "In reply to your letter of December 6th, I am writing to advise you that I cannot accept one or both of the positions suggested in your letter of April 4th."

The timing of the announcements about Metcalf's hiring gives the appearance that he was hired to do the dirty work of getting rid of Stagg as coach while leaving the president's and trustees' hands clean. Arch Ward, a sports columnist for the *Chicago Tribune*, reached the same conclusion as he wrote, "President Hutchins and members of the board of trustees said that the reappointment or dismissal of Stagg as football coach was entirely up to Metcalf. That made it easy, of course, for President Hutchins and the board of trustees. Metcalf, who probably had no choice in the matter, decided for dismissal."[14]

About a month later, Stagg wrote a friend saying he had wanted to coach at least one more year because Chicago has "the best material I have ever seen.... I wanted to see if I could not produce a winning team. First, I wanted to regain some of the prestige I lost as a coach. Second, I wanted to produce a first-class team for the sake of several of our boys who are anxious to get positions as coaches but are having difficulty on account of our stock being down on account of a series of bad years."[15]

He told an *Associated Press* reporter, "I could not and would not accept a job without work. I am fit, able and willing, and refuse to be idle and merely a nuisance as I would be if I were to accept this position. I must have work to do and since I cannot be football coach, I am leaving the university."[16] He told another reporter, "I'm not fooling myself into thinking that I can live to be 100 years old, but I may be good ten or fifteen years more. I've got to be active in the field of coaching, my life work, however. When I stop coaching, I'll stop living. I can't loaf now. I'm too young."[17]

Nationwide Furor

Stagg's impending mandatory retirement created a local and national furor among fans, students, and alumni. Thirty-nine members of the freshman team signed a petition asking for Stagg's retention as football coach. Their petition included signatures from thirty-one members of the varsity team and endorsements from 198 members of eleven fraternities. It read: "We, the undersigned freshmen, entered the University of Chicago with the hope that we might play football under the 'old man.' The ideals for which he stands and their influence in associating with him were deciding factors in our choice."[18]

A *Chicago Herald and Examiner* editorial criticized university officials and published a list of seventeen world leaders who were still "in useful work" beyond the age of seventy: Pope Pius IX (75), Paul von Hindenburg (85), Oliver Wendell Holmes (91), George Bernard Shaw (76), Ignace Jan Paderewski (72), Andrew Mellon (77), Charles Schwab (70), Edwin Markham (80), Frank J. Loesch (80), Clarence Darrow (75), Jane Adams (72), Lorado Taft (70), Ralph Modjeski (71), Arthur Farwell (80), Graham Taylor (71), Mary McDowell (78), and Charles Dickinson (74). The *Herald and Examiner* concluded, "Pope Pius guides the destinies of the Roman Catholic church. Von Hindenburg holds the reins of German government in firm hands. Oliver Wendell Holmes is still the prophet of American liberalism, and he sat on the bench of the United States Supreme Court until he was 90. Shaw gibes no less bitterly for his years, and Paderewski's fingers run nimbly over the keyboard."

In response to the *Herald and Examiner*, Vice President Frederic Woodward, speaking for President Hutchins, wrote a letter to the editor: "There are occasionally men who retain their powers in full, even in very advanced years, but it is our experience that few retain sufficient mental and intellectual elasticity and alertness to continue satisfactorily the work of teaching and research.... By this unalterable rule, we provide each man with certain knowledge to his future."[19] Companies and universities gradually eliminated mandatory retirement policies in the years that followed. Congress passed the Age Discrimination in Employment Act in 1967 to prohibit discrimination against employees older than forty and amended it in 1986 to prohibit mandatory retirement policies.[20]

Stagg received dozens of letters and telegrams from all over offering support and criticizing the university's decision. Christy Walsh, a sports agent who represented Babe Ruth, Lou Gehrig, and Ty Cobb, sent a telegram to Stagg, saying, "Loyal Chicago supporters and millions of football fans in all parts of the country representing several generations will emphatically protest your removal from a position which you have held so long."[21]

John L. Griffith, the first commissioner of the Western Intercollegiate Conference (Big Ten), wrote Stagg expressing outrage over the university's action: "I know that I am safe in saying that the men in the Conference and the people of this country will not agree with the opinions of the President and the Board of Trustees of the University of Chicago.... I consider that you not only through the years have been one of the greatest coaches that the game has ever produced, but that you still are."

Harold C. Ickes, a Chicago undergraduate and law school alumnus, was Franklin Roosevelt's Secretary of the Interior. "I can say in all truthfulness that Chicago won't be Chicago without you," he wrote Stagg. "The thing of real importance was that our students had you to hold before themselves in their future lives as an ideal of manliness, courage, right thinking, and clean living.... What you have done for Chicago and what you have done for Chicago men can never be told until someone comes along who can write a real epic."[22]

Lewis Atherton from Jackson, Michigan, wrote Harold Swift, an alumnus and chair of the board of trustees and heir to the Swift meat-packing company. Atherton asked Swift: "Why was Amos O. Stagg dropped from the University of Chicago after so many years of service?" Defending the decision, Swift replied: "Mr. Stagg was not dropped from the University of Chicago but was pensioned according to the regular faculty plan. The only unusual handling of his case was that instead of being pensioned at sixty-five, which in the last ten years has been customary, he was continued until he was seventy in deference to his wishes."[23]

Hutchins and the trustees had the power to do whatever they wanted to do. They could have made an exception to the policy and allowed Stagg to continue coaching beyond the age of seventy. Board minutes record that the trustees and president made an exception for Shailer Mathews, dean of the Divinity School, when they gave him the option to continue in his job past the age of seventy, but he chose to retire.[24] Mathews, who turned seventy on May 26, 1933, came to the university as a divinity school professor in 1908 and retired as dean in 1933, the same year that Stagg left.

Hutchins could be criticized for lack of transparency in the way he managed Stagg's departure. But the university's elimination of Stagg and the football program probably would have happened under any president at this era in its history. It had achieved a national reputation as a major research university, and football was no longer necessary to give it visibility. Its high academic standards made it difficult to attract the number and caliber of athletes needed to compete against other Big Ten universities.

A few months before Stagg accepted another coaching offer, Hutchins wrote Stagg to congratulate him on his upcoming "retirement." Hutchins began by saying, "Before I leave for the summer, I want to send you this personal note of appreciation of your long and faithful service to the University of Chicago." In a comment rich with irony, Hutchins concluded by saying, "I hope that in the many years which you will have in which to enjoy your well-earned leisure, you will still feel the same interest in the university which has always been characteristic of you."

Stagg's forty-one years at the university ended on June 30, 1933. During his final football season, teams from four Big Ten universities organized halftime tributes to Stagg. On October 29 at Stagg Field, the Illini Club of Chicago presented Stagg with an "I" blanket and said, "We shall ever call you a capable enemy and an ideal friend.... We present it as a tribute to your character, your sportsmanship and your ideals." The next Saturday, also at Stagg Field, President Elliot of Purdue University presented him with a "P" blanket and Boilermaker's hammer just prior to the game. On November 19, the "W" Club of the University of Wisconsin gave him an engraved plaque "in appreciation of forty-one years [of] service in the interest of amateur athletics." On November 16, three days before the Northwestern game, the "N" Club at Northwestern sent a bouquet of chrysanthemums to his home with a letter that read in part: "Many of our members have competed against your teams and all of us have observed your work. The passing years have worn away the temporary and superficial aspects of the struggle and have left in clear relief the enduring ideals for which you have consistently declared."[25]

On December 30 at its annual meeting, the NCCA gave Stagg a gold football on which was inscribed, "The National Collegiate Athletic Association to Amos Stagg in recognition of forty-one years of service in exemplifying the ideals and techniques of intercollegiate athletics, resourceful thinker, inspiring teacher, molder of men."

At the thirtieth annual "Order of the C" banquet to honor Stagg, 325 men attended including five from the 1892 team. Judge Walter Steffen, Stagg's former all–America quarterback, presented him with a bound volume of 400 personal letters of appreciation from "C" men. They had planned to give Stagg a "substantial gift," but when Stagg learned of their plans, he insisted that he wanted no gift. Steffen stated that Stagg originated the Order of the "C," an athletic honorary club that was later copied by hundreds of other college and university athletic programs.[26]

During his forty-one years of coaching football, his teams won 254 games, lost 104, and tied twenty-eight. Stagg was replaced as football coach by Clark Shaughnessy, the former coach at Tulane and Loyola-New Orleans universities. Lester wrote in *Stagg's University*, "The Maroon operation that Clark Shaughnessy inherited in 1933 was in dire straits: it had no dependable supply of raw material; its product was barely competitive; it had a decreasing share of the market; and the executives of its parent company were less sure of the value of football than any of the previous administrators had been."[27] Shaughnessy's winning percentage for the next seven years at Chicago was 17 percent. Most of Stagg Field's seats remained empty every game and Maroons football became an embarrassment. In its last season, Chicago lost eight games scoring only two points the whole season while their opponents scored an average of forty-three points per game.

Shaughnessy was, however, an excellent coach who labored at Chicago under impossible conditions. He left Chicago to become Stanford's head coach, where the team went undefeated during his first season in 1940 and ranked second in the nation. Stanford defeated the seventh-ranked Nebraska Cornhuskers 21–13 in the 1941 Rose Bowl.[28] Shaughnessy's losing record at Chicago reinforced the difficulty the university had faced since the early 1930s in attracting athletes who could compete against Big Ten teams.

Chicago Abolishes Football

Six years after Stagg left, the University of Chicago abolished college football in 1939. The trustees made the decision in a December 21 meeting and issued this statement: "Our particular interests and conditions are such that students now do not derive any benefit from intercollegiate football [but] the university will continue to promote intramural sports." Hutchins conveniently scheduled the trustees meeting and decision during Christmas break when students were not on campus. After they returned, he called a special convocation to explain the decision and said it should not be necessary to tell students that Chicago was an educational institution, not an athletic institution. "Education is primarily concerned with the training of the mind and athletics and social life, though they may contribute to education, are not the heart of it and cannot be permitted to interfere with it," he said.[29]

Chicago withdrew from the Big Ten Conference in 1946 after its basketball team lost sixty straight games. The *New York Times* reported, "The University of Chicago, a charter member and once a dominating power under Amos Alonzo Stagg, today withdrew from the 50-year-old Western conference because of athletic impotence. Long expected, the withdrawal of the faded Maroons, whose halcyon past held seven undisputed Big Ten championships, equaled only by Minnesota's modern Gophers."[30]

Led by a new athletic director, Wally Haas, football returned to the University of Chicago in 1963 as a club team, which played high schools, other club teams, and junior varsity teams. Football was upgraded to varsity status in 1969 with university support. In its first varsity game in thirty years, Chicago defeated Marquette University, 14–0. In 1973 the Maroons began competing in NCAA Division III, which is composed of small colleges and universities.[31] The Division III championship game, which also originated in 1973, was named the Amos Alonzo Stagg Bowl and is still played every year. The University of Chicago, however, has never won or participated in the bowl game that bears the name of its legendary coach.

After Stagg declined Hutchins' offer of an alternate job, his future remained in limbo for a couple of months. But as word spread of his mandatory retirement at Chicago, he began to receive coaching inquiries and offers from other universities around the country.[32] It was no time to quit.

12

Ups and Downs at College of the Pacific, 1933–1947

Success is a project that's always under construction.—Pat Summitt

Without the knowledge of the president of the College of the Pacific, the San Francisco Alumni Club president sent Stagg a telegram asking him if a coaching job on the West Coast would interest him. Everett Stark wrote, "Immediately after reaching your published declaration that you did not wish to retire but desired an active coaching position, our hopes arose that we might interest you in the oldest educational institution on the Pacific Coast...," he wrote. "You will have to look far to find another institution that maintains the high moral, cultural and scholastic standards that Pacific does, and where you will be appreciated more for the fine ideals and sterling character that you are known to possess."[1]

Stagg replied to Stark and asked for more information. As soon as he heard from Stagg, Stark reported the information to President Tulley C. Knoles. The president then wrote Stagg to say, "I would not have had the temerity to have sent you the telegram which you received from our alumni in San Francisco ... but I want to assure you I am in hearty sympathy with their action and rejoice to receive your reply."[2]

The College of the Pacific (now the University of the Pacific) was California's first chartered college in 1851, a year after it became a state. The campus moved from Santa Clara to San Jose in 1871 and Stockton in 1924. Knoles, a former history professor at the University of Southern California, became president in 1919. By 1933, the Methodist school was still virtually unknown outside California. A history of the college reported, "The football reputation of the college was nil, and its schedule consisted in playing opponents in the category of junior college teams.... High school graduates [from Stockton] were ridiculed if they thought of enrolling at the college." It also said the college was "deeply in debt and heavily mortgaged."[3]

President Knoles had been a Stagg admirer since 1894 when he was a quarterback for the University of Southern California Trojans. He watched the Stanford-Chicago game when Stagg brought the Chicago team to California that year. "I rode a bicycle thirty-eight miles to that game and always will remember how Chicago won 24 to 6. President Hoover was a student manager of Stanford's team then. I admired Mr. Stagg from that day on but never thought I would have the pleasure to be the president of the College of the Pacific and someday hire him as our football coach," Knoles told a reporter.[4]

When Knoles interviewed him on January 31, 1933, Stagg came prepared with thirty-five written questions about budget and organization of the athletic department, schedules, and duties. Negotiations went on for several weeks. After word leaked out that Stagg was considering the job, the news spread around the state like a California wildfire. George Hench, president of the alumni association, sent a telegram to Stagg: "You will have the unanimous support of the alumni as football coach and director of athletics.... The entire student body is eager to accept your leadership.... We all urge your acceptance."[5] The Stockton Merchants Alliance sent a telegram: "The Merchants Alliance of over two hundred businessmen are deeply interested in the possibilities of your coming to this city. The College of the Pacific and Stockton would feel honored with your presence."[6]

Albert Chesley, a Stockton YMCA leader, wrote, "All Stockton is agog in anticipation of your coming to the College of the Pacific.... Come to College of the Pacific and everything possible will be done to make you happy."[7] A Stockton attorney wrote, "Never have we seen such sincere and unanimous enthusiasm over the consideration of a football coach as that displayed since the mention of your name in connection with Pacific."[8] Stagg received forty-one letters and telegrams urging him to accept the job, which came from faculty, administrators, and students as well as Stockton pastors, civic leaders, and merchants. At one point, Stagg telegrammed Knoles: "Appreciate many cordial telegrams and letters. It is not necessary to send more. Satisfied I will be welcome. Decision will not turn on further expressions of good will."[9]

Stagg Accepts, California Rejoices

After agreeing to contract terms with the president, Stagg accepted the job on February 3 with a $5,000 annual salary. "I have had several offers from larger colleges and universities, but I finally decided on College of the Pacific because it is my desire to become affiliated with a small school where the spirit is splendid, and where I can aid in the development of young

Americans in a Christian way," he told the Associated Press.[10] His contract allowed him to hire a full-time assistant and spend four months of the year promoting and developing the football program. After accepting the job, the public outpouring was even larger. Stagg received sixty-nine welcoming letters and telegrams from the California governor, head football coaches at major western universities, and many well-known California citizens. Governor James Rolph wrote, "I take this opportunity of extending to you, the dean of the coaches of the United States, a most hearty welcome to this great state. Your ability to instill into athletes the spirit of good sportsmanship, which you have done over a period of many years, will bring honor and credit to the state of California."[11]

Bill Spaulding, UCLA football coach, wrote, "Your presence on the West Coast will add color and dignity to the coaching profession, and I feel it an honor to have you as one of us."[12] James Phelan, head football coach at the University of Washington, wrote, "I am very happy to have you on the Pacific coast.... I have always looked to you for football ideas, and I have enjoyed my personal acquaintance with you and realize you have elevated the coaching profession more than anyone else in the game."[13]

Upon accepting the invitation, Stagg said, "Forty years of loyalty have sunk the roots of affection down deep at the University of Chicago. I shall leave it with lumps in my throat. I went West when I was a young man. I am going West again, and I am still a young man. At seventy, men are not supposed to have ambition. But at seventy, I have the body of a middle-aged man. I have ambition, enthusiasm, will power, experience, and vitality to start on a new career and carry it on for twenty years."[14] But he also told the *Sacramento Bee* that he intended to take the Pacific team back to Chicago to challenge his old team. "I hope to take a team back to Chicago to meet the university I coached for forty-one years. When I quit Chicago, I left a challenge with the new coach, and I intend to carry it out."[15]

Arrival in Stockton

Two men rode on the west-bound train when it arrived in Sacramento on March 22, 1933. One was Herbert Hoover, who was leaving behind his old job in the White House, and Amos Stagg, who was arriving to begin a new job. The ex-President and his wife were returning to their Palo Alto home after Franklin D. Roosevelt had been inaugurated two weeks earlier. Thousands of people crowded into the station. "Mr. President," said Stagg while standing beside Hoover on the platform. "What a wonderful reception they're giving you." Hoover turned to him and said, "No, coach. They're here to greet you."[16]

A cavalcade of cars and fans escorted the Stagg couple south on Highway 99 to Stockton. "With sirens moaning, whistles shrieking, and thousands roaring welcome, Stagg came to Stockton and College of the Pacific to write another chapter in his brilliant record of achievements," the *San Francisco Examiner* reported.[17] He later recalled, "I was conducted in a continuous parade in which scores of cars participated for the forty-one miles to the city of Stockton.... I was conducted through the center of the city and then to the college where I was officially greeted at a monster pep-rally."[18]

Stagg believed the college was financially sound but soon learned it was deeply in debt. Since the Depression began in 1929, enrollment had dropped by one fourth. Unpaid campaign pledges exceeded $400,000 forcing the board to transfer money from the endowment to the operating budget, reduce all salaries by 40 percent and eliminate four faculty positions.[19]

The college was one-fifteenth the size of the University of Chicago. The football teams consistently compiled losing records and small crowds of less than 400. He later recalled, "the financial problems caused by the Great Depression had struck deep in California as they had in Chicago, and the educational institutions were feeling the full force of the panic.... The college was literally staggering under the tremendous debt because of their large building program which had not been paid for, and the college was in serious financial shape. Faculty salaries had been drastically cut and stringencies were affecting everyone."[20] Consequently, after Stagg arrived, he set two goals: first, to make the college well-known outside of central California; and second, to arrange a schedule of games that would bring a good financial return.[21]

The university was a member of the Far Western Conference, which included the University of Nevada, three California state teachers' colleges, and the California Aggies (now the University of California at Davis). Unlike Pacific, other conference schools offered free tuition, which made his recruiting much more difficult. President Knoles told Stagg in a letter, "Selected athletes are awarded tuition scholarships in order to equalize their status with those who represent other schools." He said in the same letter, "Up to the present time the games have not paid for themselves, and the college has borne all of the expenses of the coaching staff."[22]

Stagg scheduled his first spring practice on March 22, and forty-eight prospective players turned out to greet him on the football field. "The man who refuses to retire began the second job of his life today," wrote a *San Francisco Examiner* reporter.[23] Stagg had brought along Larry Apitz as his assistant coach. Apitz was an assistant coach at Chicago for four years and a star end for the Maroon football team from 1925 to 1927. In April Stagg announced that his son, Paul Stagg, would join the staff in the fall to coach the quarterbacks and running backs. Paul Stagg had also been an assistant coach at Chicago and a quarterback for the Maroons from 1929 to 1931. He had just completed a master's degree at Columbia University.[24]

In August, Stagg wrote team members a letter urging them to start practicing and getting in shape for the fall season. "I have started doing some running myself, so that I may be able to keep up with the team. I think that the coach ought to train; I always have," he told them. His letter outlined these four training rules:

1. Good habits, regular sleep, no tobacco, or alcohol.
2. Gradually develop quickness, speed, and endurance. Practice 25-yard sprints.
3. Gradually reduce surplus weight.
4. Develop muscular strength by exercise.

First Season

Pacific lost its first game to Oregon Normal 12–0 (now Western Oregon), but Oregon coach Larry Wolfe praised Stagg in his losing effort. "This was Stagg's first game on the coast, but he knew a lot about our team. He was set for every trick we had in our bag except one, and that was a left-handed passer," he told a reporter. Oregon's southpaw quarterback threw for one touchdown and intercepted a pass and ran for the other.[25] The Pacific Tigers won their second game 3–0 against the California Ramblers composed of "B" team players at the University of California–Berkeley. They played seven other games against Modesto Junior College, University of Nevada, Chico State, California Aggies, St. Mary's–California, Loyola–Los Angeles, and Fresno State. They ended the season with a 5–5 record, which included wins over the California Aggies 13–7, Chico State 14–0, and Fresno State 12–0.

Stagg's first season, compared with Pacific's 1932 season, attracted more than three times as many fans, four times as much in gate receipts, and cleared net profits of approximately $5,000. "Stagg's presence caused a great revival of College of the Pacific alumni interest and put additional pep in the undergraduate body," said one sports columnist. "The city of Stockton is now supporting the college 100 percent."[26]

During his second season in 1934, Stagg was criticized for being "cruel and unfair" to his team by scheduling games against Southern California and California-Berkeley. Yet, the team shocked everyone when it barely lost to California, 7–6, and Southern California, 6–0. After these narrow losses, the Pacific Tigers earned the nickname "giant-killers." The *San Francisco Examiner* said Pacific's narrow defeat by Southern California "astounded the football world."[27] Two weeks later, the same newspaper called the loss

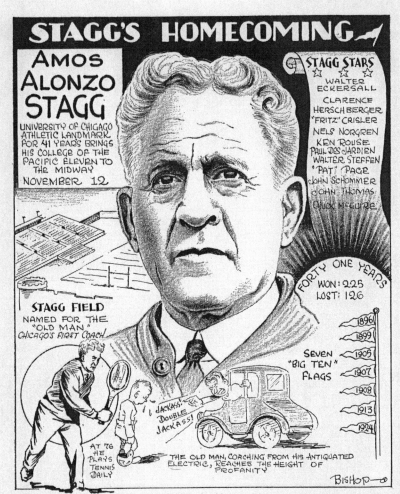

Amos Alonzo Stagg comes back to the Midway November 12 after an absence of six years. For the first time in his life he will be cast as the opponent of the Chicago team which he coached for forty-one years. On that day the "Old Man" will send his College of the Pacific Tigers against the Maroon eleven.

The game with Pacific was arranged as the University of Chicago's tribute to its greatest athletic figure in anticipation of his semi-centennial of coaching next season. The game is in recognition, too, of his great services to the development of intercollegiate athletics.

Mr. Stagg retired at Chicago in June of 1932, under the retirement regulations of the University which provide him with an annuity of $3,000. But inactivity did not appeal to him; seventy-one years young, he went west. As original and thorough a coach as ever, he has made the College of the Pacific team a respected foe even of the mighty teams of the coast.

With the "Old Man" will come Mrs. Stagg, who has been his first assistant since 1894. They both will be the guests of honor at the dinner the night before the game which the Chicago Alumni Club and the University athletic department are sponsoring. And if the "Old Man" goes home with a victory, it will be a trophy no one ever on the Midway will begrudge him.

Advertisement promoting the homecoming visit by Stagg on November 12, 1938, six years after his mandatory retirement. University of Chicago Photographic Archive, apf1-07752, Special Collections Research Center, University of Chicago Library.

to Berkeley a "moral victory" for Pacific and the "greatest aerial attack ever seen in a football game on the Pacific Coast." It said the Pacific Tigers had the Bears in "a complete state of befuddlement as the thrilling contest ended."[28] However, the great expectations did not continue for the rest of the 1934 season after the team ended with a 4–5 record.

Lonnie and Stella enjoyed some lighter moments in the summer of 1935 when they returned to Chicago to visit their daughter. On August 16, he celebrated his seventy-third birthday at a party sponsored by the Chicago Alumni Club. They presented him with a large birthday cake with the inscription: "Stagg, 73; Opponents, 0; end of first half."[29]

The 1935 season brought the Tigers an improved 5–4–1 record and the most successful of Stagg's first three seasons. Opening against Southern California, the Tigers amazed 30,000 fans as they led the Trojans for three quarters. Not until the fourth quarter did Southern California fight back to win 19–7. The Tigers went on to defeat Nevada 7–6, Chico State 20–0, and the California Aggies 26–7. After battling San Jose State to a 0–0 tie and losing to California and Stanford, they finished the season with victories over the San Diego Marines team and San Diego State—good enough for a second-place finish in the Far Western Conference.

Pacific won its first of five Far Western Conference championships in 1936 with a season record of 4–3–1. Against conference opponents Fresno State, Chico State, Nevada, and the California Aggies, the Tigers were undefeated and unscored on. They lost again to non-conference rivals St. Mary's-California and San Jose State.

Stagg celebrated his seventy-fifth birthday on August 16 shortly before the 1937 season began. The *Los Angeles Times* said, "He follows a training schedule as rigid as that prescribed for his players. Always up before 7 each morning, he runs and walks a full mile to the tennis court, where he plays for an hour. He then walks home to breakfast. Asked why he does this, he says: 'I'm keeping myself in shape just like the football players.'"[30] He told a *San Francisco Examiner* reporter, "I have taken off ten pounds during the past month by daily jogs and walks topped off with a little ball batting on the tennis courts. I hope my players feel as good as I when they report for practice September 10."[31] Despite Stagg's optimism, the team failed to meet expectations and ended the 1937 season with a 3–5–2 record.

Pacific Tigers Play Chicago Maroons

The Tigers ended the 1938 season with a 7–3 record, a conference championship, and the best record of Stagg's first six years at Pacific. Before the season began, Stagg denied rumors of any plans to retire. "If the time ever comes I'm not good enough to coach a college team, then maybe I can turn to high school coaching. I never have and never intend to give any thought to retirement," he told a reporter while vacationing in Tucson.[32]

He also fulfilled his public promised to take the team to play the University of Chicago. On November 12, 1938, the Pacific Tigers traveled to Chicago shortly after impressive wins over Nevada and Fresno State. Stagg and the team were met at the train station by Clark Shaughnessy, coach, Nelson Metcalf, athletic director, and a group of Stagg's former players. Chicago had lost five of its six previous games, including a 47–13 loss to Harvard the previous week.

Stagg addressed a group of 1,500 students, alumni, and fans at a bonfire on the campus the night before the game. "I have sorrowed in your defeats, and I have rejoiced in your victories. If you win tomorrow, it will be all right. And if the College of the Pacific wins, it will, of course, be all right.... But my feelings will not be hurt regardless of who wins the game. Yours are friendly faces—mine is the same to you."[33] A "Letter to Amos Alonzo" was published in the *Chicago Tribune* on the day of the game. "Today you return after six years of absence to the field on which a large part of your long and noble life has been spent to pit your College of the Pacific against your Maroons, and whatever the score, it will be your victory. For you have triumphed over time and defeat and neglect and the fickle spirit of the age, and your soul goes marching on."[34]

The Chicago band played during a pre-game parade that included "a strange procession of vehicles denoting the various stages in Stagg's stay at Chicago beginning with the horse and buggy of the gay '90s up to the later type automobile."[35] Stagg and Shaughnessy sat in the lead car waving to more than 10,000 fans. The procession stopped at the end of the field, where several hundred former Chicago athletes honored Stagg with a scroll "presented with love and affection by 1,100 living members of the Order of the C."[36]

The game program included ads for *Perfecto Garcia* cigars, *Chesterfield, Old Gold,* and *Camel* cigarettes, which Stagg would have never allowed if he had been in charge. It also included a full-page ad from the Drake Hotel for an evening of dinner, dancing and "delightful entertainment" by radio stars Ozzie and Harriet. In its pregame summary, the program said, "Six years after he was gone, his thousands of friends are returning not so much to watch the football game as once again to see the 'Old Man' on Stagg Field."[37]

The Pacific Tigers romped over the Chicago Maroons 32–0. Chicago never moved the ball into Pacific territory until late in the third quarter and completed only eight of twenty-one passes. Three of them were intercepted including two for touchdowns by the Tigers. Pacific completed nine of eighteen passes with no interceptions and scored three of their five touchdowns in the fourth quarter. "Even the homecoming committee thought this was overdoing the welcome home motif a trifle," according to one Chicago sportswriter.[38]

At the end of the game, members of Chicago's team carried Stagg on their shoulders off the field. The *New York Times* described the victory: "Amos Alonzo Stagg still rules the Midway today.... The man who went West a second time because he wouldn't quit coaching at seventy came back to the school he directed for forty-one years."[39]

Despite a loss against California-Berkeley, the 7–3 season was Stagg's best of his first five years at Pacific. Impressive wins came against the California Aggies, 34–6; undefeated Fresno State, 18–13; and Nevada, 51–0. The Nevada victory marked the largest score ever recorded at Pacific's stadium. Stagg told a reporter that the quality of college football had progressed considerably since he began coaching. "Thirty years ago, football was an exclusive sport for the few young men who could afford to go to college. Today it is the common man's sport.... In every department of the game, I can see a vast improvement. We have better passers today, better punters, and more of them. The boys today are bigger, faster, and more agile athletes."[40]

Stella's Scouting

By the late 1930s, Stagg's three children were grown, which gave Stella more time to be an assistant coach and team scout. A California reporter said of her, "She charts all plays at home games, keeps statistical records on the practice field and in an emergency can scout the opposition. She did this last week traveling to Davis to watch the California Aggies in action while College of the Pacific was in the Southwest to play Southern Methodist." He continued, "While A.A. was directing his team in the game with Southern Methodist last Saturday, Mrs. Stagg was in the press box at Davis, diagramming Mustang plays in their game against Humboldt State. An expert at this business of scouting, Mrs. Stagg compiled a comprehensive report not only of Aggie plays, but also on the strength or weakness of individual players."[41]

Not only did she chart games and compile statistics, she repaired the team's uniforms. When Pacific played Northwestern in 1946, the *Chicago Tribune* reported, "Athletic equipment is limited at Pacific. Mrs. Stagg's needlework salvaged many of the jerseys and blankets used yesterday."[42]

On January 1, 1938, she scouted the Sugar Bowl game between Louisiana State and the University of Santa Clara, a future opponent. Her two pages of notes revealed a detailed grasp of football plays and offensive formations. She wrote:

Santa Clara used the Notre Dame formation throughout the game ... the only variation being that once and perhaps more times they had the quarterback shift to the left of center instead of to the right on a shift right formation. L.S.U. used a single-wing formation. In addition to the single wing, L.S.U. used the double wing at least five times, four of them for forward passes, which they completed for 23 yds, 10 yds, 14 yds. and 17 yds. The running play from double wing was the wing around play. L.S.U. had a fake shovel pass. They quick kicked from single wing.[43]

After Stagg's fourth season at College of the Pacific, team members presented a trophy to Mrs. Stagg at a student assembly to recognize her many contributions to the team. They gave it to her "in appreciation of her fine constructive work during the four years she and Mr. Stagg have been at the College of the Pacific." The *San Francisco Examiner* reported, "Her name has seldom appeared on the sports pages, but all through the years she has been her husband's closest co-worker."[44]

Stella Stagg tried to steer clear of publicity and defer attention to others. "You want someone more colorful than I am for a newspaper article," she told a reporter. Yet, newspapers occasionally profiled her work during the years she was a de facto assistant coach. When Pacific played Hawaii in 1939, "Mrs. Stagg was one of the busiest persons in the press box.... She attends every College of the Pacific game armed with a stenographer's notebook and takes notes on every play. She does not merely chart the game but keeps notes on which player carried the ball, and what the other players did on the play. She also describes what the defense does. When the game is over, she turns the notes over to her husband. Mrs. Stagg knows her football from A to Z, and she certainly is a keen observer of the games."[45]

"The first lady of American football" is how an Associated Press article described her in 1942 when she was sixty-seven. It described her as "slender, retiring, almost bird-like in her movements," and continued, "Because her husband is one of the most famed football strategists in history, she lives in the background, yet her own story is worthy of a headline.... Mrs. Stagg serves as scout, statistician, historian, typist, and adviser, as well as one-woman consolation committee when things are breaking tough." When asked what part of football she liked best, she replied, "the winning part."[46]

Early Hopes Lead to Disappointment

Stagg's began his fiftieth season of coaching in 1939 when his team defeated California-Berkeley 6–0 on September 30. It marked the Pacific Tigers' first win and only their second touchdown against the

California Bears after losing for five consecutive years. "We have just seen the biggest upset of the 1939 season recorded and 15,000 people sit stunned.... No matter what happens from here on in—no matter who beats who or how—THE upset of the season has been recorded," wrote Lee Dunbar of the *Oakland Tribune*.[47]

To honor Stagg's fiftieth season, Pacific called its 1939 team the "Golden Tigers" and added tiger stripes to the uniforms. After upsetting California-Berkeley, it ended the season with a mediocre 6–6–1 record. "The COP varsity football team unquestionably took first place among the disappointments of 1939. A team that began so auspiciously by defeating the University of South Dakota and the University of California [Davis] in its first two games was, by mid-season, a house divided against itself and the golden hopes of Coach Stagg's golden year had turned to ashes," wrote the *Stockton Record*. The article also said, "One important player abandoned the team following an inter-squad tiff early in the season, and two others were dismissed for the good of the club after the tenth contest."[48]

At the beginning of the season he and Stella donated $3,000 to the College of the Pacific to purchase an adjoining twenty-one-acre tract for a future athletic field. The college planned to use the land for tennis courts, an aquatics center, baseball field, and football practice field. O.H. Ritter, comptroller, told the *Stockton Record*, "Mr. Stagg's only stipulation was that the new area should be named Knoles Field in honor of the president of the College of the Pacific."[49] Although the college ended its football program in 1995, it went against his wishes in 1988 when it renamed the stadium the "Amos Alonzo Stagg Memorial Stadium," which was used for soccer and field hockey games. However, the college demolished it in 2014 to make room for new athletic facilities.[50]

Stagg and Glenn Scobey "Pop" Warner (1871–1954), two legendary names in college football, met for the second time on opposing teams on October 20, 1939, when Pacific lost to San Jose State. Although Warner had officially retired from coaching, he was recruited by San Jose State that year to coach its offense. The last time a Stagg-coached team (Chicago) met a Warner-coached team was in 1907 when Warner coached the Carlisle Indian School and its celebrated star, Jim Thorpe. Carlisle also won that game 18–4. Between his stints at Carlisle and San Jose State, Warner was head coach at Pittsburgh, Stanford, and Temple. Danzig wrote in *The History of American Football* that Warner "won recognition as one of the two most fertile and original minds football has known, the other's being Stagg." When their teams played each other in 1939, the two coaches had a combined ninety-five years of coaching experience.[51]

In 1939, the American Football Coaches Association, which Stagg helped organize in the 1920s, awarded him a plaque at its convention

honoring his fifty years of coaching. It was the first "Stagg Award" the association has given annually to the "individual, group or institution whose
services have been outstanding in the advancement of the best interests of
football." Recipients receive a plaque which is a replica of the one given to
Stagg at the 1939 convention. The purpose of the award is "to perpetuate the
example and influence of Amos Alonzo Stagg."[52]

Stagg and Rockne in the Movies

Win or lose, Stagg was never afraid to schedule games against big-time
opponents. His games against Southern California, California, and Stanford had already boosted the tiny College of the Pacific to national acclaim.
Notre Dame came next. Notre Dame's coach and athletic director, Elmer
Layden, had invited Stagg two years earlier to bring the Pacific team to play

Cast members of the 1940 film, *Knute Rockne, All American*. From left: Henry
O'Neill (doctor); Pat O'Brien (Knute Rockne); Stella Stagg; Nick Lukats (technical advisor), and Amos Stagg. University of Chicago Photographic Archive,
apf1-07801, Special Collections Research Center, University of Chicago
Library.

in South Bend. In the first game of the 1940 season, Stagg took the Tigers to play Notre Dame, which the Fighting Irish easily won, 25–7, and ended their season with a 7–2 record.

The game, however, was not the biggest news of the day in South Bend. The movie *Knute Rockne, All American* made its national premiere at four South Bend theaters and attracted more than 4,000 local viewers. The principal actors were Ronald Reagan (who played quarterback George Gipp), Pat O'Brien (who played Rockne) and Gale Page (who played Bonnie Rockne). The actors dashed from theater to theater with police convoys to make guest appearances in South Bend. Stagg played himself in a scene with three other famous football coaches who also played themselves: Glenn "Pop" Warner, Bill Spaulding, and Howard Jones.

Knute Rockne died in a tragic plane crash in 1931, and the largely hagiographic movie portraying his life story was produced nine years later. Stagg influenced Rockne and Notre Dame directly through his former player Jesse Harper, who played Chicago football during the 1903–1905 seasons. Harper was Notre Dame's first full-time coach and coached Knute Rockne when he was a student on the team.

One movie scene begins with a cascade of newspaper headlines from various large cities such as "FOOTBALL SCANDAL ATTACKED BY NATION'S EDUCATORS" and "CRY OF PROFESSIONALISM RAISED BY COLLEGE AUTHORITIES." In the next scene, Stagg, Warner, Spalding, and Jones persuaded Rockne to speak to a conference of leading educators in New York and defend college football against its criticisms. Stagg told Rockne in this scene, "These men have come to you because you've always been a leader. They need your name and your voice to speak for them.... It's for the boys, all of them, all over the nation." In the next scene, Rockne spoke to the educators and made a vigorous, passionate defense of football against criticisms of violence and professionalism.[53]

One of Stagg's friends wrote him a few months later saying, "We went to see the movie of the life of Knute Rockne the other night and were greatly pleased to be watching what I take to be your debut in the movies. You looked as great as ever, and your voice was most familiar." Stagg replied saying, "I did this as a tribute to the memory of Rockne, [but] the scene was pure fiction."[54]

Stagg was correct. Murray Sperber wrote in *Onward to Victory*, "In the late 1930s and early 1940s, the debate on intercollegiate athletics was real and important enough for scriptwriters to create a scene that never occurred and to have their fictional Rockne speak words that the real one never uttered." He added, "No formal hearing on intercollegiate athletics ever occurred during Rockne's lifetime.... No one ever visited Rockne to urge him to attend a nonexistent hearing."[55]

The movie played fast and loose with other facts. In an affront to Stagg, the movie producers had invited him to participate in a movie that credited Rockne with football innovations that Stagg himself had pioneered. Besides the fictitious scene, the movie portrayed Rockne when he was a student who played a pass receiver and his quarterback, Gus Dorais, as inventors of the forward pass. The Notre Dame athletic website even today says that Rockne and Dorais "debuted" the forward pass.[56]

In one scene, Rockne and Dorais practiced throwing passes on a Lake Michigan beach before the 1913 season began. Rockne told Dorais, "No team has ever used the forward pass as the major thrust of its offense." After trailing Army at halftime in the next scene, Rockne asked Harper to let them use the forward pass in the second half. Rockne pled, "Let us use the forward pass. I know it will work." Harper replied, "I'm not so sure. We've never seen it in a game." Rockne said, "Neither has the Army; what can we lose?" And Harper replied, "It's your idea, Rock. If you think you can put it over, go ahead." So, in the second half Dorais completed fourteen of seventeen pass attempts as Notre Dame upset Army for a 35–13 win in a game that became legendary.

The forward pass, however, had been legalized by the Rules Committee seven years earlier in 1906, as explained in Chapter 8. Most sources credit Saint Louis University and its coach Eddie Cochems with the first legal use of a forward pass during the 1906 season. The team's quarterback threw a twenty-yard touchdown pass against Carroll College on September 5, 1906.[57] Stagg and quarterback Walter Eckersall, however, used it extensively in Chicago's 63–0 victory over Illinois on November 10, 1906. Within a year, the forward pass was widespread among college teams.

Frank P. Maggio in *Notre Dame and the Game That Changed Football* explained the origin of the forward pass. Although the forward pass didn't originate at the Army–Notre Dame game, it was the first in which a forward pass was received *on the run*.[58] "The sophisticated passing attack that Harper installed at Notre Dame had been long in the making—after being introduced to the weapon by Stagg," he wrote. Until then, pass receivers ran their routes, stopped, and turned around before the quarterback threw the ball. Harper said the team practiced the forward pass for weeks before the Army game.[59]

The movie's second error was in portraying Rockne with inventing the "Notre Dame shift" formation after he watched a team of chorus girls dancing in a theater. After watching the chorus girls perform, Rockne admired their precise timing and movements and scribbled some play diagrams on a notepad. Then he started teaching them to his team. In this formation, the entire backfield shifts right or left after the count begins, and the center hikes the ball to one of the halfbacks instead of the quarterback. The shift created many offensive variations and a surprise for the defensive team since it did not know which player would receive the ball.

However, Rockne himself credited Stagg with inventing the shift: "To Alonzo Stagg goes credit for this revolution in football that gave us the shift—the dramatic equalizer between the 'big' and 'little' teams. The shift quickly became popular. It was new and spectacular and gave the untechnical football fan a chance to see something of the game besides mass huddles, flying wedges, and stretcher-barriers," he wrote in his autobiography.[60]

Rockne said the idea came to him from Jesse Harper, who learned it while playing quarterback for Stagg at Chicago in 1905. "After the Yale debacle of 1914, Harper called me into his Pullman drawing room," Rockne later wrote. "He announced that we had to break into something new, something different, in the way of offense.… He began drawing marks on a piece of paper, describing a backfield shift similar to what Chicago had used when he was quarterbacking. Harper's variation was that he made the shift cover twice as much territory."[61]

Years after his 1931 death, Notre Dame fans were eager to see a major motion picture to preserve Rockne's heroic image. When Ronald Reagan ran for president in 1980 and 1984, he capitalized on his portrayal of star quarterback George Gipp for his campaign slogan, "Win one for the Gipper." In the movie scene while dying from a rare disease at age twenty-five, Gipp supposedly told Rockne, "Tell them to win one for the Gipper," which Rockne did after the Fighting Irish trailed Army at halftime in 1928. "Win one for the Gipper" has entered the halls of football legends, but there is no clear evidence that Gipp ever made the deathbed remark. It could be one of the exaggerated tales for which Rockne was famous.[62] Sperber said in *Onward to Victory* that Rockne's widow, Bonnie, had complete control over the movie script due to the copyright laws at the time. "The studio had to comply to her requests," Sperber wrote.[63]

Stagg Declines Film Offer

In 1952 when Stagg was coaching at Susquehanna University, MGM offered him $300,000 and 7 percent of gross receipts for the movie rights to his life story. Stagg Jr. told an interviewer in 1967, "It was to star Spencer Tracy and Katharine Hepburn, who bore marked resemblances to my father and mother. When he turned it down, we were aghast. He told us, 'It's my life, and I don't expect my sons to tell me how to run it.'"[64] Stagg Jr. recalled the experience again in 1985 when he told an interviewer that he tried to persuade his father to allow MGM to make the movie:

I said, "Father, if you make a movie, you have a chance to spread your motives and ideals to millions of people...." I discussed it over and over again with him. Now, it was a very easy sale for me. MGM offered me a thousand dollars a week for two and a half months if I would set it up and make sure everything was correct. One day out of the clear sky, he said to me, "If I got the $300,000 that they want to give me, I would give it all to Yale, perhaps some to the University of Chicago. I most certainly wouldn't give it to the children." He said it was an "odious" idea. He just didn't think he should do it on principle.[65]

Stagg received letters from several Hollywood writers and producers asking about making a movie of his life. For example, Harry Hall, a Los Angeles sports promotion representative wrote Stagg in 1944: "I was surprised to read in the paper where you refused to have your life made into a motion picture. It is common knowledge to me that you have consistently refused to capitalize financially on your fame.... If your reason for rejecting the idea is your dislike for financial gain, this 'stigma' could be erased by giving your share of the money to some War Charity. If you reconsider the idea of making a picture based on your life, I would feel highly honored in being your representative. I will render my services to you GRATIS."[66] Again, however, Stagg declined. "Thank you for your good letter," he wrote. "At the present time, the idea of having my life filmed is repugnant to me. I have not encouraged any of the six or seven people who have taken up the matter with me."[67]

One of Stagg's guiding principles was "Never to sell my name and never profit by endorsing!, something." He wrote in *Touchdown!*, "I have never capitalized on my name because I did not like the feel of it."[68] He cited this as the reason he declined to permit the movie in a talk he gave at the College of the Pacific's chapel service on May 11, 1943. In this address titled "What does Jesus mean to me?" he explained this and six other ways that his Christian faith had affected his life. He gave the example of declining a $200 offer to appear on a radio program. When coaching at Susquehanna in the early 1950s, he declined a $500 offer to appear on a national television program.[69]

Chicago Tribune columnist Arch Ward cited the Knute Rockne movie as one reason he declined the offer. "Amos A. Stagg has once again has vetoed movie company plans to make the story of his life," he wrote. "The Grand Old Man says the script would call for a romantic picture, and he isn't interested in a love story. Besides, Amos hasn't been too friendly toward the picture makers since the story of Knute Rockne was filmed and showed Rock getting his idea for the Notre Dame shift from watching a line of chorus girls. Stagg says Rockne got the shift from him."[70]

Despite Stagg's repeated refusals to authorize a movie, his children signed a six-month movie option agreement in 1964, the year before he died. The Stagg Special Collection at Stagg High School in Palos Hills, Illinois, contains a document titled "Option Agreement, re: Life Story of Amos Alonzo Stagg, Sr." and dated October 1, 1964. It was signed by Amos Alonzo Stagg, Jr., Paul Stagg, and daughter, Mrs. Ruth Stagg Lauren. In consideration of a $1,500 payment, the family conveyed to Walter Schwimmer "an option to purchase all exclusive rights with respect to the life of their father, Amo Alonzo Stagg, Sr., as depicted in the mediums of: (1) A biography currently being written by Amos A. Stagg, Jr.; (2) television programs; (3) motion pictures; (4) theatrical productions; (5) newspaper and magazine articles." Schwimmer was owner of a Chicago production company and best known as producer of the 1950 television series *The Cisco Kid*. On October 1, 1964 (the date the option was signed), the elder Stagg was 102 years old, frail, and living in a California convalescent center. He died just five months later. While there is no evidence Stagg consented to the option agreement, the option expired a month after he died, and a movie was never produced.

Fictionalizing a few scenes in a movie based on a true story is not uncommon. But the movie's use of Stagg and other famous coaches to portray themselves while crediting Rockne with football innovations he did not create is duplicitous. Rockne's tragic death in a plane crash and portrayal in the successful movie made him a pop culture legend. Stagg, however, was arguably a more successful coach than Rockne with many more football innovations and three times as many career wins. If Stagg's children had been successful in enabling the production of a movie about their father, the Stagg name might today be as widely known as Rockne's.

Stagg Protests Loss to San Jose State

Another 4–7 losing season for the Pacific Tigers came in 1941. The controversial 7–0 loss to San Jose State that season was the only game on record in which Stagg protested a loss. San Jose's fullback, Allen Hardesty, took the ball on the thirteen-yard line and drove to the one-yard line, where he was tackled by a Pacific defensive player. Hardesty appeared to be down at this point, but officials ruled that he rolled over the goal line after he was tackled, and they awarded the touchdown. "That was stoutly denied by every member of the Pacific team on the field at the time," according to the *Stockton Record*.[71] Believing that San Jose didn't earn the winning touchdown, Stagg asked the San Jose athletic director to cancel and replay the game.

"It was a touchdown," said referee Joseph Canella when contacted by a reporter after the game. "The ball rested on the goal line, and Hardesty was thrown back after making the score."[72] Yet, Stagg called San Jose athletic director Allen Hartranft and asked him "to replay the game" against Pacific. Hartranft quoted Stagg as saying, "The boys are very dissatisfied. Pictures show that Hardesty didn't score that touchdown that won the game. Won't you play the game over again?"

"No," Hartranft firmly replied. "We have a full schedule. In fact, we have to drop a game in order to make the trip to the Islands. I will leave the matter up to the authorities—the officials who handled the game."[73] In an "open letter" to Stagg published in the *Stockton Record*, Hartranft reiterated his point: "We therefore feel that any decision should be left in the hands of those trained for their jobs and paid to arbitrate such questions. If you and your players and the supporters of the College of the Pacific are, as suggested, good sportsmen, you will abide by the decision of those officials."[74] At this point, Stagg could do nothing else.

World War II Produces a Winning Season

After four consecutive losing seasons, the onset of World War II made the outlook for the 1943 season look even bleaker. More than sixty colleges had suspended their football teams and most of Pacific's male students were drafted into the military. Stagg canceled spring practice after only seven players showed up for the first practice. President Knoles suggested that Stagg cancel the season. Stagg, however, persuaded the president to let him have a team after he voluntarily reduced his salary by $2,000. Stagg said in a letter, "I have been taking care of three of my four elderly sisters for a good many years, and when the war started the college here was so hard up that I voluntarily offered to reduce my $5,000 salary to $3,000."[75]

Nevertheless, it turned out to be Stagg's most unexpected season. If World War I produced his worst team in 1918, World War II produced his best in 1943. He was able to organize an excellent team because the Navy assigned a considerable number of recruits to the College of the Pacific for special training. Between 1943 and 1946, the Navy paid tuition for more than 125,000 enlistees in 131 colleges and universities for officer training. Stagg wrote, "That [1943] season Uncle Sam furnished me the best material in his Navy V-12 program at the College of the Pacific that I had ever worked with. We had just one hour for daily practice, but the players were in such superb condition and had so much 'know-how' that all I had to do was teach them the plays and the strategies and the particular defense I wanted used for each game. It was the easiest season I ever coached."[76]

The Pacific Tigers won seven games and lost two. The two biggest wins occurred against the UCLA Bruins on October 2 followed by a victory against the California Bears the next Saturday. Pacific came from behind to defeat the Bruins 19–7 in the fourth quarter, which was "the third straight time they came from behind to achieve a victory for the white-haired pig-skin patriarch," according to the *Los Angeles Examiner.*[77] Then the team defeated the California Bears, 12–6, who were "out-passed, out-run, out-kicked, out-blocked, out-tackled and out-charged by Pacific's Tigers," according to the *Oakland Tribune.*[78]

Coach of the Year

Several honors for Stagg came at the end of the season when he was named national "Coach of the Year." W.R. Schroeder, co-founder of the Helms Athletic Foundation, was chairman of a war charities football game played between College of the Pacific and the March Field Air Force Base Team at the Los Angeles Coliseum in 1943. The Air Force Team beat Pacific, 20–0. Schroeder wrote, "After the game that night I took all of the College of Pacific players and Coach Stagg out to Hollywood for dinner at a restaurant adjoining Columbia Broadcasting studios. While we were having dinner, someone from CBS brought a wire report to me that Coach Stagg had just been chosen 'College Football Coach of the Year' in the annual poll conducted by the *New York World Telegram.* He received fifty-five votes compared with Notre Dame's Frank Leahy who received twenty and Indiana's Bo McMillin with six votes."[79]

Schroeder stood up, made an announcement, and read the wire report and then called on Stagg for comments. With tears streaming down his face, Stagg rose and said, "All of the boys of this fine College of the Pacific team were the ones who were responsible for my having been chosen Coach of the Year." Then the captain of the team immediately rose and with tears streaming down his face said, "No, Mr. Stagg, you were the one who made us the fine team which we were this year. We were not responsible for you having been chosen Coach of the Year. It is your own honor."[80]

Stagg soon received other awards and honors. A day later, he was named "Man of the Year" in a Football Writers Association poll after gathering 78 percent of the vote. John L. Griffith, Western Conference commissioner, came in second place, while Angelo Bertelli, Notre Dame quarterback, was third.[81] A week later, Stagg earned the "Comeback of the Year" award in an Associated Press poll of sportswriters. Stagg received sixty-five points, and twelve first-place votes, barely edging out professional golfer Patty Berg with sixty points and pro football player Bronko Nagurski a distant third.[82]

In 1944, he was named Grand Marshall of the Tournament of Roses Parade on January 1. He succeeded Governor Earl Warren, who was Grand

Ceremony held on October 21, 1960, to mark the naming of a Giant Sequoia in honor of Amos Alonzo Stagg. The tree stands in Alder Creek Grove, Tulare County, California. University of Chicago Photographic Archive, apf1-07856, Special Collections Research Center, University of Chicago Library.

Marshall in 1943 and preceded ex-president Herbert Hoover, the Grand Marshall of the 1945 parade.[83] Three months later, Stockton Mayor Ralph Fay proclaimed March 7, 1944, which was Arbor Day, as "Amos Alonzo Stagg Day." Stockton citizens honored him by planting a giant Sequoia tree on the Pacific campus. The plaque read, "This Sequoia Gigantea was planted on Arbor Day, March 7, 1944, by the people of Stockton in honor of Amos Alonzo Stagg, 'The Grand Old Man of Football.'" Another giant Sequoia Redwood tree, located in California's Giant Sequoia National Moment, was renamed the "Amos Alonzo Stagg Tree" in 1960 by its owner. The Stagg Tree is the world's fifth-largest tree with a height of 243 feet and an estimated age of 3,000 years.[84]

Notable Players

The College of the Pacific was small and could not compete against larger universities for the best recruits. Only two of Stagg's Pacific players became notable as successful coaches or professional athletes. **Wayne Hardin**, a Stockton High School graduate, played quarterback and halfback for the Pacific Tigers from 1946 to 1948. He was head football coach at the U.S. Naval Academy from 1959 to 1964, where he led the Midshipmen to five consecutive wins over Army. He coached at Temple University from 1970 to 1982. His Naval Academy teams produced two Heisman Trophy winners: Joe Bellino in 1960 and Roger Staubach in 1963. Hardin's Navy teams went to the Orange Bowl in 1961, losing 14–6 to the Missouri Tigers, and the Cotton Bowl in 1964, losing 28–6 to the Texas Longhorns. Hardin was inducted into the College Football Hall of Fame in 2013 after compiling a career record of 118–74–5.[85] Hardin remained a personal friend of Stagg until the end of his life and visited him at the convalescent center a couple of years before he died.

 Eddie LeBaron played as a freshman quarterback during Stagg's last season in 1946. He played another three seasons under his successor, Larry Siemering, and earned All-America honors his senior year. LeBaron, who was only five feet, seven inches tall, shattered Pacific records that included career touchdowns (59), touchdowns in a season (23), longest punt (74 yards), and total offensive yardage for three consecutive seasons. After graduation, he played pro football for the Dallas Cowboys and the Washington Redskins. In 1960, he set the NFL record for the shortest completed touchdown pass: two inches. He was chosen for the College Football Hall of Fame in 1980.[86]

 LeBaron said of Stagg, "I was a freshman there his last year in 1946 when he was eighty-four. But he was the head coach, he did it all. And if somebody tore their pants, he would take them home for his wife to sew. He didn't have any meetings. Everything was done on the practice field. He never used bad language. If you did anything wrong, he might call you a jackass."[87]

 After Stagg won "Coach of the Year" and other honors in 1943, the accolades did not last long. The next three seasons brought more disappointments. The team went 3–8 in 1944, 0–10–1 in 1945, and 4–7 in 1946. In the last game of Stagg's Pacific years and fifty-seventh year of coaching, the Tigers lost 14–13 to North Texas State in the Optimist Bowl.[88] It must have been a game for optimists since the Tigers were invited after a 4–7 losing season. Sponsored by the Houston Optimist Club, the bowl game was played only one year and never held again.

 Despite the losing seasons, Stagg's fourteen-year presence had given College of the Pacific higher attendance and more national media exposure than anyone thought possible. During those fourteen years, the college netted nearly $250,000 from its football program and paid off and burned its $300,000 mortgage.[89] Before he arrived, game attendance averaged less

Amos and Stella Stagg in 1944. University of Chicago Photographic Archive, apf1-07766, Special Collections Research Center, University of Chicago Library.

than 400. It reached 70,000 in a UCLA game in the Los Angeles Coliseum, the largest to ever see a Stagg game.[90] "He set up a football program which proved financially profitable beyond the fondest dreams of the most ardent supporters of the college when [he] arrived on the scene," according to a college history.[91]

Table 13: College of the Pacific Football, 1933–1946

Year	Wins	Losses	Ties
1933	5	5	0
1934	4	5	0
1935	5	4	1
1936	5	4	1
1937	3	5	2
1938	7	3	0
1939	6	6	1

Year	Wins	Losses	Ties
1940	4	5	0
1941	4	7	0
1942	2	6	1
1943	7	2	0
1944	3	8	0
1945	0	10	1
1946	4	7	0
Total	**59**	**77**	**7**
Source: *University of the Pacific Archives and Special Collections.*			

His fourteen-year record at COP of 59–77–7 included four winning seasons, seven losing seasons, and three break-even seasons.[92] Despite the losing seasons, the Tigers played difficult schedules against big-time California teams such as Southern California, UCLA, California-Berkeley, and San Jose State. He set the all-time coaching record in 1946 when he achieved his 314th win, which surpassed Glenn "Pop" Warner's 313 career wins. Eddie LeBaron said years later, "I guess we broke Pop Warner's record that last year [1946], but nobody ever said anything about it in those days. I never heard mention of it until years later when I read he had the most wins. I never gave it much thought until the Bear Bryant thing came up."[93] Stagg's record stood for thirty-five years until Alabama's Paul "Bear" Bryant surpassed it when he reached his 315th career wins in 1981 (more about that in the next chapter).

Déjà Vu All Over Again

After three losing seasons, calls for Stagg's resignation began to come from students and alumni. Suddenly, it was déjà vu all over again. "It's hard to believe but there is a campaign on at the College of the Pacific to get Amos Alonzo Stagg, the grand old man of football, to retire. The students and faculty still vow they love the 84-year-old mentor and admit that in his day he was one of the greatest. But they would like him to go to the sidelines and take things easy," according to one newspaper.[94]

Knoles, who now had the title of "chancellor," asked Stagg for his resignation as head football coach and offered him another position as an athletic consultant. The university tried to make it look like a voluntary decision to step aside. "Stagg has been asked by officials to make a decision, and it is believed he will resign as head football coach," Art Farey, Pacific's public relations director told the press. "We had hoped to conduct these negotiations without any publicity in the newspapers that would prove embarrassing to Mr. Stagg. However, the rumors broke out, so we had to take a stand."[95] Knoles offered Stagg an alternate position as "consultant in athletics" on November 14, similar to the position Hutchens offered him at Chicago fourteen years earlier. More déjà vu.

Stagg refused the offer and replied to Knoles: "Unfortunately, the plan does not fall in with my life's purpose, which has guided me during my forty-one years at the University of Chicago and fourteen seasons at the College of the Pacific.... I am fully convinced that the 'pearl of great price' for me is to continue my life's purpose of helping young men through the relationship of coaching. That was the reason I did not accept the proposal to remain at the University of Chicago at a large salary.... It has been hard for me to make this decision, and it is especially hard to break up my happy relationship with the college. I now feel free to accept another position for next season."[96] He told a reporter, "I'm just a man out of a job, and I'm looking for another. I still want to coach, and as far as my vitality is concerned, I think I can do a better job of it than I ever did."[97]

Chancellor Knoles and the new president, Robert E. Burns, issued a joint statement saying, "The fact that we do not believe he should continue here under the pressure of active coaching does not mean that we have forgotten what he has done to advance the identity, prestige, and resources of the college.... We are very, very sorry that Mr. Stagg does not see fit to remain with us. We would have been proud to have him stay here for we are fully cognizant of the remarkable contribution he has made to the college and to the West during the last fourteen years."[98]

Stagg wrote a friend soon after, "I thought that the College of the Pacific would be my final coaching job, but it is not to be. Knoles made me a lovely offer to remain here at a full professor's salary, which is $3,600. [He wanted] to place me in an advisory position in athletics. I came to the College of the Pacific because I wanted to keep in contact with boys through coaching. I am leaving the College of the Pacific for the same reason.... This is the fourth quarter of the game. We expect to have a lot of fun before it is finished."[99]

Father and Son at Susquehanna University, 1947–1953

We were co-equals, but he was in charge. Everybody knew that.—Amos Alonzo Stagg, Jr.

While Stagg was at the College of the Pacific, his son, Amos Alonzo Stagg, Jr., was the head football coach at Susquehanna University where he had coached for eleven years. But he needed help after his team had a string of losing seasons. Fathers usually help sons find a job, but in this case, the son helped his eighty-four-year-old father find a job.

The president of Susquehanna University in Selinsgrove, Pennsylvania, invited Stagg to become an advisory coach with his son Amos Alonzo Stagg, Jr. The president's invitation came at least partly because of alumni pressure over Susquehanna's dismal football record. Although the younger Stagg had coached football since 1935, many alumni were unhappy with the team's losing seasons. In the seven previous years, the team had won twenty-four games, lost fifty, and tied four. The *Selinsgrove Times* reported, "The record of the younger Stagg at Susquehanna is not characterized by outstanding victories. The caliber of this year's football schedule and the humiliating defeats suffered at the hands of lesser institutions prompted scores of alumni to request a change in athletic policy at SU." Some alumni even pressured the school to oust the younger Stagg after the senior Stagg was named to the position.[1]

G. Morris Smith, Susquehanna president, offered the eighty-four-year-old Stagg an annual honorarium of $1,200 for a ten-year contract to coach during the football season. "I am happy to write that at a meeting of the Executive Committee of the Board of Directors, held yesterday afternoon, they were joyfully unanimous in authorizing me to appoint you as advisory coach to your son…. My heart is warm when I think of a distinguished father and his loyal son working together in fine harmony on the campus…" he wrote in a December 1946 letter to Stagg.[2] Stagg replied four days later and accepted the offer. H.O. "Fritz" Crisler, Michigan head coach and former Chicago player, later teased Stagg, saying, "You're pretty old to be signing any ten-year contract." Stagg replied, "I'm looking forward to being able to renew it."[3]

Susquehanna is a Lutheran school in Selinsgrove on the banks of Susquehanna River north of Harrisburg. Enrollment was less than 500 students when the senior Stagg arrived. "That region of Pennsylvania is scenic and charming," he wrote. "It gave me an uplift every time I stepped out of the house and looked across the rolling hills to the mountains beyond the Susquehanna River."[4]

Susquehanna Celebrates Arrival

When Amos and Stella Stagg arrived by car in Selinsgrove on April 17, 1947, 475 cheerleaders, students, and band members met the couple on the outskirts of town and formed a parade to escort them to campus. The couple were "stolen" from their automobile and placed in a convertible as the parade proceeded to the campus. Here, they were greeted by more students, President Smith, and Stagg's son and daughter-in-law. "I'm all in a whirl," he said as he thanked the students for their warm welcome. "Both Mrs. Stagg and I appreciate your welcome, and I must say you have a beautiful campus."[5]

Stella and Amos lived in a house on faculty row with their son and his family during the football season. After the season ended, they drove back to their Stockton home until the next season began. Barbara Stagg Ecker, Amos and Stella's granddaughter, wrote in a 1999 letter: "It was my duty to drive him to football practice part of the time. My grandmother would always follow later with rubbers, coats, a blanket, etc. if it was bad weather. I attribute her care for his long, long life." Barbara Ecker reported in the same letter that Stagg declined an invitation to appear on *The People*, a popular television program during the early 1950s. "They wanted to fly him to New York and pay him $500 to be on the program. He politely declined because he had to run with the boys, his football players, in the morning," she wrote.[6]

Team practices usually began around 12:15 p.m. Monday through Thursday when father and son met with the team in a classroom to review plays and strategy for the next game. After a break, they reassembled on the field at 3:30 and practiced until about 5:45. Stella Stagg attended most practices making notes and diagrams of the formations. She also continued to chart the games as she did at College of the Pacific.[7] They were really a coaching "trio" of father, mother, and son.

Despite his title of "advisory coach," the senior Stagg was the de facto head coach. His son said, "We were co-equals, but he was in charge. Everybody knew that." Shortly before he arrived on campus, the elder Stagg told the press, "Of course, I won't have the whole say. Amos Jr. will also have some ideas. I suppose we will divide it up by using three parts of my stuff to one of his."[8] Charles Carr, a team starter from 1948 through 1951, later recalled, "There is no question in my mind that senior [Stagg] was in charge of the team." Besides coaching football, the young Stagg served as athletic director, coached the basketball, track, and tennis teams, and taught health and physical education classes. His father's coaching help was a welcome addition to an overworked schedule.

The first season led by the Stagg duo was successful. In the final minutes of the season's last game, the Crusaders came from behind to tie Allegheny and end the season with a 4–1–2 record. It was Susquehanna's best record since its undefeated 1940 season. The *Selinsgrove Times* reported, "The Crusaders made their breathtaking touchdown in the last ten seconds of play when Peters leaped high in the end zone to snare a pass from Bob O'Gara.... Using the flanker system inaugurated by Amos Alonzo Stagg, Sr. and an extensive aerial attack, the Crusaders were the stars of a thrilling performance."[9]

Even in his late eighties, Stagg could roll with the punches and demonstrate physical resilience. Stephen D. Ross, one Stagg's former players, described an incident when he was knocked over and almost injured during practice. "One of the tackles threw a block [hitting Stagg], and it wiped out the Old Man completely and knocked him down. He was eighty-nine or ninety years old at the time, and we were all horrified. We rushed over to pick him up thinking what's happened here? He got up, brushed us off, and sort of angrily said, 'Look fellows, when I'm too old to get up off the ground, I will quit coaching. So, leave me alone.' We thought we had really done some damage, but he popped right up."[10]

The Crusaders had roller-coaster seasons after 1946. Their record dipped to 2–6 in 1948 and 1–7 in 1949. Fortunes improved in 1950 when the team achieved a 4–2–1 record. Then in 1951, the team climaxed an unbeaten season after holding off a last-minute threat and defeating Ursinus College 19–14 on November 17. Other victories that season were over Johns Hopkins, Wagner, National Aggies, Juniata College, and Haverford College. Although the 1932 and 1940 teams were undefeated, this was the first undefeated and untied football season in Susquehanna's history.

Team members honored the senior Stagg with a letterman's award jacket and a jointly signed letter "to show our deepest and most sincere gratitude for coaching the 1951 Susquehanna University football team to its first undefeated, untied season in history.... To those of us who are

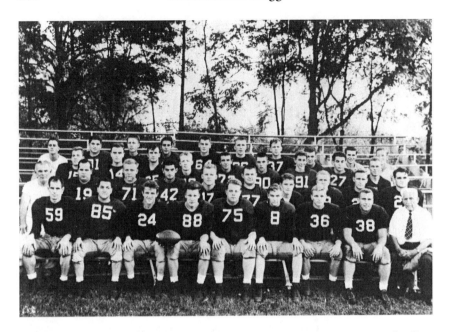

Susquehanna's undefeated 1951 football team. Amos Stagg, Sr., is on the first row, right end, and Amos Stagg, Jr., is on the second row, left end. University of Chicago Photographic Archive, apf1-11152, Special Collections Research Center, University of Chicago Library.

graduating, we must say with deep regret in our heart that we will miss you … and football more than ever next season…. We graduating seniors … would like to send along our best wishes and kindest regards to our coach, who we think is the best coach in the country."[11]

Stella Continues Scouting

Stella Stagg continued to sit in the press box and diagram plays at most games. One afternoon she took off to scout a football practice at Dickinson College in Carlisle, which was about an hour from Susquehanna. When she returned, she dropped a pile of notes on her husband's desk and said, "I decided to scout Dickinson. You can get a pass receiver behind their left halfback. He's slow on covering." The next Saturday with the score tied in the fourth quarter, Susquehanna won the game when its quarterback, following her tip, tossed a pass over the head of the left halfback.[12]

A newspaper reporter wrote in 1948, "Today a conversation between Coach and Mrs. Stagg is frequently interspersed with such frequent expressions … as 'mousetraps,' 'split backs,' and 'flankers.'" She never missed a

Susquehanna practice session and was frequently found in a quiet nook taking notes and observing her husband and son running through practice drills. She was once asked when she began taking notes to help her husband as a team scout and assistant coach. She said it was in 1933 after they left Chicago for California. "I just had to become an expert," she told a reporter. "There came a period in my life with the children reared and gone when I sort of felt the emptiness. Then I started this. Now Amos and I are working side by side again."[13] She added, "Oh, I do not think my diagrams are of any great value to my husband, who has an excellent memory. They are only refreshers. Suppose he wants to know what play of importance took place in a game two years ago. Well, we just look it up."[14]

Edward R. Murrow Comes to Town

Stagg's fame followed him to Susquehanna, where he received hundreds of speaking invitations throughout his six years but coaching always remained his first priority. During his first year at Susquehanna, he received more than 100 invitations for public appearances or engagements but accepted only two. In 1952, he was featured on a national television program. Edward R. Murrow (1908–1965) was the legendary CBS journalist and war correspondent, best known for hosting *See It Now* and *This Is Your Life* programs. His *See It Now* series, which ran from 1951 to 1958, focused on news and feature stories similar to its successor *60 Minutes*. In 1952, Murrow took his production crew to Selinsgrove to interview the father and son while they practiced with the team.

"Having a considerable fondness for small colleges and great men, we decided to go down to Susquehanna University in the foothills of the Pennsylvania mountains," Murrow announced as he began the episode. "It's a place with a registration of 400 and football squad of twenty-six. Coached by Amos Alonzo Stagg, Sr., age ninety, we went to watch the training of the football squad. We took our cameras down there on Friday."

In two scenes obviously planned for the camera, the quarterback gave the football to the running back, while the senior Stagg ran along next to the offensive team as the play progressed. In the next scene, Stagg gave the team a little pep talk. "This may be my last season here, and I want it to be a good season. I'm counting on you to do the work. You're the boys who are going to have the fun, and you're the boys who are going to get the honors. For every man, put out the best you have. That means playing the most honest and conscientious way you can, so you will be all right for the game. And come up 100 percent in manhood and courage. We're depending on you. You're not a large squad, but there's a lot of manhood here. Little men even can have more dynamite than the bigger fellows, and I want you to have 100 percent dynamite this year. Don't fail me."

Table 14: Stagg and Stagg's Susquehanna Record, 1947–1952

Year	Wins	Losses	Ties
1947	4	1	2
1948	2	6	0
1949	1	7	0
1950	4	2	1
1951	6	0	0
1952	4	3	0
Total	**21**	**19**	**3**
Source: Susquehanna University Archives.			

After this scene, Murrow asks Stagg Sr. a question: "What do you think about the whole matter of commercialization and the paying of college athletes?" Stagg replies, "I'm dead against it, and it's a very dangerous thing for the colleges. I think they are destroying the game to the extent they are taking away the value from the students themselves and the players."[15]

The Stagg coaches produced no All-America players or bowl-bound teams during those six years. However, the senior Stagg's influence was felt. Former player Stephen Ross said in a 1988 interview that although he had never played high school football, Stagg gave him a chance. He saw Ross throwing the ball in intramurals and encouraged him to try out for the varsity team. "He gave me a chance to play football, which I may not have had if I went elsewhere. He had the patience to work with men like me. He was a man of greatness, but he had a degree of humility that rubbed off on me. He took the time to work with players without great athletic ability and worked them up to their potential. I know it gave me and others a chance to feel good about themselves." Ross would later become president of Pennsylvania Blue Cross Insurance and chair of Susquehanna's board of trustees.[16]

After the 1952 season ended, Amos and Stella returned to their Stockton home. In January 1953, the ninety-year-old Stagg entered a Stockton hospital for eleven days—the longest time he had ever spent in a hospital. All his physician, Dr. Langley Collis, told the press was that Stagg suffered from an "intestinal disorder."[17] When he left the hospital on January 13, Stagg told an Associated Press reporter that he felt "first-rate" but that he would take it easy until spring when he planned to rejoin his son at

Susquehanna. The hospitalization caused Stagg to miss the annual meeting of the NCAA Rules Committee in New Orleans, which was only the third he had missed since 1904.

The most interesting aspect of this hospitalization was not the illness itself, but the press coverage it received throughout the nation including the *New York Times*.[18] Hundreds of American newspapers carried Associated Press and United Press reports quoting Stagg's doctor about his condition. His reports started on January 3 describing Stagg's intestinal disorder as "serious, but not critical" followed by "slightly improved," "improved," "out of danger," and finally "fine condition." When he was released on January 13, Collis told the United Press, "Mr. Stagg has been well for several days, but he has been staying here recuperating from the intestinal disorder."[19]

Surpassing Bear Bryant?

Before coming to Susquehanna, Stagg's Chicago and Pacific teams compiled 314 wins, the most ever recorded by a football coach. His team won twenty-one games at Susquehanna University. In November 1981 after a 28–17 win over Auburn, Alabama's Paul "Bear" Bryant surpassed Stagg with his 315th career victory. Following an 8–4 season in 1982, Bryant retired.[20] Shortly after that, Stagg Jr. and Susquehanna alumnus Jack Thorp of Norwalk, Connecticut, led the campaign to persuade the NCAA to credit Stagg's twenty-one wins to his father's record, which would enable him to keep his first-place ranking. Thorp wrote to the NCAA, "Once the team got on the field, there was absolutely no doubt as to who was head coach. Amos Alonzo Senior ran the pre-game warmup, gave the pep talk before kickoff, made substitutions, sent in plays and ran the whole damn show."[21]

"There is no question in my mind that senior was in charge of the team," said Charles Carr, a team member from 1948 through 1951. "The old man would do the talking before the game. He would talk for hours on long rides back from games. I can still see him at the age of eighty-nine on the practice field, and he was showing us how to run with the ball. He fell down during making a move, but when we tried to help him up, he said he didn't need any help."[22]

The NCAA turned a deaf ear to their appeal. During the six years Susquehanna sent athletic records to the NCAA, Stagg Jr. was listed as the school's "head coach" and his father was listed as "advisory coach." Steve Boda of the NCAA reported on the decision, "The president of the school never did name him as head coach, and all of our records show Stagg Jr. as head coach. We just can't recognize Stagg Sr. thirty-two years later."

Shortly after that, Susquehanna named its football field "Stagg Field" for the elder Stagg. All three universities where the senior Stagg had coached named athletic fields after him before or after he left. So did Exeter Academy and West Orange (N.J.) High School. "That's exactly the way it should be. I was proud to be associated with him," said Amos Alonzo Stagg, Jr., in a 1985 interview.[23]

Stella's Health Declines

Between football seasons at Susquehanna, the Stagg couple returned to Stockton from January through August to spend the off-season. He was planning to return to coach the Susquehanna team in August 1953 but wrote President Smith that he and Stella would have to remain in California because of her health problems. "You are mighty good, President Smith, to send us an invitation to return next fall. I am sorry to write that very unfortunately we will not be able to accept.... About two months ago, Stella had a breakdown which has kept her under the doctor's care and in bed most of the time," he told Smith.[24] President Smith wrote back to Stagg and gave him a standing offer to return if Stella's health improved.

At that point, the ninety-year-old Stagg thought he might retire. The Associated Press reported, "Amos Stagg, Football's Grand Old Man, to retire because of the nervous breakdown Stella suffered several months earlier." Stagg told the Associated Press, "My buddy, the mainstay and center of my life for fifty-nine years needs me. I will stay by her. I have had sixty-three years of coaching; If I can't have another, it's all right. I won't be faithless to my buddy. It would be nice to continue coaching, but it seems unlikely."[25]

He told the *New York Times,* "If I don't coach this

Amos Stagg celebrating his 90th birthday on August 16, 1952. University of Chicago Photographic Archive, apf1-07883, Special Collections Research Center, University of Chicago Library.

year, I may coach the next. It depends on Mrs. Stagg's health. I'm in good condition now and won't give up the game. But I'll stick by her first."[26] A few years earlier he had told a friend what a devoted wife Stella was and how much she had helped him as a coach: "She has submerged her personal ambitions, and quietly and loyally and effectively, devoted herself to her family and to her husband…. As the children, one by one broke their home ties, more and more she has entered into helping me fulfill my responsibilities. She has made a business of studying and learning the science of football from the standpoint of helping her husband. She has made a specialty of charts and keeping a running account of the games."[27]

Stagg's ninety-first birthday arrived on August 16, 1953. When asked by a reporter how he planned to celebrate, he said, "It will be just a quiet day at home with my wife, Stella."[28] This birthday was his first since 1890 when he didn't have a job.

14

Fourth Quarter in Stockton, 1953–1965

No man has the right to retire as long as he can work and produce something that will be of benefit to his fellow-men.—Amos Alonzo Stagg

Although Stagg was "unemployed" for about a month, he didn't wait long to get back to work. The *San Francisco Examiner* reported, "The Grand Old Man of football isn't through yet. At the age of ninety-one, Amos Alonzo Stagg yesterday accepted an offer that will keep him in his beloved football coaching field for the sixty-fourth consecutive year." On September 7, he began a part-time coaching position with Stockton College (now San Joaquin Delta College), a four-year school that included two years of high school and two years of junior college. Head coach Earl Klipstein, who played for Stagg at the College of the Pacific, offered him a job coaching the team's punters, kickers, and assisting with their offensive strategy. Stagg told the press his first priority was still to look after Mrs. Stagg. "But after that I will give the best I can to football."[1] Coach Klipstein told a reporter, "Mr. Stagg will be in charge of the passing and the punting. He will install his famed punt formation.... He has stayed sharp by being active in football.... He can help us, and we'll surely enjoy having him."[2]

Beginning his new job on Monday, September 7, 1953, Stagg spent about two hours every afternoon coaching punters and kickers of the Stockton Mustangs. Stagg's physical resilience was still not deterred by his age. In 1954, he was instructing some team members on ball snapping when center Romer Berr charged into him and knocked him unconscious for five minutes. Before an ambulance arrived, Stagg recovered, got up, and told the players, "You don't have to worry about me. I know how to take care of myself." He continued to drill the players for another ninety minutes. "It was all my fault," he explained later. "I was just trying to tell them not to charge so fast after passing the ball back on punt formation, and Berr didn't hear me."[3]

Three years later, the Associated Press reported, "Stagg, still hale and hearty after sixty-five years of coaching, has no plans to retire. Even at home, Stagg refused to slow down. Stagg does all the yard work at his moderate-size Stockton home but still craves more exercise. So twice a day he swings a golf club—100 healthy swings at a time."[4]

Return to Chicago

Stagg and his wife returned by train to Chicago in 1955 to celebrate the fiftieth anniversary of the 1905 Chicago football and track teams, which both won conference championships. The 1905 football team gained fame for defeating Michigan 2–0 and ending its five-year winning streak. Players from the championship teams crowded around them at Chicago's Union Station as the couple stepped off the train.[5] Stagg greeted most of them by name. It was "Hello, Mark" and "Great to see you, Art," as Mark Catlin and Art Badenoch stepped forward. As the crowd walked through the station, someone asked Stagg about how he would feel if Chicago restored football. "I'd throw up my hands and toss my hat in the air and jump with joy," he replied. Twenty former track and football players attended the reunion. "It has never happened before. Imagine a fellow my age returning to meet my former students, some now seventy or more years old," Stagg remarked at the dinner.[6]

In 1957, Stagg and Stella took the train to New Orleans to attend his fiftieth NCAA Rules Committee meeting. He began attending the meetings in 1904 and missed only three between 1904 and 1957. The chairman of the 1957 committee was Michigan's Fritz Crisler, who had played for Stagg at Chicago and was Chicago's assistant coach from 1922 through 1929.[7]

In his final years in Stockton, Stagg attended numerous birthday and special recognition dinners up through his 100th birthday. In 1957, 200 members of the College of the Pacific family recognized Stagg and Stella in an event honoring his upcoming birthday, her recent birthday, and their upcoming sixty-third anniversary. They received a seven-foot high, 200-pound cake. "This gathering is a beautiful idea," Stagg told the crowd. "It gets hold of your heart and your soul. We all belong to one another. I don't know how long this will continue, but I want to live long enough to look after Stella, and Stella wants to live long enough to look after me. We're in love with one another. That is sufficient."[8]

In 1958, the *San Bernardino County Sun* reported that the Stockton College's Mustangs had "the oldest football mentor in the world on their staff." The article reported that Stagg "acts as chief advisor and technical coach for the Mustangs." Athletic Director Mike Garrigan said although Stagg did not travel with the team, he attended "all of the Mustang's workouts."[9] That same year Stagg was inducted into the College Football Hall of Fame as a coach after he had been inducted as a player in its inaugural year of 1953. Two of his former Chicago football players were also inducted that year: Walter Eckersall, who played from 1903 to 1906, and Jay Berwanger who played from 1933 to 1936. The three were recognized in a halftime ceremony at the Chicago-Knox College game on February 1, 1958. Berwanger was present to accept his award while ninety-five-year-old Stagg wired regrets from California that he could not attend. Eckersall had died in 1930 at the age of forty-three after a long struggle with alcoholism.

When Stagg celebrated his ninety-sixth birthday on August 16, 1958, he cashed in the full value of a $10,000 life insurance policy. He had purchased it in 1908 when he was forty-six and coaching at the University of Chicago. Stagg's insurance company said the odds of living fifty years after the age of forty-six and collecting the full value of the policy were 100,000 to three. The Northwestern Mutual Life salesman who sold it to him was Harold Ickes, Stagg's friend at the University of Chicago who later became Secretary of the Interior for President Franklin D. Roosevelt from 1933 to 1946.[10]

Time *Magazine's Cover Story*

In a story about the secrets of aging, Stagg appeared on the cover of *Time* magazine in 1958. With the title "Adding Life to Years," the story included quotes from scientists, geriatric physicians, and four well-known Americans who were living successful lives during their advanced years. While most of the story focused on Stagg, it included profiles of former president Herbert Hoover (eighty-four), former General Motors president Alfred P. Sloan, Jr. (eighty-three), and inventor and engineer Charles F. Kettering (eighty-two).[11]

The story began: "Every afternoon last week, a gray 1951 Chevrolet threaded through the streets on the edge of town, pulled up alongside the field where the Stockton College red-and-blue jerseyed Mustangs worked out under the gentling fall sun of California's Central Valley. The team's kickers and punters broke from the rest of the team and gathered with Stagg where he coached them on proper kicking techniques. 'Heads down, boy, eyes up,' he shouted at number eighty-four. Turning aside, he leaned to demonstrate the proper kicking posture, saying, 'Relax boys and don't be awkward.'"

Reflecting on his childhood, Stagg told *Time*: "We used to give one or two cents as our church contribution. Food was plain but plentiful; home grown vegetables dominated the table, eked out with home-fattened hogs." When he was in high school, *Time* wrote, "Stagg was almost a zealot about exercise—he ran the mile between home and school both ways." At age ninety-six, Stagg remained "an active practitioner of the cult of physical exercise." Every morning, he does a routine of bending and stretching exercises that included push-ups and pull-ups on a fig tree in his back yard. He does 100-yard runs, cuts his own lawn with a manual push mower, and rakes his own leaves. His weight of 150 pounds "has not changed in three-score years." *Time* contrasted Stagg's exercise regimen with that of Sloan and Kettering, who proclaimed that they have "never taken a lick of exercise in their lives." Although both said they used the stairs at work, "on level ground, the farthest they walk is from office or apartment door to car or from car to plane."

Seeking a common thread in their lives, *Time* concluded, "The one common denominator that sociologists, psychiatrists, gerontologists, and geriatricians see in all actively productive oldsters ... is a keen continuing interest in some activity, which carries with it a revitalizing sense of participation in life.... The oldster, like the human being of any age, must feel that what he is doing is useful, needed, and appreciated." Some would say Stagg's passion was football, but he often said it was helping and influencing young men through the activity of football.[12]

Many articles were written during Stagg's later years about his using a push mower to mow his lawn. In 1959, Herbert "Fritz" Crisler was athletic director at the University of Michigan and a former Chicago player and assistant coach. Crisler drove to Stockton to visit Stagg when he was ninety-six. "I found him mowing his lawn with a hand mower, as chipper and spry as a frisky squirrel. A neighbor had come over and told Stagg that some kids were playing on his lawn daily, kicking it up. 'You'll never raise grass that way,' the neighbor said. Stagg laughed, 'Thank you. But I'm more interested in raising boys,'" Crisler wrote in a *Reader's Digest* article.[13] When Stagg died, Crisler told the *Chicago Daily News*: "He was never profane nor a fire-eater, but he was the toughest kind of taskmaster. Chicago teams worked longer hours and harder than any other conference team.... He was a keen psychologist in handling men. He knew which players to be firm with, which to 'gentle' along, but he did it in a manner that did not bring out jealousies."[14]

On his ninety-seventh birthday in 1959, Stagg told a reporter, "Last year I used to do some running to keep in shape, but I'm not as young as I used to be. I mowed the lawn this morning because the grass is getting a little high." He wrote a friend that same year, "For the last twenty-six years, ever since we came to Stockton, the house and yard furnish me plenty of exercise in mowing the lawn and raking the leaves from ten trees. Stella and I usually end the day by taking a fifteen to twenty-minute walk before going to bed." They did not own a television. "We enjoy reading, and we do an awful lot of it," Stagg told a reporter.

Friends at the College of the Pacific wanted to do something to help him on his ninety-eighth birthday and ordered a new power mower to replace the push-mower. He shipped it back promptly with the note: "I can still use the old one, and besides, I need the exercise. Mowing the lawn under my own power keeps me in condition."[15]

Stagg's "secrets" for a long life were not really secrets but habits that researchers have repeatedly verified as contributing to longevity. He had a passion for living and reason to get up every morning. Starting in his childhood, he was physically active. He ran to and from school in West Orange and to and from football practice at Yale besides playing on the football and baseball teams. In Chicago, he played tennis or golf almost daily when weather permitted and practiced with the teams he coached. His diet was mostly vegetarian during his later years, and he never smoked or consumed alcoholic beverages. He had a stable family life and a wife who did everything she could to make him happy and successful. Stagg's faith contributed to his purpose for living and a supportive social network. A 2019 study by Ohio State University researchers found that persons with a religious affiliation live up to nine years longer than those without one.[16]

A "Great Living American"

In 1959, William McDonnell, president of the U.S. Chamber of Commerce, wrote Stagg informing him of his selection as one of seven "Great Living Americans." McDonnell wrote, "You have been chosen by the Chamber of Commerce of the United States as one of the 'Great Living Americans' to be honored at a dinner on Monday, April 27, 1959, on the occasion of the Chamber's 47th annual meeting. The panel of judges chose you for this recognition because of your contribution to athletics and the beneficial influence over the young men of America for so many years."[17]

He invited Stagg to the recognition dinner in Washington, D.C., on April 29, which Stagg declined, citing the difficulty of the long trip from California. The program for the dinner cited Stagg, "For the inspiring example of sportsmanship, fair play and religious faith he has set for college athletes, first as a performer himself and for most of his life as a coach." Stagg sent a recorded message to be broadcast at the dinner, thanking them for the honor and saying, "God has been good to me in allowing me to live as long as I have. When I was a young man, I promised my Creator that I would work with youth as long as I was able."[18] The six others who received the Chamber's honor were Harry Byrd, U.S. Senator; Helen Hayes, actress; Frank H. Knight, economics professor; Henry Cabot Lodge, U.S. Ambassador; Louise Williamson, corporate executive; and Robert E. Wood, retired chairman of Sears, Roebuck and Company. That same year Yale President A. Whitney Griswold sent Stagg a telegram informing him that he was Yale's oldest living graduate. Stagg replied, saying, "Thanks for your good telegram telling me of the distinction…. I shall try to behave myself for the rest of my days so that dear old Yale will not suffer."[19]

Stagg said on many occasions that his primary aim was to build character through coaching. Years earlier, he had told a reporter, "The first duty of intercollegiate athletics is to build character. If intercollegiate athletics do not build character, then our aim is not properly leveled…. Of what use is this institution called intercollegiate athletics if we lose sight of our primary aim? And what is our primary aim? If it is not the development and molding of character, then what is it?"[20]

Stagg and 222 guests, including many former players, celebrated his 98th birthday on August 16, 1960, in Stockton, where he was presented the Gold Medal award from the National Football Foundation and Hall of Fame. "Every football man could use his life as a pattern," said Chester LaRoche, foundation president and former Yale quarterback, in a speech about Stagg's career. The medal's inscription read, "Presented to Amos Alonzo Stagg, football pioneer, master strategist, embodiment of the football ideal through many decades; builder of men in mind, body and spirit; his legacy a golden heritage to the American youth."[21] LaRoche read a telegram from President Dwight Eisenhower, a former West Point football player, which said, "On your birthday I am delighted to send greetings to you and best wishes to all gathered in your honor. You have won the respect of sportsmen everywhere." Eisenhower and General Douglas MacArthur, were the only two previous recipients of the Gold Medal award.[22]

Final Retirement (Really)

Stagg's eyesight began to fail while he was ninety-seven. A few days before his ninety-eighth birthday, a *New York Times* reporter visited with Stagg and described him: "The old gentleman's eyes are beginning to dim. He has cataracts on both eyes. His hands and occasionally his face twitch with uncontrollable tremors of age. But his mind is as alert as ever and his basic physical vigor keeps asserting itself." Stagg chuckled when he told the reporter, "When I was ninety-five, I faded a bit; I stopped running."[23]

A month after his ninety-eighth birthday, Stagg retired from coaching for the third and final time, saying, "I guess it's about time to quit. I have already coached for seventy years." His seventy years of coaching consisted of coaching seventy years of football, thirty-two years of track, twenty years of baseball, and four years of basketball.[24] He wrote Stockton Coach Larry Kentera, "It is with a deep feeling of regret that I write you that I will not be able to accept your invitation to come for football practice this year. For the past seventy years, I have been a coach. At ninety-eight years of age, it seems a good time to stop. I appreciate your courtesy in inviting me to help again as last year. I had a lot of fun working with you and your punters and your staff," Stagg wrote. "In addition to his fine advice, Mr. Stagg helped us a great deal as a morale builder. We want him to feel that he is always welcome to join us at any time in any capacity he may desire," Kentera told a reporter.[25]

In a film produced for his 100th birthday celebrations held in several cities, Stagg described the reasons for giving up active coaching but also said he would continue coaching through a "football correspondence school." He said, "At ninety-eight, we were so far behind in our

August 16, 1961

Dear Friend:

Thank you very much for remembering me. At 99, one looks like this -- and writes like this.

Gratefully,

Amos Alonzo Stagg

Stagg created this card to respond to hundreds of birthday cards and greetings on his ninety-ninth birthday, August 16, 1961. University of Chicago Photographic Archive, apf1-07866, Special Collections Research Center, University of Chicago Library.

correspondence that I decided I would have to give up coaching on the field for coaching on the desk. In all sincerity, I felt I could keep my faith with my dedication to God by conducting a football correspondence school. Until the present moment, we have been busy writing letters, entertaining visiting coaches, and greeting dignitaries."[26]

He and Stella tried to reply to hundreds of cards and notes he had received. "They keep coming in. I don't know how many—bunches of them—and we're not equipped for a job like that." Their son, Paul, and granddaughter came from Oregon for three days to help them answer the mail. During this three-day period, Stagg dictated 300 replies that he gave his granddaughter for typing. Stagg had to depend on Stella to read his letters and newspapers. In reply to a letter-writer who had asked for an autograph for his grandson, Stagg wrote, "Of course, I am glad to send my autograph for your grandson. Please tell him that all the extra flourishes on my autograph are caused by the fact that I have cataracts in my eyes and cannot see what I am writing."[27]

High Schools Named After Stagg

Two high schools, one in Stockton and the other in Palos Hills, Illinois, were built and named for Stagg before he died. The Stockton Board of Education voted to name its proposed new high school, the Amos Alonzo Stagg High School and dedicated it on February 25, 1959. Stagg and Stella attended with a crowd of 2,000 for the dedication. Dr. Clark Kerr, president of the University of California system, was the keynote speaker.[28]

In 1963, Chicago Consolidated School District 230 announced plans to build Amos Alonzo Stagg High School in Palos Hills. The school district had a policy of naming new schools after "great people who got their greatness in the Midwest." It had already named a school for poet Carl Sandburg and entrepreneur Victor J. Andrew. A press release announced that the district chose Stagg because of "his unparalleled service in teaching the young to shoot and shoot square for seventy years; the spartan ruggedness and simplicity of his life in devotion to an ideal, and the granite-like integrity that never compromised for victory." In a letter to the school district, Yale President Whitney Griswold congratulated the school district for naming the school after a Yale alumnus. His letter mentioned that Stagg was the only Yale alumnus who had contributed to its fund every year since it was founded in 1890.[29]

After obtaining Stagg's permission for the naming, Superintendent William O. Fisher traveled to Stockton several months before he died to visit him in a convalescent center. He also visited Mrs. Stagg who was still living in their Stockton home. "He knew I was coming and seemed prepared with a multitude of questions. He was mentally as sharp as a fifty-five-year-old person [and] the conversation flowed very nicely," Fisher recalled in a 1985 interview. He said during the first hour of conversation, Stagg asked many questions about the students, teachers, curriculum, and what kind of extra-curricular activities would be offered. During the second hour, Fisher asked Stagg about some of his most memorable experiences as a coach. As Fisher was starting to leave, Stagg called him back to his bedside and said, "Mr. Fisher, in all my life, I've achieved a lot of honors." Then he said, "I've received all these awards but naming the Amos Alonzo Stagg High School after me is the greatest honor I've ever had."[30] The school opened on September 27, 1964, and continues to honor its namesake with an "Amos Alonzo Stagg Room" filled with historic photos and football memorabilia.

Stagg Turns 100

Two months before he turned 100 on August 16, 1962, Stagg and Stella entered a convalescent center in Stockton, where they lived for their remaining years. When Stagg reached his 100th birthday, recognition came from throughout the country, and celebrations were held in twelve cities. California governor Edmond Brown (1905–1996) was keynote speaker at a 100th birthday celebration at the Stockton Civic Auditorium attended by 500 guests. Though frail and partly blind, Stagg made an unexpected appearance and perked up when greeted by former players and friends. While the crowd sang "Happy Birthday," a three-feet high birthday cake with 100 candles was wheeled into the room. "I didn't think I'd make it, but I did. I'm 100 years old today. Some way or another, it's hard to believe," he said. A year earlier he had told a reporter, "Time is running out for me. I don't know if I'll make it to the century mark. But it would be nice."[31]

Stagg's life-long abstinence from alcohol caused a last-minute shift in plans for the event. Original plans called for a cocktail reception preceding the dinner. Arriving guests were greeted with this sign: "Sorry, folks, no alcohol being sold here tonight. Let us remember that the man we are honoring this evening has refrained from the use of alcohol for 100 years. Therefore, let each of us pay him a personal tribute by toasting him instead with a drink of punch or soda."[32] Other cities holding celebrations included Annapolis, Maryland; Boston, Springfield and East Hampton, Massachusetts; New York, Philadelphia, Chicago, Seattle, San Francisco, and West Orange, New Jersey.[33] Wayne Hardin, coach at the U.S. Naval Academy team and one of Stagg's former players, hosted the Annapolis event. The special fifteen-minute film, *100 Years and Forever*, was shown at all of the dinners. Stagg wrote the script of the film telling the story of his own life against a backdrop of photographs, news stories, and film clips from his life.

The keynote speaker at the Springfield College event was Jackie Robinson, Brooklyn Dodgers Hall of Fame pitcher and the first African American player to break the color barrier in professional baseball. Robinson praised the moral standards set by Stagg and how much they had influenced a generation of coaches and players of all sports. "Mr. Stagg never smoke or drank in his lifetime, and it's pretty obvious to me that this played a big part in his life and his athletics. My coaches told me a long, long time ago that if I expected to develop my body, expected it to grow as I wanted it to, and to compete in athletics as I wanted to, I could not mix alcohol, nicotine, and sports. It just wouldn't work," Robinson told the crowd.[34]

In San Francisco, KCBS Sports Director Don Klein served as emcee at a banquet held at the Fairmount Hotel, where Jack Curtis, head football coach at Stanford, was the keynote speaker. The theme for the evening was "Parade of Champions" and 100 champions from various sports attended the event to honor each year of Stagg's life. Stagg and his wife spent most of the day receiving well-wishers at the convalescent center where they had been confined for several months.[35] They received more than 500 letters from well-wishers. "And that's not counting telegrams," Stella told a reporter.[36] She held up one from President John F. Kennedy that read:

> I am delighted to join with All-Americans in paying tribute to Amos Alonzo Stagg on the occasion of his 100th birthday. The banquets which are being held across the country this evening are but a symbol of pride and affection we have for Mr. Stagg. His character and career have been an inspiration since his own undergraduate days for countless Americans of all ages. Few men in our history have set so persuasive and shining example as teacher, coach, and citizen. His integrity and dedication to all of the goals he has set for himself are unmatched.[37]

That same year, the Stagg Foundation published *The Unreconstructed Amateur: A Pictorial Biography of Amos Alonzo Stagg* by Bob Considine, an American sports journalist and author of a dozen books. Proceeds from the book and the celebration dinners were used to build the Amos Alonzo Stagg Physical Fitness Center at the University of the Pacific.[38]

Amos Alonzo Stagg, Jr., said his father left an unpublished autobiography titled *Stagg of Yale*. Stagg Jr. told the *New York Times* the day after his father died, "Dad has written about two-thirds of his autobiography, and I have nearly finished it for possible publication…. I know after all those years at Chicago that title may sound strange. But Dad and I decided he came from Yale where he was a great athlete and that was the best title."[39]

Although the autobiography was never published, the manuscript was kept at the Stagg High School Archives in Palos Hill, Illinois, and used in research for this book.[40]

The End

At the age of 101, the *Oakland Tribune* reported in June 1964, "Stagg amazes his doctors." His nurse at Hillhaven Convalescent Center told the reporter "he is doing fine" and his health was "normal" for a man his age. The article said that his doctors "continued to be amazed at the way he is doing ... [and] Mrs. Stagg comes in every afternoon and spends several hours with her husband. Old friends stopped by three or four times a week."[41]

Six weeks after the article was published, Stella died of a kidney ailment at age eighty-eight on July 22, 1964. Her *New York Times* obituary said, "Mrs. Stagg was said to have been the greatest living woman expert on football during her husband's career." Wayne Hardin was quoted in the obituary as saying, "One day at practice we noticed Mrs. Stagg sitting on a log beside the field taking notes. We were all curious, so I was elected to ask her why she had been taking these notes all week. She said, 'Young man, I'm just deciding whether you start Saturday or not.'"[42] In a 1961 interview, Stagg was asked to name his "most satisfactory accomplishment in the world of sports." He told the reporter, "I couldn't pick any one thing. But I'll say this: When I married Stella, I got the top prize."[43]

She was one of fifty recipients the Alumni Association on the University of Chicago honored on the university's fiftieth anniversary in 1941. The "Public Service" citation honored her as "Useful Citizen, Homemaker, and 'Mother to a Thousand Men.'" The *Chicago Alumni Magazine* said at the time of her death, "She had a photographic memory ... and her knowledge of football was professional." Chicago President George W. Beadle said in a condolence message, "Mrs. Stagg was loved and respected by thousands of our students and was an integral part of the great Stagg tradition that brought so much honor and dignity to the University."[44]

The *San Francisco Examiner* reported that Stagg celebrated his 102nd birthday "quietly" on August 16, 1964, a month after Stella died. Paul Stagg told a reporter that his father was unaware that it was his birthday and that he hadn't been able to communicate with anyone since Stella's death on July 22. Among the telegrams congratulating the "Grand Old Man of Football" were some from Yale University, the University of Chicago, the Football Hall of Fame, and the New York Yankees.[45]

Amos Alonzo Stagg died in his sleep at 10:45 a.m. on March 17, 1965, eight months after Stella. He had been in fragile health for two years and took a turn for the worse after developing a fever. He had also been suffering for months from uremic poisoning, which leads to kidney failure. Besides being the oldest Yale graduate at the time of his death, Stagg was the last surviving member from the University of Chicago's original faculty from 1892.

The Rev. Myron Herrell conducted the funeral at Central Methodist Church in Stockton and emphasized the quality of Stagg's life rather than his athletic accomplishments: "If the Stagg shelves held just so many trophies for so many games won, we might have mere records set for succeeding generations to break. But it was the quality of his life that wrote meaning into his great accomplishments," he said.[46]

More than 400 friends and family members attended the funeral, including many of Stagg's former players. He was buried at Park View Cemetery in Manteca, California. A month after he died, the Chicago Board of Trustees unanimously adopted a lengthy tribute to Stagg, which was inscribed in the permanent records of the university. The statement read in part:

> The Old Man—"the Grand Old Man"—is dead. His going symbolizes the passing of an era in the University's history, for as the last survivor of the original faculty, he was a link from its beginning to the present, a reminder of a great and triumphant aspiration that brought the University into being. He came to Chicago because he shared in that aspiration and labored mightily for its realization with a competence, dedication, and unflagging effort that was entirely selfless.[47]

What enabled him to live and stay active for more than 100 years? Researchers have conducted hundreds of studies of factors contributing to a long life. He met six of those frequently cited in research studies: (1) healthy eating habits that lean toward vegetarianism; (2) regular exercise three or four times a week; (3) marriage, especially a happy marriage; (4) religious faith and practice; (5) strong social network; and (6) strong purpose for living.[48]

This long life contributed to his enormous influence on college athletics and especially football. The three most influential coaches on modern football are probably Stagg, Walter Camp, and Glenn "Pop" Warner. While Knute Rockne is more widely known, he was more of a popularizer and promoter of college football than an innovator. The list in Chapter 8 includes twenty-nine of Stagg's football innovations and inventions. The success of his University of Chicago football teams gave the university a rise to national prominence. *Sports Illustrated* wrote of him in 1957: "If any single individual can be said to have created today's game, Stagg is the man. He either invented outright or pioneered every aspect of the modern game from such grammar school basics as the huddle, shift and tackling dummy to such refinements as T-formation strategy."[49]

But his influence extends beyond football to baseball, basketball, and track. He made interscholastic track and basketball meets a national attraction at the University of Chicago while coaching its football, track, baseball, and basketball teams. He coached the U.S. track team at the 1924 Paris Summer Olympics and served on seven U.S. Olympics committees. He helped organize the Big Ten Conference and shape modern football with fifty years of service on the NCAA Rules Committee.

Amos Alonzo Stagg, Sr., may be remembered for rising from poverty to prominence. He may be remembered for his selection to the Football and Basketball Halls of Fame. He may be remembered for his athletic versatility and genius. He may be remembered for his Christian faith and character. He may be remembered for a happy marriage lasting almost seventy years. He may be remembered for coaching until he was ninety-eight. Shortly before he turned 100, however, a *Sports Illustrated* reporter visited Stagg at the convalescent center and later wrote, "Stagg, dressed in his plaid flannel bathrobe and plaid slippers, sat in the Stockton sun the other day and, haltingly, expressed a wish. 'I would like to be remembered,' he said quietly, 'as an honest man.'"[50]

Appendix 1:
University of Chicago
Football, 1892–1932

Not included are high school opponents, 1892–1897,
and non-collegiate opponents, 1918–1919

Year	Wins	Losses	Ties
1892	4	4	1
1893	6	4	2
1894	10	7	1
1895	8	3	0
1896	10	2	1
1897	8	1	0
1898	9	2	0
1899	12	0	2
1900	7	5	1
1901	5	5	2
1902	11	1	0
1903	10	2	1
1904	8	1	1
1905	10	0	0
1906	4	1	0
1907	4	1	0
1908	5	0	1
1909	4	1	2
1910	2	5	0
1911	6	1	0

Year	Wins	Losses	Ties
1912	6	1	0
1913	7	0	0
1914	4	2	1
1915	5	2	0
1916	3	4	0
1917	3	2	1
1918	1	5	0
1919	5	2	0
1920	3	4	0
1921	6	1	0
1922	5	1	1
1923	7	1	0
1924	4	1	3
1925	3	4	1
1926	2	6	0
1927	4	4	0
1928	2	8	0
1929	7	3	0
1930	2	5	2
1931	2	6	1
1932	3	4	1
Total	**227**	**112**	**26**
Source: UChicago Department of Athletics and Recreation.			

Appendix 2:
Big Ten Conference
Championships Under
Amos Alonzo Stagg

Year	Overall Record	Conference Record
1899	12–0–2	4–0
1905	9–0	7–0
1907	4–1	4–0
1908	5–0–1	5–0
1913	7–0	7–0
1922*	5–1–1	4–0–1
1924	4–1–3	3–0–3

*Conference title shared with Iowa and Michigan

Source: UChicago Department of Athletics and Recreation.

Appendix 3:
University of Chicago
Presidents, 1891–1951

William Rainey Harper	1891–1906
Harry Pratt Judson	1907–1923
Ernest DeWitt Burton	1923–1925
Max Mason	1925–1928
Robert Maynard Hutchins	1929–1951

Chapter Notes

Preface

1. *Collier's*, Oct. 25, 1930, 25.
2. Allison Danzig, "Alonzo the Magnificent," *NYT*, Dec. 28, 1933.
3. "Mrs. Amos Alonzo Stagg, wife of football coach, dead," *NYT*, July 24, 1964, 27.
4. Arch Ward, "In the wake of the news," *CT*, Aug. 28, 1948, 15.
5. "Inflation Calculator," U.S. Official Inflation Data, Alioth Finance, Aug. 12, 2020, https://www.officialdata.org/.

Chapter 1

1. "Three killed, 82 injured in flaming wreck on Valley Daylight," *SFE*, Feb. 5, 1947, 1.
2. "Friends, admirers, flock around Stagg," *The Sacramento Bee*, Feb. 5, 1947, 11.
3. Associated Press, "Stagg, 61, says he will not quit coaching until he is 70," *NYT*, Nov. 29, 1922, 21.
4. "Amos Alonzo Stagg dies at 102," *Chicago American*, Mar. 17, 1965, 42.
5. AAS and Stout, *Touchdown!* (New York: Longmans, Green and Co., 1927), 299.
6. AAS to N.C. Plimpton, Oct. 4, 1922, box 10, folder 13, AASP.
7. AAS to J.E. Raycroft, July 26, 1901, box 12, folder 1, AASP. See also "Amos Alonzo Stagg, legendary grid coach, dies," *CT*, Mar. 18, 1965, 3.
8. John Underwood, "Amos Stagg: A century of honesty," *Sports Illustrated*, Aug. 13, 1962, 43.
9. "Mrs. Stagg is winner," *CT*, Aug. 28, 1898, 7.

10. "Mrs. Stagg victorious again," *CT*, Aug. 30, 1898, 4.
11. AAS Jr., videotaped interview with Dominic Bertinetti, Jr., Feb. 22, 1985. Stagg Special Collection.
12. *Ibid.*
13. Bob Considine, *The Unreconstructed Amateur: A Pictorial Biography of Amos Alonzo Stagg* (San Francisco: Amos Alonzo Stagg Foundation, 1962), 20. See also AAS and Stout, *Touchdown!*, 106.
14. AAS to Harold H. Swift, April 17, 1925, box 10, folder 15, AASP.
15. AAS to Harry A. Baldwin, Dec. 31, 1941, box 3, folder 5, AASP.
16. AAS to Samuel D. Barnes, July 31, 1952, box 3, folder 5, AASP.
17. Allison Danzig, *The History of American Football* (Englewood Cliffs, NJ: Prentice-Hall, 1956), vii.
18. Victor Wisner, "Coach, adviser, pal—that's the Midway's Grand Old Man," *CT*, Feb. 5, 1928, 29.
19. "Stagg wins at Jackson Park," *Chicago Inter Ocean*, July 30, 1899, 9.
20. "Stagg, 69 today, beats his son at tennis," *NYT*, Aug. 16, 1931, 22.
21. Considine, *The Unreconstructed Amateur*, 141.
22. "Stagg in close golf match," *NYT*, Dec. 5, 1913, 12.
23. Tim Cronin, *Golf Under the Clock Tower, One Hundred Years of Olympia Fields* (Olympia Fields, IL: Olympia Fields Country Club, 2015), 1.
24. J.G. Davies, "Olympia Fields tourney," *CT*, June 15, 1916, 18.
25. AAS, "Olympia, as it is, as it will be," Olympia Fields Country Club, *The Olympian*, August 1917, 7.

26. Lochinvar, "Western Department," *American Golfer*, 15, 6 (April 2016), 433–441.

27. Edwin Pope, *Football's Greatest Coaches*, Tupper and Love, Inc., 1956, 234.

28. AAS to W.A. Davenport, July 2, 1926. box 1A, folder 15, AASP.

29. AAS and Henry L. Williams, *Scientific and Practical Treatise on American Football*. Originally published by Harper and Brothers, 1894. Reprinted in *The American Football Trilogy* by The Lost Century of Sports Collection (LostCentury.com), 2015, 43–44.

30. "Dried apples, nuts, prunes, and water for the Maroon team," *Chicago Inter Ocean*, Sept. 18, 1907, 4.

31. AAS to Henry L. Stimson, Feb. 17, 1944, box 6, folder 13, AASP.

32. Edwin Pope, *Football's Greatest Coaches*, 1955, 234.

33. "Coach A.A. Stagg will go south for the Winter," *Chicago Inter Ocean*, Nov. 23, 1904, 4.

34. "Alonzo Stagg, who stands for honesty, pureness, and fairness in college athletics," *CT*, Nov. 20, 1904, 15.

35. "Stagg coaches from his bed," *CT*, Jan. 19, 1906, 10.

36. AAS to William S. Harman, Dec. 16, 1947, box 4, folder 4, AASP.

37. AAS to F.G. Baumgartner, April 6, 1923, box 1a, folder 12, AASP.

38. Geenburg, *Winning the Biggest Game of All*, 52.

39. "Stagg's burden too heavy," *CT*, Jan. 29, 1913, 14.

40. AAS and Stout, *Touchdown!*, 242.

41. Office of Public Relations, University of Chicago, April 6, 1962, Stagg Special Collection. See also "Stagg's famed electric car to go to museum," *CT*, Feb. 17, 1933, 21.

42. Stan Hochman, "Hardin remembers Mr. Stagg," *Philadelphia Daily News*, Feb. 20, 1981, 119.

43. "$12,300,000 ad bill to boost cigarettes," undated clipping, box 107, folder 6, AASP.

44. AAS to Walter K. Towers, Aug. 10, 1916, box 107, folder 5, AASP.

45. AAS, "The University of Chicago and tobacco," *The Instructor*, 1919, box 107, folder 5, AASP.

46. Ida B. Cole, "What Coach Stagg says of tobacco and athletes," *The Young Crusader*, undated, box 107, folder 5, AASP.

47. Rev. W.F. Baldwin to AAS, April 15, 1915, box 107, folder 6, AASP.

48. AAS to Rev. W.F. Baldwin, undated, box 107, folder 6, AASP.

49. Lenna Lowe Yost to AAS, April 3, 1936, box 105, folder 3, AASP.

50. AAS, "Proposed Speech of Amos Alonzo Stagg Before Committee of the United States Senate Investigating the Prohibition Law and Effect of the Volstead act," April 27, 1926, box 107, folder 3, AASP.

51. L.C. Speers, "The testimony on Prohibition summed up," *NYT*, May 2, 1926, 5.

52. "Prohibition hailed by Stagg as check on post-war students," *NYT*, Mar. 14, 1930, 1. See also "Students contradict Stagg," *NYT*, Mar. 15, 1930, 3.

53. "Stagg backs Prop 3," *Sacramento Bee*, Oct. 27, 1958, 4.

54. Sol Butler to AAS, May 7, 1926, box 1A, folder 12, AASP.

55. AAS to Sol Butler, May 10, 1926, box 1A, folder 12, AASP.

56. "Excerpts from A.A. Stagg's Letters," Nov. 17, 1892, Stagg Special Collection.

57. AAS and Amos Alonzo Stagg, Jr., *Stagg of Yale*, 34. (unpublished manuscript, c. 1958). Stagg Special Collection.

58. John W. Boyer, *The University of Chicago: A History. Chicago* (University of Chicago Press, 2015), 121.

59. "Football for half a century," *New Orleans Times*, Dec. 28, 1937.

60. AAS to Mr. and Mrs. Charles W. Gilkey, Aug. 28, 1943, AASP.

61. Florence M. Seder to AAS, Aug. 14, 1929, box 105, folder 1, AASP.

62. AAS to Florence M. Seder, undated, box 105, folder 1, AASP.

63. AAS to James L. Brader, April 24, 1928, box 1A, folder 12, AASP.

Chapter 2

1. John Greenburg, *Winning the Biggest Game of All: The Story of Amos Alonzo Stagg* (Amazon Kindle, 2000).

2. AAS and Amos Alonzo Stagg, Jr., *Stagg of Yale* (unpublished manuscript, c. 1958), 20. Stagg Special Collection.

3. Stagg Family Record, box 105, folder 1, AASP.

4. AAS and Amos Alonzo Stagg, Jr., *Stagg of Yale*.

5. Considine, *The Unreconstructed Amateur*, 20. See also *Touchdown!*, 48.
6. AAS Jr. videotaped interview with Dominic Bertinetti, Jr., Feb. 22, 1985. Stagg Special Collection.
7. AAS and Amos Alonzo Stagg, Jr., *Stagg of Yale*, 25.
8. Francis J. Powers, *Amos Alonzo Stagg* (St. Louis: C.C. Spink and Son, 1946), 5.
9. AAS and Amos Alonzo Stagg, Jr., *Stagg of Yale*, 9.
10. *Ibid.*
11. "Boyhood Life of Amos Alonzo Stagg," Stagg Special Collection.
12. *"Ibid.*
13. Van Varner, "Amos Alonzo Stagg," *Guidepost*, August 1959, 3.
14. AAS and Amos Alonzo Stagg, Jr., *Stagg of Yale*, 6.
15. AAS to Rev. Joseph C. Hazen, Jan. 26, 1925, box 2, folder 6, AASP.
16. "Excerpts from A.A. Stagg's Letters, Nov. 17, 1892," Stagg Special Collection.
17. Francis J. Powers, *Life Story of Amos Alonzo Stagg, Grand Old Man of Football* (St. Louis: C.C. Spink and Son, 1946), 6. See also AAS and W.W. Stout, *Touchdown!* (New York: Longmans, Green and Company, 1927), 50.
18. AAS and Stout, *Touchdown!*, 69.
19. AAS and Amos Alonzo Stagg, Jr., *Stagg of Yale*.
20. AAS Jr. videotaped interview with Dominic Bertinetti, Jr., Feb. 22, 1985. Stagg Special Collection.
21. AAS and Stout, *Touchdown!*, 72.
22. AAS and Amos Alonzo Stagg, Jr., *Stagg of Yale*.
23. *Ibid.*

Chapter 3

1. AAS and Amos Alonzo Stagg, Jr., *Stagg of Yale*, 35.
2. *Ibid.*
3. Erin Ann McCarthy, "Making Men: The Life and Career of Amos Alonzo Stagg, 1862–1933" (PhD diss., Loyola University Chicago, 1994), 31.
4. AAS and Stout, *Touchdown!*, 71–72.
5. *Ibid.*
6. AAS to Ida Stagg, April 4, 1884, box 1, folder 1, AASP.
7. AAS to H.D. Everett, June 21, 1910, Stagg Special Collection.

8. Quindecennial Report, Class of 1988, Yale (New Haven: Dorman Lithography Co., 1904), 31. Cited in McCarthy, "Making Men," 67.
9. AAS and Stout, *Touchdown!*, 73
10. Ellis Lucia, *Mr. Football: Amos Alonzo Stagg* (New Brunswick, NJ: A.S. Barnes, 1970), 57.
11. "Forty years on the Midway," *CT*, Oct. 14, 1931, 17. See also *Touchdown!*, 77.
12. "Yale's dandy twirler," *Baseball Record*, May 27, 1887, box 266, folder 6, AASP.
13. "Twenty men struck out," *NYT*, May 27, 1888, 1.
14. AAS and Stout, *Touchdown!*, 107.
15. "Yale's great victory over Harvard," June 26, 1888, box 269, folder 4, AASP.
16. *The Boston Globe*, April 5, 1891, 12.
17. AAS and Stout, *Touchdown!*, 109. See also "Chronological Record of Amos Alonzo Stagg's Contributions to the Game of Football," Stagg Special Collection.
18. Quoted in Ruth Sparhawk, "A Study of the Life and Contribution of Amos Alonzo Stagg to Intercollegiate Football" (EdD diss., Springfield College, December 1968), 36.
19. Quoted in McCarthy, "Making Men," 62.
20. *Ibid.*, 64.
21. Jim O'Rourke to AAS, June 3, 1888. Cited in Sparhawk, "A Study of the Life and Contribution of Amos Alonzo Stagg to Intercollegiate Football," 36.
22. H. B. Jewett to Stagg, May 19, 1887, box 1a, folder 2, AASP.
23. Considine, *The Unreconstructed Amateur*, 29.
24. AAS and Stout, *Touchdown!*, 106.
25. "George Washington Woodruff, 1864–1934," University of Pennsylvania Archives and Records Center, https://archives.upenn.edu/exhibits/penn-people/biography/george-washington-woodruff. See also G.W. Woodruff, "Stagg and Dr. Williams," *CT*, Nov. 29, 1902, 6.
26. McCallum, *Ivy League Football Since 1872*, 27.
27. AAS and Stout, *Touchdown!*, 78. See also Stagg quoted in "Stagg to Reach 99 Tomorrow," Associated Press, *CT*, Aug. 15, 1961, 45.
28. "1889 Yale Bulldogs," SportsReference.com, https://www.sports-reference.com/cfb/schools/yale/1889-roster.html.

29. Quoted in Danzig, *The History of American Football*, 124.

30. AAS to William Fay, *Collier's Magazine*, Oct. 26, 1949. Amos Alonzo Stagg, Sr. & Jr., Susquehanna University Archives, Section 3, RG 2.2.7.

31. Paul Stagg, "The Development of the National Collegiate Athletic Association in Relationship" (PhD diss., New York University, 1946). See also AAS and Stout, *Touchdown!*, 60.

32. AAS and Stout, *Touchdown!*, 74.

33. Tim Cohane, *The Yale Football Story* (New York: G.P. Putnam's Sons, 1951), 27.

34. John McCallum, *Ivy League Football Since 1872*, 37.

35. AAS and Stout, *Touchdown!*, 57.

36. Quoted in Roger R. Tamte, *Walter Camp and the Creation of American Football* (Champaign: University of Illinois Press, 2018), 66.

37. *Ibid.*, 63.

38. Cohane, *The Yale Football Story*, 34.

39. Walter Camp, https://www.nndb.com/people/106/000165608/.

40. Q&A with Roger R. Tamte, University of Illinois Press Blog, Aug. 6, 2018, http://www.press.uillinois.edu/wordpress/qa-with-roger-m-tamte-author-of-walter-camp-and-the-creation-of-american-football/.

41. Tamte, *Walter Camp and the Creation of American Football*, 135. Whitney is quoted as first describing Camp as "the father of American football" on p. 99.

42. AAS and Stout, *Touchdown!*, 109.

43. *Ibid.* See also McCarthy, "Making Men," 67–68.

44. AAS and Stout, *Touchdown!*, 105.

45. AAS to Pauline Stagg, Sept. 1884, box 1, folder 1, AASP.

46. Harvey T. Woodruff, "A.A. Stagg, coach and sportsman," *CT*, May 19, 1912, 8.

47. G.H. Dickinson to AAS, box 1A, folder 4, AASP.

48. A.J. Johnson to AAS, April 4, 1892, box 1A, folder 7, AASP.

49. Joseph Shipley to AAS, Nov. 15, 1890, box 1A, folder 5, AASP.

50. AAS to Marshall Bartholomew, Sept. 3, 1958, box 5, folder 1, AASP.

51. AAS to Paul Stagg, Jan. 15, 1889. box 1, folder 9, AASP.

52. Undated newspaper clipping, box 266, folder 7, AASP.

53. "With Stagg as a model," undated newspaper clipping, box 269, folder 4, AASP.

54. Tony Ladd and James A. Mathisen, *Muscular Christianity: Evangelical Protestants and the Development of American Sport* (Grand Rapids: Baker Books, 1999), 59.

55. Peter Iverson Berg, "A Mission on the Midway; Amos Alonzo Stagg and the Gospel of Football" (PhD diss., Michigan State University, 1996), 38.

56. Ladd and Mathisen, *Muscular Christianity*, 53.

57. AAS to Ida Stagg, Feb. 20, 1886, box 1, folder 2, AASP.

58. AAS to Pauline Stagg, Jan. 30, 1887, box 1, folder 6, AASP.

59. Quoted in McCarthy, "Making Men," 88.

60. AAS to Walter Camp, Jan. 15, 1925, Stagg Special Collection.

61. AAS and Stout, *Touchdown!* 130.

62. "Pitcher Stagg faces Harvard men in a new role," *Boston Globe*, Mar. 27, 1891, 6.

63. "Semi-Annual Examination, Junior Class, June 1887, box 266, folder 8," AASP.

64. AAS to Pauline Stagg, Mar. 8, 1890, box 1, folder 1, AASP.

Chapter 4

1. "100 Years and Forever, A Film by and about Amos Alonzo Stagg, 1962," Springfield College Archives, https://cdm16122.contentdm.oclc.org/digital/collection/p15370coll2/id/20992/rec/78.

2. AAS and Stout, *Touchdown!*, 131.

3. Yale men were surprised," *NYT*, Dec. 13, 1890, 3.

4. John McCallum, *Ivy League Football Since 1872*, appendix.

5. *Ibid.*, 138.

6. "Harvard defeats Stagg's team," *NYT*, Nov. 1, 1891, 3.

7. Amos Alonzo Stagg Collection, Springfield College Digital Archives, Springfield, Mass.,
https://cdm16122.contentdm.oclc.org/digital/collection/p15370coll2/id/20992/rec/78.

8. Quoted in Danzig, *The History of American Football*, 23.

9. "James Naismith," Kansas Historical Society Kansapedia, https://www.kshs.org/kansapedia/james-naismith/12154.

10. AAS to Ruth Stagg, undated, Stagg Special Collection.

11. "Basket Football Game," *The Springfield Republican,* Mar. 12, 1892, Springfield College Digital Collections. The Springfield Digital Collections includes this addendum: "This has long been considered the first public game of basketball or at least one of the first time the game was mentioned in the newspapers, but this is in dispute. An early listing of the game has since been found. That said, this is definitely the most famous listing of the game." https://cdm16122.contentdm.oclc.org/digital/collection/p15370coll2/id/22034/rec/67.

12. "Amos Alonzo Stagg," Naismith Memorial Basketball Hall of Fame, http://www.hoophall.com/hall-of-famers/amos-alonzo-stagg/.

13. John Miller, *The Big Scrum: How Teddy Roosevelt Saved Football* (New York: HarperCollins, 2015), 40.

14. Berg, "A Mission on the Midway," 77.

15. "Excerpts from A.A. Stagg's letters, Chicago, Feb.6, 1893," Stagg Special Collection.

16. "A great athlete," *Minneapolis Star-Tribune,* Sept. 24, 1892, 2.

17. "Excerpt from letter from A.A. Stagg to a friend, Dayton, Ohio," Jan. 29, 1892, Stagg Special Collection.

18. Quoted in Theodore Morrison, *Chautauqua: A Center for Education, Religion, and the Arts in America* (University of Chicago Press, 1974), 74–75.

19. "Excerpt from letter from A.A. Stagg to a friend, Chautauqua, N.Y., July 19, 1892," Stagg Special Collection.

20. *Ibid.,* July 30, 1892. Stagg Special Collection.

21. *Ibid.,* July 12, 1892. Stagg Special Collection.

22. Email to the author, Dec. 19, 2017.

23. Berg, "A Mission on the Midway," 80.

Chapter 5

1. "Dr. Harper and Mr. Stagg," *University of Chicago Magazine,* Nov. 1964, 8.

2. William Rainey Harper, 1891–1906, University of Chicago, Office of the President, https://president.uchicago.edu/directory/william-rainey-harper.

3. Harper to Board of Trustees, Feb. 16, 1891. University of Chicago Special Collections Research Center, Digital Photo Collection for William Rainey Harper.

4. AAS and Stout, *Touchdown!,* 143–144.

5. John W. Boyer to author, Aug. 20, 2020.

6. Robin Lester, *Stagg's University: The Rise, Decline, and Fall of Big-Time Football at the University of Chicago* (Urbana: University of Illinois Press, 1995), 10.

7. Thomas Wakefield Goodspeed, *A History of the University of Chicago: The First Quarter Century* (University of Chicago Press, 1916), 498.

8. Chicago Baptists became increasingly unhappy with the liberal direction of the Divinity School and in 1913 established the Northern Baptist Theology Seminary. The trustees gradually distanced the university from its Baptist roots and in 1944 eliminated all denominational requirements for the president and board of trustees. However, the board adopted a statement stating its "sincere desire to insure the continuance of the university forever as a Christian institution" and directed that all future trustees should receive copies of the statement. See Minutes of the Board of Trustees, April 13, 1944, and Boyer, *The University of Chicago: A History* (Chicago: University of Chicago Press, 2015).

9. Morrison, *Chautauqua: A Center for Education, Religion, and the Arts in America,* 77.

10. Thomas Wakefield Goodspeed, *A History of the University of Chicago,* 124.

11. Boyer, *The University of Chicago: A History,* 53.

12. Morrison, *Chautauqua: A Center for Education, Religion, and the Arts in America,* 74–75.

13. Boyer, *The University of Chicago: A History,* 122.

14. AAS to Harper, Nov. 25, 1890, box 14, folder 38, AASP.

15. Brian M. Ingrassia, *The Rise of Gridiron University: Higher Education's Uneasy Alliance with Big-Time Football* (Lawrence: University Press of Kansas, 2012), 42.

16. "Excerpt from a letter to Pauline" (Stagg's sister), Jan. 27, 1891, Stagg Special Collection.

17. "Stagg to stick by Yale," *Boston Daily Globe,* Nov. 28, 1891, 2.

18. "Stagg called to Hopkins," *Boston Daily Globe,* Dec. 6, 1890, 6.

19. *Ibid.*

20. AAS to Harper, Nov. 28, 1891. box 14, folder 1, AASP.

21. AAS, President's Report, 1897–1898, box 18, folder 10, AASP.

22. AAS to Harper, Mar. 8, 1892. box 14, folder 38. AASP.

23. "Extracts from A.A. Stagg's Letters, Dec. 24, 1892," Stagg Special Collection.

24. AAS to Harper, undated, box 14, folder 38, WRHP.

25. Goodspeed, A History of the University of Chicago, 377–378.

26. "Address delivered by A.A. Stagg at the laying of the cornerstone of the gymnasium," Carnegie Institute of Technology, June 13, 1923, Stagg Special Collection.

27. "Coach Stagg's 'Theory and elements' brings out some unexpected gridiron candidates," CT, June 28, 1906, 6.

28. Berg. "A Mission on the Midway," 106.

29. John W. Boyer to author, Aug. 20, 2020.

30. Gerald Parshall, "The Great Panic Of '93," U.S. News & World Report, Nov. 2, 1992, 70.

31. William Rainey Harper (1891–1906), http://www-news.uchicago.edu/president/history/harper.shtml.

32. AAS and Stout, Touchdown!, 169.

33. Ibid., 146–147.

34. Bernard Berelson, Graduate Education in the United States (New York: McGraw-Hill, 1960), 15.

35. Ingrassia, The Rise of Gridiron University, 3,

36. Goodspeed, A History of the University of Chicago, 486.

37. AAS and Stout, Touchdown!, 155–156.

Chapter 6

1. "Excerpts of letters written by Stagg to his family," Stagg Special Collection.

2. AAS, undated letter, box 29, folder 1, AASP.

3. Ibid., 157.

4. Team Records, University of Chicago, in McCallum, Big Ten Football Since 1895, 246.

5. Interview with A.A. Stagg, Jr., April 21, 1967, quoted in Sparhawk, "A Study of the Life and Contribution of Amos Alonzo Stagg to Intercollegiate Football," 56.

6. See www.worldsfairchicago1893.com for more information. The interested reader can also find YouTube videos with motion picture footage from the fair and music by the Columbian Choir and Columbian Orchestra.

7. "Extracts from A.A. Stagg's Letters, Oct. 21, 1892," Stagg Special Collection.

8. "Excerpts from A.A. Stagg's letters, Chicago," Dec. 1, 1892, Stagg Special Collection.

9. Gerald Parshall, "The Great Panic Of '93," U.S. News & World Report, Nov. 2, 1992, 70.

10. George Britt, Forty Years—Forty Million. The Career of Frank A. Munsey (New York: Farrar and Rinehart Co., 1935), 88.

11. AAS and Stout, Touchdown!, 169.

12. Ibid.

13. AAS, "Athletic Field" in Annual Report to the President, 1894, box 18, folder 10, AASP.

14. AAS and Stout, Touchdown!, 170.

15. "Chicago's eleven are quartered in the city all night," San Francisco Morning Call, Dec. 24, 1894, 10.

16. Francis J. Powers, Life Story of Amos Alonzo Stagg, Grand Old Man of Football (St. Louis: C.C. Spink and Son, 1946), 11.

17. AAS and Stout, Touchdown!, 191.

18. "Will leave for the coast today," CT, Dec. 19, 1894, 5.

19. Ibid., AAS and Stout, Touchdown!, 194.

20. Ibid., 192.

21. "Chicago's eleven are quartered in the city all night," San Francisco Morning Call, Dec. 24, 1894, 4.

22. Advertisement, San Francisco Morning Call, Dec. 29, 1894, 4.

23. "Chicago won it," San Francisco Morning Call, Dec. 26, 1894, 10.

24. "Got a licking, Stanford ignominiously defeated," CT, Dec. 26, 1894, 1.

25. "Chicagoed by Oakland," SFE, Jan. 2, 1895, 4.

26. Berg. "A Mission on the Midway," 106.

27. A.C. Jones, "Tomorrow is 95th birthday for football's Grand Old Man," The Capital Journal (Salem, OR), Dec. 24, 1956.

28. AAS and Amos Alonzo Stagg, Jr., Stagg of Yale, 47–49.

29. AAS Jr. videotaped interview with Dominic Bertinetti, Jr., Feb. 22, 1985. Stagg Special Collection.

30. AAS and Amos Alonzo Stagg, Jr., *Stagg of Yale,* 48–49.
31. AAS, "A Sonnet," Jan. 14, 1894, box 2, folder 17, AASP.
32. Stella Robertson, "Written at Sunset," Feb. 27, 1894, box 2, folder 17, AASP.
33. Lester, *Stagg's University,* 21.
34. Greenburg, *Winning the Biggest Game of All.* See also McCarthy, "Making Men," 166.
35. "Amos Alonzo Stagg, legendary grid coach, dies," *CT,* Mar. 18, 1965, 52.
36. Greenburg, *Winning the Biggest Game of All.*
37. "Excerpts from A.A. Stagg's Letters, Sept. 3, 1894," Stagg Special Collection.
38. "Extract from letters of A.A. Stagg, Chautauqua, New York, Aug. 2, 1892," Stagg Special Collection.
39. "Excerpt of letter from A.A. Stagg, Hamline, Minn., Sept. 26, 1892," Stagg Special Collection.
40. AAS and Williams, *A Scientific and Practical Treatise on American Football for Schools and Colleges.* Originally published by Harper and Brothers, 1894. Reprinted in *The American Football Trilogy* published by the Lost Century of Sports Collection, 2015 (LostCentury.com).
41. *Ibid.,* 262–264.
42. "Excerpts from A.A. Stagg's letters, Nov. 17, 1892," Stagg Special Collection.
43. "Yellow on all sides," *Chicago Examiner,* Nov. 2, 1892, box 2, folder 53, AASP.
44. AAS to D.A. Robertson, Dec. 10, 1915, box 10, folder 2. AASP. See also AAS and Stout, *Touchdown!,* 161.
45. AAS to Pauline, Oct. 9, 1982, Stagg Special Collection." See also McCarthy, "Making Men," 160.

Chapter 7

1. All win-loss season records for Chicago were compiled by the author from the appendix of McCallum's book, *Big Ten Football Since 1895,* 246–249.
2. Boyer, *The University of Chicago: A History,* 160.
3. Everts Wrenn, "Chicago team claimed as one of the best in the country," *CT,* Dec. 10, 1899, 18.
4. AAS and Wesley Winans Stout, *Touchdown!* (New York: Longmans, Green and Co., 1927), 163. See also "The

Grand Old Man of Football," *Selinsgrove Times-Tribune,* Nov. 18, 1948, and
Victor Wisner, "Coach, adviser, pal—that's the Midway's Grand Old Man," *CT,* Feb. 5, 1928, 29.
5. Ray Robinson, *Rockne of Notre Dame* (New York: Oxford University Press, 1999), 39.
6. John McCallum, *Big Ten Football Since 1895,* 5.
7. Mervin D. Hyman and Gordon S. White, Jr., *Big Ten Football: Its Life and Times, Great Coaches, Players and Games* (New York: MacMillan, 1977), 28–30.
8. *Ibid.,* 25, 26.
9. H.P. Judson to AAS, Nov. 6, 1907, box 9, folder 17, AASP.
10. Carl D. Voltmer, *A Brief History of the Intercollegiate Conference of Faculty Representatives* (Menasha, WI: George Banta Publishing Company, 1935), 25–26.
11. The NCAA did not have national jurisdiction, and the Southeastern Conference began offering athletic scholarships since after it was organized in 1932.
12. "History of sports scholarships," http://sportStagg Special Collection-scholarship.com/about/history-of-sports-scholarships/.
13. Voltmer, *A Brief History of the Intercollegiate Conference of Faculty Representatives,* 67.
14. AAS to M.J. Casey, Sept. 24, 1900, box 13, folder 2, AASP.
15. AAS to Charles Harney, Mar. 4, 1899, box 13, folder 2, AASP.
16. AAS to J.V. Cole, Mar. 7, 1900, box 13, folder 2, AASP.
17. Letter from Stagg, Jan. 17, 1910, box 13, folder 9, AASP.
18. John Kryk, *Stagg vs. Yost: The Birth of Cutthroat Football* (Lanham, MD: Rowman & Littlefield, 2015), 64, 184.
19. AAS to Harper and Harper to AAS, both Aug. 17, 1904, box 10, folder 9, WRHP. Cited in Lester, *Stagg's University,* 90.
20. "Correspondence with athletes, June 20, 1899," box 13, folder 2, Department of Athletics and Physical Culture Papers, University of Chicago Archives and Special Collections.
21. "Stagg will change his policy," *Chicago Inter Ocean,* Nov. 26, 1902, 4.
22. "Chicago wants 'prep' athletes," *CT,* Nov. 26, 1902, 6.
23. *Ibid.*

24. Dean Vincent to Stagg, June 14, 1906, box 10, folder 16, AASP. Raycroft to Stagg, Stagg to Judson, Jan. 27, 1906, box 12, folder 5, AASP.

25. Ibid., 71.

26. McCarthy, "Making Men," 257. See also Lester, Stagg's University, 177–179, and Luther Fernald, managing editor of The Daily Maroon, to Stagg, April 11, 1908, box 9, folder 18, AASP.

27. McCarthy, "Making Men," 201.

28. Harper to AAS, April 27, 1895, box 9, folder 1, AASP.

29. AAS, handwritten note, undated, box 18, folder 1, AASP.

30. "Resist Mr. Stagg's demands," CT, Jan. 30, 1896, 7.

31. "H.G. Gale steps down and out," CT, Jan. 15, 1896, 8.

32. "Captain in name only," Chicago Inter Ocean, Jan. 20, 1896, 4.

33. Graham Kernwin to Ruth M. Sparhawk, May 10, 1967, quoted in Sparhawk, "A Study of the Life and Contributions of Amos Alonzo Stagg to Intercollegiate Football," 79.

34. AAS telegram to H.O. Page, Feb. 26, 1913, box 11, folder 16, AASP.

35. Lester, Stagg's University, 46.

36. "Stagg stands solid," Chicago Inter Ocean, Mar. 16, 1899, 8.

37. "Boycott the Maroons, CT, Mar. 14, 1899, 4.

38. "Stagg makes reply," Chicago Inter Ocean, Mar. 20, 1899, 4.

39. "Maroons prove one of the greatest surprises of football year," Chicago Inter Ocean, Dec. 10, 1899, 44.

40. "Chicago is ready for Michigan game," Chicago Inter Ocean, Nov. 15, 1901, 4.

41. Lester, Stagg's University, 79.

42. Cited in McCarthy, "Making Men."

43. Lester, Stagg's University, 113–115.

44. Ibid., 53.

45. Harper to AAS, Feb. 9, 1897, box 9, folder 2, AASP.

46. Harper to AAS, Feb. 1, 1900, box 9, folder 3, AASP.

47. Ray Robinson, Rockne of Notre Dame, The Making of a Football Legend (New York: Oxford University Press, 1999), 227.

48. McCallum, Big Ten Football Since 1896, 236. Chicago shared the conference championship in 1922 with Iowa and Michigan, while Michigan shared the title with other teams in 1903, 1904, 1906, 1918, 1922, 1923, 1926, 1930, and 1931.

49. "Chicago knew the signals," CT, Nov. 30, 1894, 5.

50. "Chicago knew no signals," CT, Dec. 1, 1894, 6.

51. "Michigan Fight Song," June 29, 1909, https://mgoblue.com/news/2009/6/29/Michigan_Fight_Song.aspx.

52. Quotes about Yost are from Danzig, The History of American Football, 159.

53. Kryk, Stagg vs. Yost: The Birth of Cutthroat Football (New York: Rowman & Littlefield, 2015).

54. "Chicago-Michigan football rivalry," https://en.wikipedia.org/wiki/Chicago%E2%80%93Michigan_football_rivalry.

55. "McGugin is said to be ineligible," CT, Nov. 14, 1802, 6.

56. Kryk, Stagg vs. Yost: The Birth of Cutthroat Football, 119.

57. "Michigan, 28; Chicago, 0," NYT, Nov. 27, 1903, 10.

58. AAS and Stout, Touchdown!, 233. See also Kryk, Stagg vs. Yost, 111.

59. Kryk, Stagg vs. Yost, 236.

60. Lester, Stagg's University, 69.

61. Robin Lester, "Michigan-Chicago 1905: the first greatest game of the century," Journal of Sport History (Summer 1991), 18, 2.

62. Lester, Stagg's University, 70–71.

63. The training table was really a misnomer. They were basically athletic dormitories in which players lived, ate, and slept.

64. Greenburg, Winning the Biggest Game of All.

65. AAS to John W. Heisman, Mar. 30, 1928, box 25, folder 1, AASP.

66. Associated Press, "All-American idea absurd, says Stagg," NYT, Dec. 27, 1928, 26.

67. AAS, "Excerpts of letters of A.A. Stagg to his sisters, July 20, 1931," Stagg Special Collection.

68. University of Chicago Department of Athletics and Recreation, https://athletics.uchicago.edu/sports/fball/record-book-fb.pdf.

69. Arthur Farey, "Bring out the best of boys," Together, Aug. 1957, 16.

70. AAS to Walter Eckersall, Oct. 4, 1907, Stagg Special Collection.

71. Quoted in Ruth M. Sparhawk, "A Study of the Life and Contribution of Amos Alonzo Stagg to Intercollegiate Football," 36.

72. A complete list of their names and professional teams is available at https:// athletics.uchicago.edu/sports/fball/record-book-fb.pdf.

73. AAS to "All Friends of College Football," Oct. 26, 1923, box 25, folder 2, AASP. See also "Pro elevens hurt sport, says Stagg," *NYT*, Nov. 2, 1923, 21.

74. AAS to Frederick Gillies, Nov. 22, 1922, box 22, folder 22, AASP.

75. AAS and Stout, *Touchdown!*, 296.

76. *Ibid.*, 278.

77. *Ibid.*, 276.

78. The speech was given on June 8, 1933, shortly before he left to accept the position at the College of the Pacific.

79. John P. Long interview with Dominic Bertinetti, Jr., July 19, 1989, Stagg Special Collection. Interviews with Long, Thomson, and Stagg, Jr., were conducted by Dominic Bertinetti, Jr., in 1985 as part of an oral history project for the Stagg Special Collection at Amos Alonzo Stagg High School in Palos Hills, Illinois.

80. John P. Long to Ruth M. Sparhawk, May 10, 1967, quoted in Sparhawk, "A Study of the Life and Contributions of Amos Alonzo Stagg to Intercollegiate Football," 78.

81. Interview with Frank W. Thomson conducted by Dominic Bertinetti, Jr., Nov. 18, 1985, Stagg Special Collection.

82. AAS and Stout, *Touchdown!*, 284.

83. Interview with Amos A. Stagg, Jr., conducted by Dominic Bertinetti, Jr., Feb. 22, 1985, Stagg Special Collection.

84. AAS and Stout, *Touchdown!*, 290–293.

85. AAS to Harper, Nov. 30, 1904. box 105, folder 1, AASP. See also *Touchdown!*, 215.

86. "Convocation exercises of the University of Chicago, *Chicago Inter Ocean*, April 3, 1900, 4.

87. Lester, *Stagg's University*, 41.

88. Harper to AAS, 22–23 Nov. 1897, box 9, folder 2, AASP.

89. AAS and Stout, *Touchdown!*, 203.

90. "Athletics promote honesty and morality," *CT*, Jan. 18, 1903, 11.

91. AAS to Harper, March 24, 1896, box 9, folder 2, AASP.

92. AAS to Harper, April 7, 1896, box 9, folder 2, AASP.

93. Harper to AAS, Nov. 21, 1905, box 9, folder 11, AASP.

94. AAS to Harper, July 6, 1905, box 9, folder 10, AASP.

95. "President Harper dead after 3 years' illness," *NYT*, Jan. 12, 1906, 9.

96. Harper to AAS, Nov. 14, 1904, box 10, folder 9, WRHP.

97. Quoted in Lester, *Stagg's University*, 83.

98. AAS, Annual Reports to the President, 1896–97 through 1931–32, box 17, folders 10–31, AASP.

99. McCallum, *Big Ten Football Since 1895*, 206.

100. "Hugo Bezdek and the 1909 Razorbacks, University of Arkansas Athletics, Nov. 7, 2014, https://arkansasrazorbacks.com/hugo_bezdek_and_the_1909_razorbacks_204785125/.

101. "Favors forward pass only to ends in football," *Indianapolis Star*, Mar. 30, 1910, 8.

102. "Practice began in Arkansas," *Northwest Arkansas Times*, Aug. 31, 1972.

103. Danzig, *The History of American Football*, 244. See also "Hugh Bezdek," in Michael MacCambridge, ed., *ESPN Big Ten College Football Encyclopedia* (ESPN Enterprise, 2007), 60, 45–46.

104. AAS and Stout, *Touchdown!*, 200.

105. "X-Rays an aid in football," *CT*, Nov. 7, 1897, 30.

106. McCallum, *Big Ten Football Since 1895*, 185.

107. AAS and Stout, *Touchdown!*, 207.

108. Ray Robinson, *Rockne of Notre Dame: The Making of a Legend* (New York: Oxford University Press, 1999), 18.

109. Edward Burns, "Eckersall … football immortal," *CT*, undated, box 9, folder 10, AASP.

110. *Ibid.*, 96–97.

111. "Legends of the fall," *University of Chicago Magazine*, October 1995, http://magazine.uchicago.edu/9510/October95Legends4.html.

112. "J.C. Harper dead, football coach," Associated Press, *NYT*, Aug. 1, 1961, 31.

113. "Jesse Harper," National Cowboy and Western Heritage Museum, https://nationalcowboymuseum.org/hall-of-great-westerners/.

Chapter 8

1. AAS to David S. Merriam, Dec. 14, 1913, box 11, folder 10, AASP.

2. "The Tragedy of Von Gammon," University of Georgia Digital Lab, https://digilab.libs.uga.edu/scl/exhibits/show/covered_with_glory/von_gammon. See also "Letter from Gammon's Mother," *Atlanta Constitution*, Nov. 5, 1897, 5, and "Enough of Football," *Atlanta Journal*, Nov. 1, 1897.

3. "Change the football rules," Dec. 2, 1893, *NYT*. On the history of the wedge, see John Sayle Watterson, *College Football: History, Spectacle, Controversy*, 12–13.

4. "Football unfit for college use," *NYT*, Jan. 31, 1892, 6.

5. Cynthia Crossen, "When football began, football injuries were frequent and even drew fans," *Wall Street Journal*, Dec. 1, 2004.

6. Voltmer, *A Brief History of the Intercollegiate Conference of Faculty Representatives*, 16.

7. Theodore Roosevelt, "The functions of a great university," address at Harvard, June 28, 1905, from *The Works of Theodore Roosevelt* (New York: Charles Scribner's Son, 1926), vol. XVI, 324–325.

8. Smith, *Big-Time Football at Harvard 1905*, 194.

9. "President opens war on brutality in college game," *CT*, Oct. 10, 1905. For details about this meeting, see John J. Miller, *The Big Scrum: How Teddy Roosevelt Saved Football*, 184–191.

10. *Ibid.*, 195.

11. Smith, *Big-Time Football at Harvard 1905*, 194.

12. "Westerners not invited," *Chicago Record-Herald*, Oct. 11, 1905.

13. "Football reform by abolition," *The Nation*, Nov. 30, 1905, 437–38.

14. McCarthy, "Making Men," 229.

15. University Senate Minutes, Dec. 2, 1905. Cited in Lester, *Stagg's University*, 84.

16. "Senate endorses idea of suspending game," *Chicago Record-Herald*, Feb. 4, 1906.

17. "Chicago votes to drop football," *CT*, Feb. 2, 1906, 3.

18. AAS to Board of Trustees, Jan. 24, 1906, box 9, folder 16, AASP.

19. H.P. Judson to AAS, Mar. 30, 1906, box 9, folder 16, AASP.

20. Voltmer, *A Brief History of the Intercollegiate Conference of Faculty Representatives*, 18.

21. *Ibid.*, 19, 45.

22. AAS to George Stagg, Mach 27, 1906, box 1, folder 1, AASP.

23. AAS to H.P. Judson, Nov. 28, 1907. AASP.

24. Ronald A. Smith, *Pay for Play: A History of Big-Time College Athletic Reform* (Urbana: University of Illinois Press, 2011), 49. *Pay for Play* offers the most detailed explanation of football reforms that took place between 1905 and 1910. An earlier edition of *Pay for Play* is Ronald A. Smith, *Sports and Freedom: The Rise of Big-Time College Athletics* (Oxford University Press, 1988).

25. Danzig, *The History of American Football*, 33.

26. *Ibid.*, 30.

27. *Ibid.*, 53.

28. Smith, *Pay for Play: A History of Big-Time Athletic Reform*, 51.

29. AAS, "Chronological record of Amos Alonzo Stagg's contributions to the game of football," Stagg Special Collection. See also Bernie McCarty, "Eckersall to Steffen—Football's First Great Passing Combo," *College Football Historical Society Newsletter* 18, 2 (Feb. 2005), 11–13. https://digital.la84.org/digital/collection/p17103coll10/id/8645/rec/58.

30. McCallum, *Big Ten Football Since 1895*, 247.

31. AAS, Annual Report to the President, 2007–2008, box 18, folder 15, AASP.

32. Cited in Danzig, *The History of American Football*, 33.

33. Harold Keith, "Pioneer of the forward pass," *Esquire*, Nov. 1944. The most detailed information about Cochems and the St. Louis team's development of the forward pass is in Wikipedia, https://en.wikipedia.org/wiki/Eddie_Cochems.

34. Danzig, *The History of American Football*, 33–36. Danzig contains a detailed history of the origins and early use of the forward pass.

35. John Greenburg, *Winning the Biggest Game of All*.

36. "A chronological record of Amos Alonzo Stagg's contributions to the game of football," Stagg Special Collection.

37. "Maroons victor over Illini, 63–0," *CT*, Nov. 6, 1918.

38. *Chicago Record Herald*, Nov. 18, 1906. Clipping in Stagg Special Collection.

39. Danzig, *The History of College Football*, 37.

40. "The Football Death-Roll," *Tampa Tribune*, Nov. 13, 1909, 6.

41. "Gridiron deaths hard on football," *Bismarck (ND) Tribune*, Nov. 7, 1909, 7.

42. "Is football to be reformed again?" *NYT*, Nov. 14, 1909, 3.

43. "Radical changes in football rules," *NYT*, Aug. 18, 1910, 7.

44. AAS to John Doyle, Feb. 28, 1941, AASP.

45. AAS to Anthony Serge, Dec. 28, 1931, box 2, folder 15, AASP.

46. Danzig, *The History of American Football*, 118.

47. *Ibid.*, 57, 118.

48. *Milwaukee Sentinel*, Nov. 21, 1913, Sec. 3, 8. See also A.M. Weyand, *American Football: Its History and Development* (New York: Appleton and Company, 1926), 319, and Danzig, *The History of American Football*, 73.

49. Smith, *Big-Time Football at Harvard*, 49.

50. Danzig, *The History of American Football*, 175.

51. Edwin Pope, *Football's Greatest Coaches*, 232. See also Sparhawk, "A Study of the Life and Contributions of Amos Alonzo Stagg to Intercollegiate Football," 219.

52. Lester, *Stagg's University*, 103.

53. J.B. Griswold, "You don't have to be born with it," *The American Magazine*, Nov. 1931.

54. Quoted in Danzig, *The History of American Football*, 98.

55. *Ibid.*, 99.

56. AAS, "Annual Report to the President, 1908–1909," box 13, folder 16, AASP.

57. *Ibid.*

58. Quoted in Goodspeed, *A History of the University of Chicago*, 381–382.

59. Harvey T. Woodruff, "Why not call it Stagg Field?" *CT*, Oct. 26, 1931, 21.

60. "Vote to change U. of C. grounds to Stagg Field," *Chicago Inter Ocean*, Nov. 20, 1913, 13.

61. AAS, President's Report, 1927–1928, box 18, folder 29, AASP.

62. "Scientists' writings reveal fears, fateful decisions behind 1942 experiment," *University of Chicago News*, Oct. 23, 1017, http://news.uchicago.edu/story/race-first-nuclear-chain-reaction.

63. "The Joseph Regenstein Library," 1100 E. 57th Street, University of Chicago, https://www.lib.uchicago.edu/spaces/joseph-regenstein-library/.

64. McCarthy, "Making Men," 295.

65. AAS, "Annual Report to the President, 1918–1919," box 13, folder 16, AASP.

66. *Christian Science Monitor*, April 12, 1917, 1.

67. Phil Thompson, "1918 in Chicago sports," *Chicago Tribune*, May 14, 2020. See also Tony Barnhart, "The pandemic and college football: a look back at the 1918 season," *Sports Illustrated*, May 5, 2020, https://www.si.com/college/tmg/tony-barnhart/spanish-flu.

68. AAS and Winans, *Touchdown!*, 323.

69. Thompson, "1918 in Chicago Sports," *Chicago Tribune*, May 14, 2020.

70. "Army officials deny intention to stifle sports," *CT*, Sept. 14, 1918, 12. See also AAS to W.W. Roper, Oct. 19, 1918, box 19, folder 5, AASP.

71. AAS, "Athletes and Leadership," *National Defense*, undated, Stagg Special Collection.

72. Danzig, *The History of American Football*, 305.

73. "Princeton's defeat first for big three against westerners," *Boston Sunday Globe*, Oct. 21, 1921.

74. Mark F. Bernstein, *Football, the Ivy League Origins of an American Obsession* (Philadelphia: University of Pennsylvania Press, 2001), 120.

75. AAS Jr. videotaped interview with Dominic Bertinetti, Jr., Feb. 22, 1985. Stagg Special Collection.

76. McCallum, *Ivy League Football Since 1872*, 92.

77. William F. Osburn to AAS, Feb. 27, 1931, box 2, folder 10, AASP.

78. AAS to William F. Osburn, box 2, folder 10, AASP.

79. These statistics and Chicago's annual team records are based on the official University of Chicago Football Record book, https://athletics.uchicago.edu/sports/fball/record-book-fb.pdf.

80. "Red Grange," National Football Foundation Hall of Fame, https://football foundation.org/hof_search.aspx?hof=1410.

81. Associated Press, "Red Grange alone prevents Chicago team from winning," *Baltimore Sun*, Nov. 9, 1924, 17.

82. AAS and Stout, *Touchdown!*, 348.

83. *CT*, Dec. 31, 2002, 2–4.

84. Leroy Wayne Crew, "A Historical Review of the Contributions of Amos Alonzo Stagg to Amateur Athletics Between 1915 and 1929" (M.A. Thesis, University of Southern California, 1968).

85. Lewis Perry to AAS, Mar. 22, 1924, box 2, folder 12, AASP.

86. "Baseball," Phillips-Exeter Academy, Exeter, N.H., https://www.exeter.edu/teams/baseball-v/19sp.

87. Walter Steffen, National Football Foundation Hall of Fame, https://football foundation.org/hof_search.aspx?hof=1220.

88. "Stagg in happy mood," *CT*, Oct. 11, 1905, 10.

89. Ray Robinson, *Rockne of Notre Dame*, 183.

90. "Harlan 'Pat' Page" University of Chicago Athletics Hall of Fame, https://athletics.uchicago.edu/about/history/hof/page?view=bio.

91. Frank B. Hutchinson, Jr., "Stagg's warriors trample Minnesota 29–0," *Chicago Inter Ocean*, Nov. 1, 1908, 17.

92. "The life story of Amos Alonzo Stagg," box 125, folder 7, AASP.

93. Pat Page to AAS, May 2, 1913, box 11, folder 16, AASP.

94. Pat Page to AAS, undated, box 11, folder 16, AASP.

95. AAS to Pat Page, Dec. 15, 1916, box 11, folder 16, AASP.

96. "Herman James Stegeman," University of Georgia Athletics Hall of Fame, http://gshf.org/pdf_files/inductees/coach/herman_james_stegeman.pdf.

97. "Paul des Jardien," University of Chicago Athletics, https://athletics.uchicago.edu/about/history/hof/des_jardien?view=bio.

98. "Des Jardien praised by Camp," *Sequoyah County Democrat,* Oct. 23, 1914.

99. AAS to Albion Holden, Dec. 18, 1925, box 11, folder 12, AASP.

100. Herbert "Fritz" Crisler, University of Chicago Athletics Hall of Fame, https://athletics.uchicago.edu/about/history/hof/crisler?view=bio.

101. Tim Cohane, *Great College Football Coaches of the Twenties and Thirties* (New Rochelle, NY: Arlington House, 1973).

102. Gerald Holland," The man who changed football," *Sports Illustrated*, Feb. 3, 1964, https://vault.si.com/vault/1964/02/03/the-man-who-changed-football.

103. Danzig, *The History of College Football*, 403.

104. Dan Dunkin, "Hinkle, 92, dies in his sleep," *Indianapolis Star*, Sept. 23, 1992, 36.

105. Berg, "Mission on the Midway," 226.

106. AAS to Stella Stagg, Feb. 22, 1925, box 19, folder 12, AASP. Cited in McCarthy, "Making Men," 342.

107. *The University of Chicago Song Book* (Chicago: Undergraduate Council, 1921, 1927), 16. Quoted in Lester, *Stagg's University*, 141.

108. East trails west in college football crowds," *CT*, Dec. 3, 1924, 22.

Chapter 9

1. Howard J. Savage, *American College Athletics* (New York: Carnegie Foundation for the Advancement of Teaching, 1929), 168.

2. McCarthy, "Making Men: The Life and Career of Amos Alonzo Stagg," 370.

3. "Referee erred at Ohio, Stagg tells alumni," *CT*, Nov. 3, 1927, 21.

4. Harvey Woodruff, "Din of former years missing at U. of C. fete," *CT*, Nov. 13, 1930, 21.

5. Ellen Schrecker, "The bad old days: how higher education fared during the great depression," *Chronicle of Higher Education*, June 16, 2009, https://www.chronicle.com/article/The-Bad-Old-Days-Higher-Ed/44526.

6. AAS to "All of the coaches," box 11, folder 12, AASP.

7. AAS, President's Report, 1927–1928, box 18, folder 29, AASP.

8. *Big Ten Weekly*, box 113, Swift Papers.

9. Lester, *Stagg's University*, Appendix 2, 211–212.

10. Berg, "Mission on the Midway," 275.

11. "Adds course in athletics leading to the A.B. degree," *CT*, July 18, 1922, 2.

12. *Ibid.*, 135–136.

13. William H. McNeill, *Hutchins' University: A Memoir of the University of Chicago, 1929–1950*. (Chicago: University of Chicago Press, 1991).

14. Lester, *Stagg's University*, 147.

15. Frank W. Thomson interview with Dominic Bertinetti, Jr., Nov. 18, 1985, Stagg Special Collection.

16. AAS and Stout, *Touchdown!*, 12.

17. Bertrand Russell, "Football history," *NYT*, Oct. 2, 1927, 20.

18. Associated Press, "City honors Chicago eleven for its 'good sportsmanship,'" *NYT*, Feb. 14, 1928.

19. AAS to Joe Leib, undated, box 25, folder 1, AASP.

20. Associated Press, "Chicago schedules Yale eleven in 1931," *NYT*, Dec. 28, 1928.

21. "Jay Berwanger, first winner of the Heisman Trophy," University of Chicago News, http://www-news.uchicago.edu/releases/02/020627.berwanger.shtml.

22. *Ibid.*

Chapter 10

1. Baseball results, 1892–1933, box 6, folders 1–10, Physical Education and Athletics Records. See also the Department of Athletics and Recreation website for historical records.

2. AAS and Stout, *Touchdown!*, 164.

3. "But one safe hit off Stagg," *CT*, May 28, 1893, 7.

4. Steve Salerno, "Life in America's batting cages," *Missouri Review*, Winter 2004, https://longreads.com/2014/03/05/the-feel-of-nothing-a-life-in-americas-batting-cages/.

5. "Baseball Batting Cage," U.S. Patent Office, Patent 3222067, Dec. 7, 1965.

6. "To practice in an outdoor cage," *CT*, Mar. 19, 1896, 8.

7. Bill Savage, "Out of the Ballpark," *The Core College Magazine*, Summer 2016. This article contains a detailed description and several photos about Chicago's 1910 visit to Japan. http://thecore.uchicago.edu/Summer2016/departments/out-ballpark.shtml.

8. Lester, *Stagg's University*, 110.

9. AAS to Iso Abé, June 20, 1910, box 63, folder 5, Physical Education and Athletics Records.

10. Savage, "Out of the Ballpark," http://thecore.uchicago.edu/Summer2016/departments/out-ballpark.shtml.

11. AAS and Stout, *Touchdown!*, 165.

12. AAS to Iso Abé, June 20, 1910, box 63, folder 3, AASP.

13. Iso Abé to AAS, April 18, 1910, box 63, folder 6, Physical Education and Athletics Records.

14. Iso Abé to AAS, April 8, 1910, box 53, folder 3, Physical Education and Athletics Records.

15. Bill Savage, "Out of the ballpark; U. Chicago demonstrated the glory of gentlemanly sports." *Core: The College Magazine*, 2016, http://thecore.uchicago.edu/Summer2016/departments/out-ballpark.shtml.

16. "I prophesy he will hit your curves," https://baseballhistorydaily.com/tag/fred-merrifield/.

17. J.J. Pegues, "Japan invades America," *Collier's*, April 5, 1911.

18. H.O. Page, "Japan in the U.S.A," undated, box 63, folder 5, Physical Education and Athletics Records.

19. AAS, "Annual Report to the President, 1915–16," box 18, folder 23, AASP.

20. H.O. Crisler, "Informal report on 1920 Japanese trip," box 63, folder 5, Physical Education and Athletics Records.

21. "Maroons leave a 100-year baseball legacy," https://www.uchicago.edu/features/20080324_baseball/.

22. "Baseball: 2008 Blog," University of Chicago Department of Athletics, https://athletics.uchicago.edu/about/history/travel_blogs/baseball_japan_2008_blog.

23. Associated Press, "Stagg quits track coaching," *NYT*, Dec. 27, 1928, 26.

24. Voltmer, *A Brief History of the Intercollegiate Conference of Faculty Representatives*, 55.

25. "Moloney resigns, Stagg has unique coaching method," *Chicago Inter Ocean*, April 7, 1905, 4.

26. "Rah, rahs ready for Stagg today," *CT*, April 21, 1905, 6.

27. "Busy week ahead on Midway," *CT*, April 24, 1905, 8. See also "Stagg returns to Midway," *Chicago Inter Ocean*, April 22, 1905, 4.

28. "Stagg now directs track aspirants," *Chicago Inter Ocean*, Jan. 14, 1914, 13. See also "Maroon track men humble the purple," *Chicago Inter Ocean*, Feb. 1, 1914, 19.

29. AAS, "Dual meet held in Bartlett Gymnasium," Feb. 14, 1920, box 70, folder 4, AASP.

30. "Lightbody saved for Olympics," *CT*, Jan. 31, 1906, 8.

31. "Victory for Americans in Olympic games," *NYT*, May 1, 1906, 10.

32. "Henry Binga Dismond," Blackpast, https://www.blackpast.org/african-

american-history/dismond-henry-binga-1891–1956/.

33. "A chronological record of Amos Alonzo Stagg's contributions to the game of football," Stagg Special Collection.

34. McCarthy, "Making Men," 176.

35. AAS and Stout, *Touchdown!*, 227–228.

36. *Ibid.*

37. AAS to Ned A. Merriam, Dec. 24, 1928, box 11, folder 11, AASP. See also Associated Press, "Stagg quits track coaching," *NYT*, Dec. 27, 1928, 26.

38. "Basketball," *St. Louis Globe-Democrat*, Jan. 19, 1896, 11.

39. Greenburg, *Winning the Biggest Game of All.*

40. "Maroon alumni seek expansion of sport policy," *CT*, Feb. 3, 1921, 18.

41. *Ibid.*

42. "A.A. Stagg explains basket defeats in hot reply to critics," *CT*, Feb. 4, 1921, 14.

43. "Basket critics reply to Stagg in campus daily, *CT*, Feb. 5, 1921, 10.

44. AAS and Stout, *Touchdown!*, 168.

45. "Indoor meets are marked success," *Chicago Inter Ocean*, Mar. 20, 1905, 6.

46. Robert Pruter, *The Rise of American High School Sports and the Search for Control 1880–1930* (Syracuse: Syracuse University Press, 2013), 80. Most of the information about the interscholastic tournaments came from this book. See also Pruter's article, "Early interscholastic track and field meets, Illinois High School Association," https://www.ihsa.org/NewsMedia/IllinoisHStoric/IllinoisHStoricArticle.aspx?url=/archive/hstoric/track_boys_early.htm.

47. Program, "Twenty-sixth Annual Interscholastic Track and Field Games," Stagg Special Collection.

48. George W. Scott, "Grand Old Man of football," *Listen, a Journal of Better Living* (July-August 1948), 19.

49. "Speed, stamina of 'prep' world for Stagg meet," *CT*, May 23, 1922, 17.

50. Pruter, *The Rise of American High School Sports and the Search for Control 1880–1930*, 237.

51. Lester, *Stagg's University*, 110.

52. Pruter, *The Rise of American High School Sports and the Search for Control 1880–1930*, 296.

53. "Maroons abandon national basketball meet," *CT*, Dec. 9, 1930, 25.

54. Lester, *Stagg's University*, 153.

Chapter 11

1. AAS to Max Mason, May 14, 1926, box 10, folder 9, AASP.

2. Max Mason to AAS, May 24, 1926, box 10, folder 9, AASP.

3. Jeff S. Rasley, "Marooned," *Chicago Magazine*, June 6, 2007.

4. Robert M. Hutchins with Milton Mayer, *Robert Maynard Hutchins: A Memoir* (University of California Press, 1993), 139, https://publishing.cdlib.org/ucpressebooks/view?docId=ft4w10061d;query=;brand=ucpress.

5. Lester, *Stagg's University*, 147.

6. Hutchins and Mayer, *Robert Maynard Hutchins: A Memoir*, 139.

7. Robert M. Hutchins, "College football is an infernal nuisance," *Sports Illustrated*, Oct. 18, 1954, https://www.si.com/vault/1954/10/18/546757/college-football-is-an-infernal-nuisance.

8. Mervin D. Hyman, *Big Ten Football, Its Life and Times, Great Coaches, Players, and Games*, 52.

9. "An open letter to the 'Old Man,'" *Chicago Daily Maroon*, Oct. 2, 1931.

10. Robert M. Hutchins to AAS, April 4, 1932, box 117, folder 13, Swift Papers.

11. "Keep Stagg as coach? O.K. says Hutchins," *CT*, Oct. 29, 1932, 19.

12. Associated Press, "New athletic director will not recommend reappointment of Stagg as football coach," *NYT*, Dec. 5, 1932, 22.

13. Robert M. Hutchins to Stagg, Dec. 6, 1932, box 117, folder 3, Swift Papers.

14. Arch Ward, "Talking it over," *CT*, Dec. 27, 1932, 13.

15. AAS to "Wardner and Dimple," January 26, 1933, Stagg Special Collection.

16. Charles Dunkley, "Stagg through with U. of C.; rejects post," *Chicago Herald-Examiner*, Dec. 6, 1932, box 117, folder 13, Swift Papers.

17. The Associated Press, "[Stagg] has new desire to stick as coach after physical exam," box 117, folder 13, Swift Papers.

18. Associated Press, "39 freshmen petition that Stagg remain," *NYT*, Oct. 26, 1932, 21.

19. Dr. Woodward tells why U. of C. retires all teachers at 70," *Chicago Herald and Examiner*, undated, box 117, folder 13, Swift Papers.

20. "Age Discrimination," U.S.

Department of Labor, https://www.dol.gov/general/topic/discrimination/agedisc.

21. Christy Walsh to AAS, October 14, 1932, box 96, folder 1, AASP. For biographical information on Walsh, see https://en.wikipedia.org/wiki/Christy_Walsh_(sports_agent).

22. Harold C. Ickes to AAS, March 7, 1933, box 96, folder 1, AASP.

23. Harold H. Swift to Lewis O. Atherton, November 2, 1934, box 117, folder 13, Swift Papers.

24. Minutes, Board of Trustees, Oct. 13, 1932. At the Feb. 11, 1932, trustee meeting, Shailer Mathews was included in a list of professors recommended to continue their year-by-year appointments. Cited in Lester, *Stagg's University*, 149.

25. Sparhawk, "A Study of The Life and Contributions of Amos Alonzo Stagg to Intercollegiate Football."

26. "Letter winners, young and old, acclaim Stagg," *CT*, June 9, 1933, 29.

27. Lester, *Stagg's University*, 153.

28. "1941 Rose Bowl," https://www.revolvy.com/page/1941-Rose-Bowl.

29. Hutchins and Mayer, *Robert Maynard Hutchins, A Memoir* (University of California Press), https://publishing.cdlib.org/ucpressebooks/view?docId=ft4w10061d;query=;brand=ucpress.

30. Associated Press, "Chicago withdraws from Big Ten Conference because of weak athletic teams," *NYT*, Mar. 9, 1946, 21.

31. Jess S. Rasley, "Marooned," *Chicago Magazine*, June 6, 2007.

32. Associated Press, "Stagg will coach eleven on coast," *NYT*, Feb. 5, 1933. See also "Stagg accepts coaching job with College of Pacific," *CT*, Feb. 5, 1933, 17.

Chapter 12

1. Greenburg, *Winning the Biggest Game of All.*

2. Tulley Knoles to AAS, Dec. 9, 1932, box 97, folder 2, AASP.

3. "Resume of Coach Stagg's fourteen years of coaching at the College of the Pacific, 1933–1946." Stagg Special Collection.

4. Associated Press, "Stagg will coach eleven on coast," *NYT*, Feb. 5, 1933, 1.

5. George M. Hench to AAS, undated, box 96, folder 4, AASP.

6. Merchants Alliance to AAS, Dec. 16, 1932, box 96, folder 4, AASP.

7. Albert M. Chesley to AAS, Dec. 17, 1932, box 107, folder 5, AASP.

8. Edward P. Foltz to AAS, Dec. 28, 1932, box 96, folder 4, AASP.

9. AAS to Tully Knoles, Dec. 21, 1932, Pacific Stagg Collection, folder 1.5a.7.

10. Associated Press, "Stagg signs as College of Pacific Coach," *Sacramento Bee*, Feb. 4, 1933, 21.

11. James Rolph to AAS, undated, box 96, folder 4, AASP

12. Bill Spaulding to AAS, Mar. 31, 1933, Stagg Special Collection.

13. James Phelan to AAS, undated, Scrapbook 327, AASP.

14. Warren Brown, "Stagg on new adventure," *SFE*, Feb. 5, 1933, 21.

15. Wilbur Adams, "Stagg given welcome to state here," *Sacramento Bee*, Mar. 22, 1933, 13.

16. Burkey Walter, "Was A.A. Stagg cheated of 21 wins?" *SFE*, Sept. 6, 1981, 38.

17. William Leiser, "Thousands turn out in roaring welcome to Stagg in Stockton," *SFE*, Mar. 22, 1933, 16.

18. AAS and Amos Alonzo Stagg, Jr., *Stagg of Yale*, 253C.

19. Philip N. Gilbertson, *Pacific on the Rise: The Story of California's First University* (Stockton: University of the Pacific, 2016), 124. http://scholarlycommons.pacific.edu/pacific-pubs/1.

20. AAS to Salmon Levinson, July 11, 1954. box 4, folder 13, AASP. See also AAS and Amos Alonzo Stagg, Jr., *Stagg of Yale*, 27.

21. "Resume of Coach Stagg's fourteen years of coaching at the College of the Pacific, 1933–1946," Stagg Special Collection.

22. Tully C. Knoles to AAS, Jan. 14, 1933, box 97, folder 2, AASP.

23. William Leiser, "Ex-Chicago grid mentor surprises all," *SFE*, Mar. 23, 1933, 15.

24. Associated Press, "New aide to handle backs in fall work, *SFE*, April 27, 1933, 17.

25. "Stagg happy despite of defeat, *SFE*, Sept. 24, 1933, 23.

26. Stagg draws praise," *CT*, Dec. 24, 1933, 16.

27. Harry Hayward, "Smart Stagg boys may give Bears battle," *SFE*, Oct. 13, 1934, 19.

28. Harry Hayward, "California barely ekes 7–6 victory over Pacific," *SFE*, Oct. 14, 1934, 27.

29. "A.A. Stagg is 73 today, hold party for coach," *CT*, Aug. 16, 1935, 23.

30. Braven Dyer, "The Sports Parade," *CT*, Sept. 25, 1937, 26.

31. Associated Press, "A.A. Stagg celebrates 75 years old," *SFE*, Jan. 21, 1937, 19.

32. Associated Press, "'Coach until I am 100,' Stagg says," *SFE*, Aug. 16, 1938, 20.

33. "Maroons and Stagg's team meet today," *CT*, Nov. 12, 1938, 19.

34. "Letter to Amos Alonzo," *CT*, Nov. 12, 1938, 10.

35. T.C. Hart, "'Old Man' comes home," *Chicago Daily Herald*, Nov. 17, 1938, 12.

36. *Ibid.*

37. "Chicago vs. College of the Pacific," Nov. 12, 1938, folder 2.5.12, Pacific Stagg Collection.

38. Edward Burns, "Stagg's team routs Chicago 32–0 in closing periods," Nov. 13, 1938, *CT*, 31.

39. "Chicago set back by Stagg team," *NYT*, Nov. 13, 1938, 86.

40. Associated Press, "Current gridders best, says Stagg," *San Pedro News-Pilot*, Oct. 6, 1938, 8.

41. "Mrs. Stagg gets scout report on Aggies," *Stockton Record*, Oct. 14, 1941. box 250, AASP.

42. William Fay, "Hit 'em low still the cry of Coach Stagg," *CT*, Oct. 27, 1944, 64.

43. Stella Stagg, "Sugar Bowl game, Jan. 1, 1938," box 97, folder 8, AASP.

44. Associated Press, "Grid squad gives Mrs. Stagg trophy," *SFE*, Jan. 9, 1937, 18.

45. "Don Watson's sport comment," *Honolulu Star Bulletin*, Dec. 18, 1939. box 249, AASP.

46. Russ Newland, "Mrs. Stagg part of American football," Associated Press, *Stockton Record*, Nov. 30, 1942.

47. Lee Dunbar, "Stagg's team upsets mighty California," *Oakland Tribune*, Oct. 1, 1939.

48. John J. Peri, *Stockton Record*, Dec. 30, 1939.

49. John Peri, *Stockton Record*, Sept. 8, 1939.

50. "Stagg Stadium Photo Gallery," https://www.pacific.edu/about-pacific/media-galleries/university-media-gallery/stagg-stadium-photo-gallery.html.

51. Danzig, *The History of American Football*, 222.

52. "Amos Alonzo Stagg Award," American Football Coaches Association," https://www.afca.com/category/awards/amos-alonzo-stagg-award/.

53. *Knute Rockne, All American*, Warner Brothers movie, 1940. For a detailed analysis of the movie and its historical flaws, see chapter 4, "Hollywood and *Knute Rockne, All American*" in Murray Sperber, *Onward to Victory, The Crises that Shaped College Sports* (New York: Holt and Company, 1988).

54. Dick Hurd to AAS, Nov. 28, 1940; AAS to Dick Hurd, Feb. 26, 1941, box 4, folder 4, AASP.

55. Sperber, *Onward to Victory, The Crises that Shaped College Sports*, 38–39.

56. "This Day in History," https://125.nd.edu/moments/this-day-in-history-the-forward-pass-1913-vs-army/.

57. Frank P. Maggio, *Notre Dame and the Game That Changed Football* (New York: Carroll and Graf Publishers, 2007), 77. See also "Forward Pass," https://en.wikipedia.org/wiki/Forward_pass.

58. Maggio, *Notre Dame and the Game That Changed Football*, 98–101.

59. *Ibid.* See also "1913 Fighting Irish football team," in https://en.wikipedia.org/wiki/1913_Notre_Dame_Fighting_Irish_football_team.

60. Knute Rockne, *The Autobiography of Knute K. Rockne* (New York: Bobs-Merrill, 1931), 157.

61. Ray Robinson, *Rockne of Notre Dame*, 55.

62. *Ibid.*, 209–210.

63. Murray Sperber, *Onward to Victory: The Crises that Shaped College Sports* (New York: Henry Holt and Company, 1998), 11.

64. Interview with A.A. Stagg, Jr., April 21, 1967, quoted in Ruth M. Sparhawk, "A Study of the Life and Contribution of Amos Alonzo Stagg to Intercollegiate Football," 71.

65. AAS Jr., videotaped interview with Dominic Bertinetti, Jr., Feb. 22, 1985. Stagg Special Collection.

66. Harry Hall to AAS, Feb. 8, 1944, box 105, folder 10, AASP.

67. AAS to Harry Hall, Mar. 7, 1944, box 105, folder 10, AASP.

68. AAS and Stout, *Touchdown!*, 106.

69. AAS, "What does Jesus mean to

me?" Chapel Service, May 11, 1943, folder 3.2.11, Pacific Stagg Collection.

70. Arch Ward, "In the wake of the news," *CT*, April 21, 1948, 43.

71. John J. Peri, "San Jose Wins 7–0 on disputed touchdown," *Stockton Record*, Oct. 25, 1941.

72. "Stagg asks for replay of S.J.-Pacific game," *San Jose Mercury Herald*, Oct. 31, 1941.

73. *Ibid.*

74. Irving Martin Jr., "Answer from San Jose State," *Stockton Record*, November 3, 1941.

75. AAS to C.R. Black Jr., Nov. 26, 1943, box 3, folder 5, AASP.

76. "A chronological record of Amos Alonzo Stagg's contributions to the game of football," 15. Stagg Special Collection.

77. Bob Hunter, "Alert College of Pacific squad cashes in on bruin errors," *Los Angeles Examiner*, Oct. 3, 1943.

78. Lee Dunbar, "Cal loses 4th straight grid clash," *Oakland Tribune*, Oct. 10, 1943, 13.

79. "Stagg Coach of the Year," *NYT*, Dec. 11, 1943, 18.

80. W.R. Schroeder to Art Farey, undated, box 105, folder 1, AASP.

81. Associated Press, "Stagg named football's 'Man of the Year,'" *NYT*, Dec. 12, 1943, 1.

82. "Stagg's comeback stands out in 1943," *NYT*, Dec. 23, 1943, 1.

83. Grand Marshall of the Tournament of Roses," https://www.nndb.com/honors/469/000122103/.

84. "Amos Alonzo Stagg Tree, Giant Sequoia National Moment," U.S. Forest Service, https://www.fs.usda.gov/Internet/FSE_DOCUMENTS/fseprd615789.pdf, accessed Oct. 25, 2019.

85. Daniel E. Slotnik, "Wayne Hardin, Hall of Fame football coach at Navy, dies at 91," *NYT*, April 4, 2017, B5.

86. "Eddie LeBaron, a star in the NFL, dies at 85," *NYT*, April 2, 2015, A20.

87. "Amos Alonzo Stagg: He wrote the book," *Fort Myers News-Press*, Nov. 17, 1981, 35.

88. Associated Press, "Stagg loses in farewell," *SFE*, Dec. 22, 1946, 15.

89. AAS to William France Anderson, Dec.15, 1946, box 3, folder 4, AASP.

90. "A.A. Stagg hits top and bottom," *Fresno Bee*, Nov. 11, 1944.

91. A chronological record of Amos Alonzo Stagg's contributions to the game of football," Stagg Special Collection.

92. "Pacific Football Record Book, June 2002," University of the Pacific Scholarly Commons, https://scholarlycommons.pacific.edu/ua-promo/.

93. UPI, "NFL executive recalls record-setter for Stagg," *The Record-Herald* (Provo, UT), Sept. 7, 1981, 7.

94. Hal Wood, "Monday morning experts seek scalps of many coast grid coaches," *Hanford Morning Journal*, Dec. 3, 1946, 4.

95. United Press, "Stagg asked to resign," *NYT*, Dec. 3, 1946, 44.

96. "AAS to Tully Knoles, Dec. 6, 1946, UPSC, folder 1.5a.20. See also "Stagg quits COP post," *SFE*, Dec. 8, 1946, 25–26.

97. Quoted in Considine, *The Unreconstructed Amateur*, 150.

98. Associated Press, "Stagg resigns at COP to accept Susquehanna job," *Sacramento Bee*, Dec. 7, 1946, 8.

99. AAS to William France Anderson, box 3, folder 4, AASP.

Chapter 13

1. Marion Schoch, "Pa Stagg will protect junior's job," *Selinsgrove Times*, Dec. 12, 1946, 1. See also "Move by Susquehanna grads to oust Stagg is belittled," *SFE*, Dec. 25, 1946, 16.

2. G. Morris Smith to AAS, Dec. 7, 1946, box 103, folder 5, AASP.

3. Crisler, athletic director at the University of Michigan, told this anecdote in the article, "My Most Unforgettable Character: Alonzo Stagg," *Reader's Digest*, Dec. 1962, 120–123.

4. AAS to W.H. Ball, Feb. 2, 1948, AASP.

5. Associated Press, "A.A. Stagg arrives in aid in coaching Susquehanna gridders," *York Gazette and Daily*, April 18, 1947.

6. Barbara Stagg Ecker to Bob Boyd, July 5, 1999, Stagg Special Collection.

7. Dick Westerfield, Susquehanna Press Office to Pennsylvania Legislative Correspondents Association, Oct. 6, 1949, Amos Alonzo Stagg Sr. & Jr., Susquehanna University Archives, Section 3, RG 2.2.7.

8. "Amos or Bear?" *Philadelphia Inquirer*, Aug. 10, 1981, 27.

9. "Crusaders conclude successful

season," *Selinsgrove Times*, Nov. 20, 1947, 5.

10. Stephen D. Ross videotaped interview with Dominic Bertinelli, Jr., Nov. 18, 1988, Stagg Special Collection.

11. 1951 Football Team to AAS, Mar. 13, 1952, box 103, folder 2, AASP.

12. "Wife Stagg's aide," *The Chicago Magazine*, Mar. 18, 1965, box 125, folder 9, AASP.

13. Curley Grieve, "Mrs. Stagg stands out like a bright beacon," *SFE*, Aug. 16, 1962, 53.

14. "The Grand Old Man of Football," *Selinsgrove Times-Tribune*, Nov. 18, 1948, 1.

15. Edward R. Murrow, CBS Television "See It Now" videotape, 1952, Stagg Special Collection.

16. Stephen D. Ross interview with Dominic Bertinetti, Nov. 18, 1988, Stagg Special Collection.

17. Associated Press, "Ailing Stagg, 90, goes to hospital," *Sacramento Bee*, Jan. 3, 1953, 8.

18. Associated Press, "Coach Stagg in hospital," *NYT*, Jan. 4, 1953, 151, and "Stagg Continues to Improve," *NYT*, Jan. 7, 1953, 27.

19. United Press, "Stagg to leave hospital bed," *Deseret News*, Jan. 13, 1953, 11.

20. Mike Puma, "Bear Bryant simply the best there ever was," ESPN Classic, https://www.espn.com/classic/biography/s/Bryant_Bear.html.

21. George Vecsey, "A quiet crusade, *NYT*, July 27, 1981, 32.

22. George Vecsey, New York Times Service, "Son tries to add to senior Stagg's list of victories, *Minneapolis Tribune*, Aug. 2, 1981, 8C.

23. *Ibid.*

24. AAS to G. Morris Smith, July 28, 1953, box 103, folder 5, AASP.

25. Associated Press, "Amos Stagg, football's Grand Old Man, to retire," *Visalia Times Daily*, Aug. 3, 1953.

26. "Stagg not to coach this fall," *NYT*, Aug. 3, 1953, 20.

27. AAS, "Comments of Amos Alonzo Stagg about his wife," July 15, 1948, folder 3.2.17, Pacific Stagg Collection.

28. Associated Press, "Stagg 91 today, plans a quiet day with wife," *CT*, Aug. 16, 1953, 41.

Chapter 14

1. Don Selby, "Stagg returns to football," *SFE*, Sept. 8, 1953. See also "Stagg at 96 will help coach Stockton's eleven," *NYT*, Sept. 8, 1953, 40.

2. Don Selby, "Stagg joins staff in Stockton," *SFE*, Sept. 8, 1953, 39. See also "Stagg will celebrate 91st birthday quietly at home," *SFE*, Aug. 16, 1953, 45.

3. Associated Press, "Stagg revives after being knocked out," *CT*, Sept. 15, 1954, 68.

4. Associated Press, "Stagg, 95 today, still in harness," *San Rafael Daily Independent Journal*, Aug. 16, 1957, 12.

5. Howard Barry, "Stagg recalls life's work: development of young men," *CT*, June 3, 1955. See also "1905 Chicago stars greet Coach Stagg," *CT*, June 2, 1955, 77.

6. Associated Press, "Stagg, 92, to attend reunion of 1905 Chicago U. champs," *SFE*, May 27, 1955, 28.

7. Associated Press, *SFE*, Jan. 11, 1957, 36. See also "Stagg, 94, goes to 50th football rules meeting," *CT*, Jan. 11, 1957, 39.

8. Associated Press, "COP group fetes Stagg," *SFE*, Aug. 11, 1957, 48. See also Considine, *The Unreconstructed Amateur*, 103.

9. "Stagg serves as chief adviser," *San Bernardino County Sun*, Dec. 6, 1958, 28.

10. "Stagg beats the odds," *Chicago Sun-Times*, Aug. 19, 1958.

11. "Adding life to years," *Time*, Oct. 20, 1958, 62.

12. *Ibid.*

13. Herbert O. Crisler, "My most unforgettable character: Alonzo Stagg," *Reader's Digest*, Dec. 1962, 120–123.

14. *Chicago Daily News*, Mar. 19, 1965. Quoted in Sparhawk, "A Study of the Life and Contributions of Amos Alonzo Stagg," 109.

15. Considine, *The Unreconstructed Amateur*, 101.

16. Laura E. Wallace, et al, "Does religion stave off the grave? Religious affiliation in one's obituary and longevity," *Social Psychological and Personality Science* 10, 5 (2019), 662–670.

17. William McDonnell to AAS, Feb. 2, 1959, box 105, folder 13, AASP.

18. "Chamber honors seven as 'Great,'" United Press International, *NYT*, April 28, 1959.

19. Associated Press, "Stagg: 'I'll try to

behave,'" *SFE*, Dec. 8, 1959, 43.

20. Harry Costello, "Stagg cites college aim: 'molding of character,'" *Detroit News*, Feb. 18, 1922.

21. National Football Foundation Hall of Fame Gold Medal Award, Oct. 24, 1960, box 3, folder 14, AASP.

22. Associated Press, "Stagg feted on 98th Birthday," *SFE*, Aug. 17, 1960, 55.

23. Bill Becker, "Stagg nearing another goal at 98," *NYT*, Aug. 14, 1960, 5.

24. The archival records at the University of Chicago are not clear about the years that Stagg coached the basketball team between 1894 and 1896.

25. John J. Peri, "70 seasons are enough; Stagg quits coaching," *Stockton Record*, Sept. 16, 1960, 29. Pacific Stagg Collection, box 1.3.5.

26. "100 Years and Forever, A film by and about Amos Alonzo Stagg, 1962," Springfield College Archives, https://cdm16122.contentdm.oclc.org/digital/collection/p15370coll2/id/20992/rec/78.

27. AAS to George L. Emery, Oct. 27, 1960, box 3, folder 14, AASP.

28. AAS to Mrs. Bob Coe, Sept. 27, 1956, box 105, folder 1, AASP. See also "Stagg School Dedicated," Associated Press, *SFE*, Feb. 26, 1959, 34.

29. District 230, "School named for Stagg," Dec. 12, 1962. Stagg Special Collection.

30. William O. Fisher interview with Dominic Bertinetti, Jr., Feb. 11, 1985, Stagg Special Collection.

31. United Press International, "Stagg feared he would never make it," *CT*, Aug. 17, 1962, 43.

32. Associated Press, "This Stagg party was a dry one," *Oakland Tribune*, Aug. 17, 1962.

33. United Press International, "12 cities will honor Stagg on his birthday," *CT*, Aug. 3, 1962, 3,

34. "Transcript of Jackie Robinson speech at Amos Alonzo Stagg 100th birthday celebration," Aug. 12, 1962, Springfield College Digital Collections, https://

cdm16122.contentdm.oclc.org/digital/collection/p15370coll2/id/16430/rec/80.

35. Associated Press, "Can't keep Stagg down," *SFE*, August 17, 1962, 55.

36. "Amos Alonzo Stagg fetes 'Century of Life' tonight," *Daily Independent Journal* (San Rafael, CA), Aug. 16, 1962, 17.

37. John F. Kennedy telegram to F.H. Busher, Aug. 15, 1962. Stagg Special Collection.

38. Bob Considine, *The Unreconstructed Amateur*, 1962.

39. Associated Press, "Wrote 'Stagg of Yale,'" *NYT*, Mar. 18, 1965, 30.

40. AAS and Amos Stagg, Jr., *Stagg of Yale* (Unpublished manuscript, c. 1958), Stagg Special Collection.

41. Ed Schoenfeld, "Stagg amazes his doctors," *Oakland Tribune*, June 2, 1964.

42. "Mrs. Amos Alonzo Stagg, wife of football coach, dead," *NYT*, July 24, 1964, 27.

43. Hal Wood, UPI, "Stagg: 'My Maroons could win today,'" *SFE*, Aug. 15, 1961, 47.

44. "Stella Robertson Stagg," *Chicago Alumni Magazine*, October 1964, box 125, folder 9, AASP.

45. Associated Press, "Quiet 102nd birthday for Stagg," *SFE*, Aug. 17, 1962, 53

46. The Rev. Myron Herrell, "Untarnished trophy" (funeral sermon), March 16, 1965, Stagg Special Collection.

47. Walter V. Leen, board secretary to Dr. Paul Stagg, April 13, 1965, Stagg Special Collection.

48. These studies are easily accessible online by using the search terms "Longevity and..." with the words: nutrition, exercise, marriage, religion, social network, and purpose.

49. SI staff, "Pat on the back," *Sports Illustrated*, Sept. 23, 1957, https://www.si.com/vault/1957/09/23/623343/pat-on-the-back.

50. John Underwood, "A century of honesty," *Sports Illustrated*, Aug. 13, 1962, 43, https://vault.si.com/vault/1994/08/29/a-century-of-honesty.

Bibliography

Abbreviations

Special Collections

AASP: Amos Alonzo Stagg Papers, University of Chicago Special Collections Research Center and Archives.

Physical Education and Athletics Records: Department of Physical Education and Athletics Records, 1892–1999, University of Chicago Special Collections Research Center and Archives.

WRHP: William Rainey Harper Papers, University of Chicago Special Collections Research Center and Archives.

Pacific Stagg Collection: Amos Alonzo Stagg Papers, Holt-Atherton Special Collections and Archives, University of the Pacific, Stockton, California.

Stagg Special Collection: Amos Alonzo Stagg Special Collection in the Media Center at the Amos Alonzo Stagg High School, Palos Hills, Illinois. The Stagg Special Collection documents are not systematically organized into boxes and folders.

Swift Papers: Harold Swift Papers (trustee), University of Chicago Special Collections Research Center and Archives.

Newspapers

CT: CT
LAT: Los Angeles Times
NYT: New York Times
SFE: San Francisco Examiner

Archives

Amos Alonzo Stagg High School, Palos Hills, Illinois, Media Center, Stagg Special Collection.

Springfield College, Springfield, Massachusetts. Digital Collections, Amos Alonzo Stagg Collection.

Susquehanna University Archives, Selinsgrove, Pennsylvania. Blough-Weiss Library, Amos Alonzo Stagg Junior and Senior Collection.

University of Chicago Library, Chicago, Illinois. Special Collections Research Center and Archives, Amos Alonzo Stagg Papers, 1866–1964.

University of the Pacific, Stockton, California, Holt-Atherton Special Collections, Amos Alonzo Stagg Collection.

Books

Bernstein, Mark F. Football: The Ivy League Origins of an American Obsession. Philadelphia: University of Pennsylvania Press, 2001.

Berry, Elmer. The Forward Pass in Football. New York: A.S. Barnes, 1921.

Boyer, John W. The University of Chicago: A History. Chicago: University of Chicago Press, 2015.

Brooks, Philip L. Forward Pass: The Play That Saved Football. Yardley, PA: Westholme, 2014.

Cohane, Tim. Great College Football Coaches of the Twenties and Thirties. New Rochelle, NY: Arlington House, 1973.

_____. The Yale Football Story. New York: Putnam and Sons, 1951.

Considine, Bob. The Unreconstructed Amateur, A Pictorial Biography of Amos Alonzo Stagg. San Francisco: Amos Alonzo Stagg Foundation, 1962.

Danzig, Allison. The History of American Football: Its Great Teams, Players, *and Coaches*. Englewood Cliffs, NJ: Prentice-Hall, 1956.

Gilbertson, Philip N. *Pacific on the Rise: The Story of California's First University*. Stockton, CA: University of the Pacific, 2016.

Goodspeed, Thomas Wakefield. *A History of the University of Chicago: The First Quarter Century*. Chicago: University of Chicago Press, 1916.

Greenburg, John. *Winning the Biggest Game of All: The Story of Amos Alonzo Stagg*, Amazon Kindle, 2000.

Hyman, Mervin D., and Gordon S. White. *Big Ten Football, Its Life and Times, Great Coaches, Players, and Games*. New York: Macmillan, 1977.

Ingrassia, Brian. *The Rise of Gridiron University: Higher Education's Uneasy Alliance with Big-Time Football*. Lawrence: University Press of Kansas, 2012.

Kryk, John. *Stagg vs. Yost: The Birth of Cutthroat Football*. Lanham, MD: Rowman & Littlefield, 2015.

Ladd, Tony, and James A. Mathisen. *Muscular Christianity: Evangelical Protestants and the Development of American Sport*. Grand Rapids: Baker Books, 1999.

Lester, Robin. *Stagg's University: The Rise, Decline, and Fall of Big-time Football at Chicago*. Urbana: University of Illinois Press, 1999.

Lucia, Ellis. *Mr. Football: Amos Alonzo Stagg*. South Brunswick: A.S. Barnes, 1970.

Maggio, Frank P. *Notre Dame and the Game That Changed Football: How Jesse Harper Made the Forward Pass a Weapon and Knute Rockne a Legend*. New York: Carroll and Graf, 2007.

McCallum, John D. *Big Ten Football Since 1895*. Radnor, PA: Chilton, 1976.

_____. *Ivy League Football Since 1872*. New York: Stein and Day, 1977.

McNeill, William H. *Hutchins' University: A Memoir of the University of Chicago, 1929–1950*. Chicago: University of Chicago Press, 1991.

Miller, John J. *The Big Scrum: How Teddy Roosevelt Saved Football*. New York: Harper Perennial, 2012.

Pope, Edwin. *Football's Greatest Coaches*. Atlanta: Tupper and Ware, 1955.

Powel, Harford. *Walter Camp: The Father of American Football: An Authorized Biography*. Boston: Little, Brown, 1926.

Powers, Francis J. *Life Story of Amos Alonzo Stagg, Grand Old Man of Football*. St. Louis: C.C. Spink and Son, 1946.

Pruter, Robert. *Pay for Play: A History of Big-Time College Athletic Reform*. Urbana: University of Chicago Press, 2011.

_____. *The Rise of American High School Sports and the Search for Control 1880–1930*. Syracuse: Syracuse University Press, 2013.

Reprinted in *The American Football Trilogy* by the Lost Century of Sports Collection, LostCentury.com, 2015.

Robinson, Ray. *Rockne of Notre Dame, The Making of a Football Legend*. New York: Oxford University Press, 1999.

Savage, Howard J. *American College Athletics*. New York: Carnegie Foundation for the Advancement of Teaching, 1929.

Solberg, Winton U. *Creating the Big Ten: Courage, Corruption, and Commercialization*. Urbana: University of Illinois Press, 2018.

Sperber, Murray A. *Onward to Victory: The Crises That Shaped College Sports*. New York: Henry Holt, 1998.

Stagg, Amos Alonzo, and H.L. Williams. *A Scientific and Practical Treatise on American Football for Schools and Colleges*. New York: D. Appleton and Company, 1894.

Stagg, Amos Alonzo, and Wesley Winans Stout. *Touchdown!* New York: Longman, Green, 1927.

Stagg, Amost Alonzo, and Amos Alonzo Stagg, Jr. *Stagg of Yale* (unpublished autobiography, c. 1958). Stagg Special Collection, Amos Alonzo Stagg High School, Palos Hills, Illinois.

Tamte, Roger R. *Walter Camp and the Creation of American Football*. Urbana: University of Illinois Press, 2018.

Underwood, John. *The Death of an American Game: The Crisis in Football*. Boston: Little, Brown, 1979.

Voltmer, Carl. *A Brief History of the Intercollegiate Conference of Faculty Representatives*. Menasha, WI: George Banta, 1935.

Watterson, John Sayle. *College Football: History, Spectacle, Controversy*. Baltimore: The Johns Hopkins University Press, 2000.

Webb, Bernice. *The Basketball Man, James Naismith*. Lawrence: University of Kansas Press, 1973.

Weyand, Alexander M., and Parke H. Davis. *American Football, Its History and Development.* New York: D. Appleton, 1926.

Theses and Dissertations

Berg, Peter Iversen. *A Mission on the Midway: Amos Alonzo Stagg and the Gospel of Football.* PhD diss., Michigan State University, 1996.

Crew, Leroy Wayne. *A Historical Review of The Contributions of Amos Alonzo Stagg To Amateur Athletics Between 1915 and 1929.* Master's thesis, University of Southern California, 1968.

McCarthy, Erin Ann. *Making Men: The Life and Career of Amos Alonzo Stagg, 1862–1933.* PhD diss., Loyola University Chicago, 1994.

Newsome, Ron. *Amos Alonzo Stagg: His Football Coaching Career at the University of Chicago.* PhD diss., East Texas State University, 1988.

Sparhawk, Ruth. *A Study of The Life and Contributions of Amos Alonzo Stagg to Intercollegiate Football.* PhD diss., Springfield College, 1968.

Stagg, Paul. *The Development of the National Collegiate Athletic Association in Relationship to Intercollegiate Athletics in the United States.* PhD diss., New York University, 1946.

Index

Numbers in *bold italics* indicate pages with illustrations